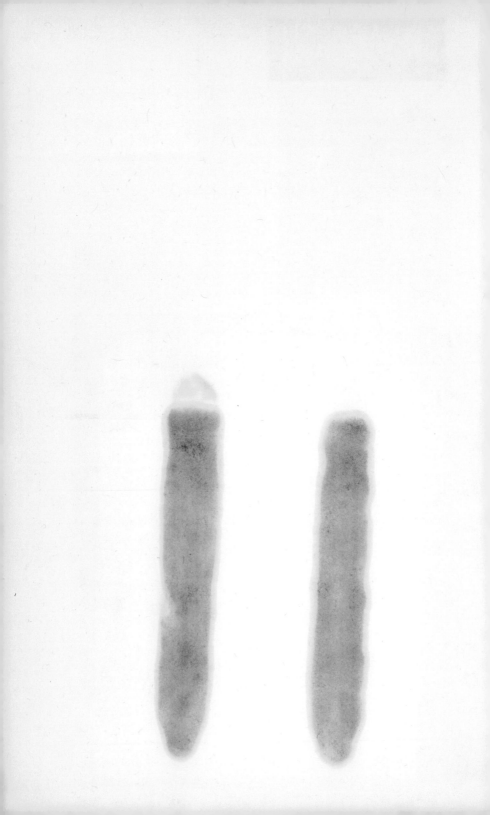

PROBABILITY, TIME, AND SPACE IN
EIGHTEENTH-CENTURY LITERATURE

PROBABILITY, TIME, AND SPACE IN
EIGHTEENTH-CENTURY LITERATURE

edited by
Paula R. Backscheider

AMS Press
New York

c 1979

Library of Congress Cataloging in Publication Data
Main entry under title:

Probability, time, and space in eighteenth-century literature.

Papers, most of them revised, of the 1973–76 sessions
of a Modern Language Association group.
Includes bibliographical references and index.
1. English literature—18th century—History and
criticism—Addresses, essays, lectures.
2. Philosophy, Modern—18th century—Addresses, essays,
lectures. 3. Literature and science—Addresses, essays,
lectures. I. Backscheider, Paula. II. Modern
Language Association of America.
PR442.P68   820'.9'005   78-20850
ISBN 0-404-16046-8

MANUFACTURED IN THE UNITED STATES OF AMERICA

Contents

Introduction

Paula R. Backscheider

From a modest beginning in 1967, the Modern Language Association group which produced these essays has grown to a membership of more than 250 scholars and survived three name changes imposed by the reorganizations of the MLA. The group whose session or seminar is titled "Problems in Eighteenth-Century Evidence" is dedicated to the investigation of theoretical problems and to experimentation with new approaches. Each session incorporates a variety of genres, material from a number of periods within the 1660–1800 rubric, and illustrates several different approaches to the theoretical concept.

The group members receive papers in November, and the MLA session is devoted to vigorous discussion and debate. Correspondence and conversation about the papers often extends over the next few months. The papers in this volume represent the topics for 1973–1976; most have been revised for publication.

The Restoration and eighteenth-century person was not cultured if he was ignorant of science. Science engaged his interest and imagination as psychology and communication theory do our own age. Bacon and Descartes had challenged man to master the entire natural world, and scientific development in the period was truly extraordinary. Poets and ordinary men thrilled to man's potential. Pope wrote,

> Go, wondrous creature, mount where Science guides.
> Go, measure earth, weigh air, and state the tides,
> Instruct the planets in what orbs to run
> Correct old Time, and regulate the Sun.[1]

The secularization of the idea of history and of change, the mathematization of thinking about natural phenomena, and the growth of empirical science revolutionized thought. Mathematics seemed to offer a certainty which philosophy and science had not. Descartes expressed both the idea and the satisfaction:

> Most of all was I delighted with Mathematics because of the certainty of its demonstrations and the evidence of its reasoning; but I did not yet understand its true use, and, believing that it was a service only in the mechanical arts, I was astonished that, seeing how firm and solid was its basis, no loftier edifice had been reared thereupon.[2]

Around 1660, Pascal, Huygens, Leibnitz, Hudde, de Witt, Wilkins, and Graunt independently discovered and applied basic ideas of probability. The probability that emerged was both statistical and epistemological.[3] Representing the lines of inquiry and ordering the universe, both paths of probability developed simultaneously; most probablists, in fact, were concerned with both, although they did not necessarily make the distinction. Rapid developments in the physical sciences threatened and challenged thinkers. Accompanying the desire to know more came the desire to assign degrees of certainty or credibility to statements of belief lacking statistical content.

By the late seventeenth century, man lived in a Newtonian universe. Pope's "Epitaph. Intended for Sir Isaac Newton, In Westminster Abbey" epitomizes the praise accorded him: "Nature, and Nature's Laws lay hid in Night./ God said, *Let Newton be!* and All was *Light.*"[4] Gravitational and inertial forces which could be described in formulae explained the natural and manmade world. Planets, seasons, hours were mechanical. The revolution in thinking about time can be compared to the impact of relativity theory. A few could grasp the ramifications, but all were affected and had to grapple with the ideas. To Plato, time was a "moving image of eternity," to Aristotle, "the number of motion with respect to before and after," to Augustine, the "distension of soul" and, therefore, sensible duration. In the eighteenth century, Chambers in his *Cyclopaedia* defined astronomical time as "that taken purely from the motion of the heavenly bodies, without any other regard. Civil time is the former time accommodated to civil uses." Newton regarded absolute time as the perfect measure of movement because it was independent of motion; those before him puzzled over time as a quality of movement. Later Kant was to reconcile physical and psychological time by defining it as an *a priori* form of inner sense "empirically real and transcendentally ideal." Today the revolution in calculating time is just as great, and the grappling just as difficult. Time is now measured according to the constancy of atomic structures.

Thinking about space was equally revolutionary. Rather than simply marking the end or boundary of an object, space became a concept, like time, in which objects exist or move. An essential quality of an object is space; it had shape, density, and motion, all expressible in mathematical terms.[5] Space, like time and probability, became a way of understanding and ordering the world and part of new conception of causality. In a universe which is a mathematical structure, all phenomena are co-existent. This principle reinforced man's new power and his limitations. Through mathematics, he could predict because mathematical relationships are pre-existent and universal; but because he could comprehend events only sequentially through his senses, he could explain events only in cause-effect terms. That the greatest scientists of the time attempted to use their scientific knowledge to argue for the existence of God is recognition both of their power and of their fears.

The toys of science gave men and women pleasure and adorned their drawing rooms. Magnifying glasses were the rage.[6] Many numbers of contemporary periodicals were devoted to explaining science and experiments. Fontenelle's *Entretiens sur la pluralité des mondes* was a best seller for women. The Royal Society was a flourishing and prestigious institution and people petitioned to be invited.[7] The show put on for Margaret Cavendish displayed respectable experiments combined with the wonder of the magician's craft.[8]

The literature of the period also demonstrates the incorporation of and preoccupation with science: Swift's Academy of Projectors, Pope's *Essay on Man*, Sterne's *Tristram Shandy*, Wesley's hymns—but that is the subject of the essays in this volume.

Notes

1. Alexander Pope, *Essay on Man* II, 19-22.

2. Rene Descartes. *Discourse on the Method of Rightly Conducting Reason*, translated by Elizabeth Haldane and G. R. T. Ross in *Descartes. Spinoza. Great Books of the Western World.* Robert M. Hutchins, ed. (Chicago: William Benton, 1952), 43. For Descartes' definition of mathematics see Rule IV, *Rules for the Direction of the Mind*, p. 5.

3. Ian Hacking, *The Emergence of Probability* (Cambridge: Cambridge University Press, 1975), pp. 11-12.

4. In *English Literature in the Early Eighteenth Century 1700-1740* (Oxford: Clarendon, 1968), Bonamy Dobree says, "By the time of Newton's death in 1727 it became almost obligatory to mention Newton in a poem, on whatever subject, so much so that Somerville rounded off with some lines upon him even that agreeable hunting poem *The Chase*," pp. 500-501.

5. Morris Kline, *Mathematics in Western Culture* (Oxford: Oxford University Press, 1972), p. 106.

6. Stella and Mrs. Pepys were among the women who enjoyed their own magnifying glasses. See for example, *Journal to Stella*, Letter XXVII, 22 August 1711, I, 38, edited by Harold Williams (Oxford: Basil Blackwell, 1974). Gerald Meyer, *The Scientific Lady in England 1650-1760* (Berkeley: University of California Press, 1955) and Marjorie Hope Nicolson, *The Microscope and English Imagination* (Northampton, Mass.: Smith College Studies in Modern Languages, 1935) as well as such general studies as A. R. Hall's *The Scientific Revolution, 1500-1800: The Formation of the Modern Scientific Attitude* (London: Longmans, Green, 1954) which discuss the influence of science on the ordinary man and woman.

7. Significantly, the *Philosophical Transactions* of the Society began appearing in print in 1665.

8. For a description of Margaret Cavendish's visit and the experiments performed see Samuel I. Mintz, "The Duchess of Newcastle's Visit to the Royal Society," *JEGP*, 51(1952), 168–176.

List of Contributors

PAUL K. ALKON is Professor of English at the University of Minnesota. In addition to shorter studies of topics in eighteenth-century literature, he has written *Samuel Johnson and Moral Discipline* (1967) and *Defoe and Fictional Time* (forthcoming).

LEWIS WHITE BECK is Professor of Philosophy at the University of Rochester and has been Chairman of the Board of Officers of the American Philosophical Society, President of the Eastern Division of the American Philosophical Association, and President of the Northeastern American Society for Eighteenth-Century Studies. He is author of numerous articles and books including *Early German Philosophy: Kant and his Predecessors* (1969) and *Essays of Kant and Hume* (1978).

RAYMOND F. HILLIARD is Assistant Professor of English at the University of Richmond. His 1976 doctoral dissertation was on the development of Jane Austen's psychological realism. He has read papers at meetings of NEMLA and NEASECS and is currently at work on essays on Austen and on Mary Wollstonecraft.

PAUL J. KORSHIN, Associate Professor of English at the University of Pennsylvania, served as Executive Secretary of the American Society for Eighteenth-Century Studies and is active on the eighteenth-century Short Title Catalogue project. He has written *From Concord to Dissent: Major Themes in English Poetic Theory, 1640-1700* (1973) and numerous articles on Restoration and eighteenth-century literature and intellectual history, and edited several books including *Studies in Change and Revolution.* He is completing a book-length study of typology.

IVOR LeCLERC, Professor of Philosophy at Emory University, is author of *Whitehead's Metaphysics* (1958) and *The Nature of Physical Existence* (1972) and is at present engaged in an inquiry in ontology, *The Theory of Being.* He has published many papers on the philosophy of nature, on metaphysics, on the philosophy of society, and on individual thinkers. He is editor of *The Relevance of Whitehead* (1961) and *The Philosophy of Leibniz and the Modern World* (1973).

LOUIS T. MILIC has been Professor of English and Chairman of the Department at Cleveland State University since 1969. His major scholarly interests are eighteenth-century prose and stylistics. He is the author of *A Quantitative Approach to the Style of Jonathan Swift* (1967), *Style and Stylistics* (1967), *Stylists on Style* (1969), and numerous articles and papers.

ROBERT MOYNIHAN, an Associate Professor of English at SUNY, Oneonta, has written and published on a number of topics including the "Yale Critics," modern thought and criticism, and the eighteenth-century novel. He is at work on a book concerning dialectical form in seventeenth- and eighteenth-century poetry.

MAXIMILLIAN E. NOVAK is Professor of English at UCLA. In addition to continuing work on Dryden, Congreve and Defoe, he is at work on a book about the changing modes of fiction from 1660 to 1840.

MARGARET J. OSLER is Associate Professor of History at the University of Calgary; her special area of interest is the history and philosophy of science. She has published several articles on seventeenth-century theories of matter and scientific method.

RICHARD B. SCHWARTZ, Professor of English and former Associate Dean of the Graduate School at the University of Wisconsin, Madison, is the author of *Samuel Johnson and the New Science* (1971), *Samuel Johnson and the Problem of Evil* (1975), and *Boswell's Johnson: A Preface to the LIFE* (1978). He has published numerous articles on eighteenth-century literature. With the aid of H. I. Romnes and ACLS fellowships, he is now preparing a study of the texture of life in Johnson's London.

The late HOPEWELL SELBY was Assistant Professor of English at the University of Illinois, Chicago Circle. She had published articles on Swift.

DAVID TARBET is associate Professor of English at SUNY, Buffalo. He has published a number of essays on eighteenth-century literature and philosophy and is currently writing about the journals of James Boswell.

HOYT TROWBRIDGE, now Emeritus Professor of English at the University of New Mexico, served as Chairman of the department and, for eight years, as Dean of the College of Arts and Sciences. He has been active since the organizations's foundation in the affairs of the American Society for Eighteenth-Century Studies and is a regular contributor to its journal and to the annual bibliography of current scholarship which it sponsors. He is the author of *From Dryden to Jane Austen: Essays on English Critics and Writers, 1660-1818* and numerous articles and review essays.

I. PROBABILITY

Certainty, Scepticism, and Scientific Optimism: The Roots of Eighteenth-Century Attitudes Toward Scientific Knowledge

Margaret J. Osler

Two apparently contradictory epistemologies of science held sway in the eighteenth century. The spectacular successes of rational mechanics led a number of natural philosophers to maintain that, at least in the field of mechanics, science can penetrate the secrets of nature with certainty. Despite the resounding achievements in mathematical physics, eighteenth-century philosophers of science persisted in the attempt to establish epistemological foundations for the methods of science. Whereas the physicists believed themselves to be approaching the position of Laplace's omniscient intelligence, the philosophers came to abandon the hope that scientific methods can lead to certainty or even penetrate the veil of appearances.[1]

Was this apparent contradiction in eighteenth-century attitudes towards scientific knowledge genuine; What were its sources? In the following pages I will argue that these divergent attitudes arose from two different epistemological traditions current in the seventeenth-century, traditions which converged on the mechanical philosophy and produced in turn the apparently contradictory attitudes toward scientific knowledge.

3

Specifically, I will argue that while the physicists regarded mechanics as a science of primary qualities, the philosophers viewed natural philosophy as a science of secondary qualities. I will trace the physicists' optimism to Copernicus' insistence that astronomical theory describe reality; the mitigated scepticism of Locke and his followers stemmed from the sceptical crisis that followed on the heels of post–Reformation discussions about criteria for determining a rule of faith. Resolution of these divergent attitudes toward scientific knowledge was not possible until Hume developed techniques of philosophical analysis sufficiently powerful to expose the real problems separating the physicists from the philosophers.

I

The problems addressed by the physicists and their attitudes toward scientific knowledge both originated in the Copernican revolution. By insisting that astronomy describe the real system of the heavens, in contrast to the Greek and medieval attitude that astronomical theories need only save the phenomena, Copernicus presented the physicists with the problems that were to occupy them for the following century and a half. The realism of Copernican astronomy demanded answers to physical questions: What keeps the planets in their orbits? How can we account for the observed behavior of projectiles, given the diurnal and annual motions of the earth? The search for answers to these questions led to the formulation of a new physics, culminating in the Newtonian synthesis at the end of the seventeenth-century.

The mechanical philosophy which dominated seventeenth-century scientific thinking became the focus of the physicists' optimism. Whatever the differences in the details of their systems—whether they regarded matter as atomic or infinitely divisible, whether or not they believed void to exist, which properties they considered matter to possess—mechanical philosophers agreed that all phenomena in the physical world are caused by matter and motion. Central to all versions of the mechanical philosophy was the doctrine of primary and secondary qualities. All mechanical philosophers agreed that we must distinguish between properties possessing different ontological status: Primary qualities are those which matter really possesses: secondary qualities are those which matter appears to possess due to the interaction between the primary qualities and the human senses. All of the sensible properties of bodies can thus be reduced to a small number of primary qualities which really exist. Although mechanical philosophers disagreed about the list of primary qualities—e.g. Descartes asserted that extension is the only primary quality, while Gassendi included others such as heaviness—all agreed that some qualities really belong to matter while others only appear to belong as a result of the interaction between matter and human sensory organs.[2] Given the basic tenets of the mechanical philosophy, the science of mechanics became a central element in the new philosophy of nature: the fundamental process by which change takes place in nature is the collision of particles of matter. Thus mechanics was tied to two aspects of the new science: It became a necessary adjunct to astronomy on account of the philosophical realism of Copernicus and his followers, and it provided the new philosophy of nature with its most fundamental process: impact.

The importance of impact to the mechanical philosophy further reinforced the epistemological realism inherited from astronomy. Since physicists employed only primary qualities in solving the problem of impact, one could infer that the laws of mechanics describe the real nature of things. Regardless of which properties they ascribed to matter as primary, and despite fundamental differences about the ontological status of force or the relationship of mechanics to empirical knowledge, the physicists of the period solved the problem of impact entirely in terms of primary qualities. For example, Descartes attempted to derive laws of impact by considering only the size and motion of the particles involved.[3] Size for Descartes meant extension, which was for him the only primary quality. Similarly, Huygens, who was a Cartesian, ultimately derived the laws of impact entirely on kinematic grounds, using only the magnitudes of the bodies and the directions and magnitudes of their motions.[4] When Newton derived the laws of impact in the *Principia*, he made use exclusively of properties which served as primary qualities in his philosophy of nature: mass and movability.[5] If impact and, more generally, mechanics deal only with the primary qualities of bodies, it follows that the science of mechanics deals with the real nature of things.

Examination of two solutions to the problem of impact— Colin MacLaurin's and Jean d'Alembert's—and its relationship to their theories of matter, and of attitudes toward the epistemological status of mechanics plainly reveals the close connection between the appeal to primary qualities and the physicists' optimism. In *An Account of Sir Isaac Newton's Philosophical Discoveries* (1748), Colin MacLaurin undertook to present Newtonian physics in the language of analytical mathematics. He opened the book with an optimistic assessment of scientific knowledge. "To describe the *phenomena* of nature, to explain their causes, to trace the relations and dependencies of those causes, and to enquire into the whole constitution of the universe, is the business of natural philosophy."[6] He derived the laws of impact directly from the three Newtonian laws of motion,[7] which, as MacLaurin presented them, ascribe to matter the following primary qualities: Extension, movability, figure, solidity, impenetrability, inertia, and infinite divisibility.[8] Inertia (*via inertiae*) was the pivotal quality for MacLaurin. It provided the distinction between space and matter,[9] and it raised the specter of Newtonian forces, the status of which was a critical issue for eighteenth-century philosophers and physicists. For the purposes of the present discussion, inertia raises the further question of the epistemological status of mechanics, for MacLaurin's evidence that matter possesses inertia was empirical.[10]

The ascription to matter of inertia and other empirically known primary qualities posed the question of what our knowledge of qualities tells us about the world. MacLaurin regarded such knowledge as problematic, but in the end capable of revealing the true nature of things with certainty.

In our ideas which are repetitions of other ideas, we find very different degrees of resemblance between them and those of which they are repetitions. . . . And as it is no objection against the existence of the souls of other men, that they may be very different from the notion or conception we may have formed of them; so it is no just reason against admitting the existence of body, that its inward essence, or *substratum*, may be very different from any thing we know of it. It is, however, rating out ideas of external objects by much too low to compare them to words or mere arbitrary signs, serving only to distinguish them from each other. For it is from our ideas of them that we learn their properties, relations, and their influences upon each other, and upon our minds and those of others, and acquire useful knowledge concerning them and ourselves. For example, by comparing and examining our ideas, we judge of order and confusion, beauty and deformity, fitness and unfitness, in things. The ideas of number and proportion, upon which so useful and extensive sciences are founded, have the same origin.[11]

On what grounds did MacLaurin justify his faith in the reliability of empirical knowledge?

In contrast to the Cartesians and other system builders who attempted to derive the phenomena from first principles,[12] MacLaurin believed rather uncritically that he could be sure his concepts and laws accurately revealed nature's ways because they were based directly on the phenomena. "For in any other way, we can never be sure that we assume the principles which really obtain in nature; and that our system, after we have composed it with great labours, is not mere dream and illusion."[13]

MacLaurin believed that Newton's method of always insuring that analysis precede synthesis guaranteed the success of his science.

He [Newton] has taken care to give nothing for demonstration but what must ever be found such; and having separated from this what he owns is not so certain, he has opened matter for the enquiries of future ages, which may confirm and enlarge his doctrines, but can never refute them.[14]

This methodological guarantee led MacLaurin to envisage an ever-increasing range of phenomena encompassed within the bounds of scientific truth.

MacLaurin's optimism was shared by Jean d'Alembert, although d'Alembert based his outlook on very different epistemological foundations. D'Alembert's goal for mechanics was Cartesian: he sought to deduce the laws of mechanics from clear and distinct ideas, thereby achieving certainty.[15] In the Preface to his *Traité de dynamique* (1743) and in the influential *Preliminary Discourse to the Encyclopedia of Diderot* (1751), d'Alembert drew a sharp distinction between the mathematical sciences and those which were "merely experimental."[16] Mechanics, which he regarded as one of the mathematical sciences along with geometry and algebra, proceeds from clear and distinct ideas deductively to laws of motion. D'Alembert sought deductive unity for the sciences, based on the smallest number of fundamental principles.[17] Corresponding to these goals, his stated aim in the *Traité de dynamique* was to reduce the science of mechanics to the smallest number of principles of the greatest breadth.[18]

The laws of impact, as well as the other results in d'Alembert's mechanics, follow from three basic laws: "la force d'inertie, le mouvement composé, & l'équilibre."[19] D'Alembert believed that these three laws could be couched entirely in terms of the primary qualities—extension and impenetrability—which he considered to be known clearly and distinctly, thus guaranteeing their certainty.[20] His effort to avoid causal and metaphysical notions—namely force and mass—in his derivation of these laws reveals his desire to couch his physics entirely in terms of primary qualities. Thus he tried to reduce all cases of impact to the law of equilibrium as it pertained to bodies of the same mass, thereby believing that he could eliminate mass as a relevant parameter.[21] Similarly, he tried to avoid the troublesome notion of force by claiming that the word was simply a convenient way of avoiding circumlocutions.[22] Indeed, he wanted to avoid all references to the causes of acceleration and deceleration, lest such metaphysical notions spoil the certainty of his mechanics.[23]

Different as their assumptions about matter and knowledge might be, both MacLaurin and d'Alembert attempted to deduce the laws of impact using only primary qualities as parameters in their mechanics. In both cases, the appeal only to primary qualities implied that the laws of physics describe the real nature of

the world. Their optimistic assessment of scientific knowledge
was reinforced by the successes of mathematical physics after
Newton. From the Laws of Motion, Newton himself had derived
the powerful law of universal gravitation which incorporated
the phenomena of both terrestrial and celestial physics into the
body of mathematical mechanics. He had proceeded further to
show how the phenomena of comets, lunar motions, tides, and
the precession of the equinoxes—as well as the planetary motions—followed from this basic law. In the generations that followed, gravitational theory was applied to a variety of additional
problems with astonishing success. By the end of the eighteenth
century, Laplace—in his five-volume *Traité de la méchanique
céleste* (1798–1827)—was able to demonstrate that the solar
system is a gravitationally stable Newtonian system. The law of
universal gravitation seemed to be the mathematical key to the
universe, leading Laplace to utter the classic statement of scientific optimism.

> Given for one instant an intelligence which could comprehend all the
> forces by which nature is animated and the respective situation of all
> the beings who compose it–an intelligence sufficiently vast to submit
> these data to analysis—it would embrace in the same formula the move-
> ments of the greatest bodies of the universe and those of the lightest
> atoms; for it, nothing would be uncertain and the future, as the past,
> would be present to its eyes.[24]

Whatever the specific arguments of the individual physicists,
epistemological optimism was restricted to the mathematical
sciences, particularly to mechanics and celestial mechanics. The
physicists contrasted the truth and ever-expanding scope of
mechanics with two other activities which equally consumed
the interest of eighteenth-century scientists: experimental science and mechanical hypothesis-building. Although the experimental and observational aspects of science, such as electri-
city, magnetism, and chemistry were based on a Newtonian
model—that enunciated in the *Opticks* in contrast to that elaborated in the *Principia*—these researches did not yield the same
kind of system and elegance found in mechanics. Newton had
expressed the hope that these areas would ultimately be sub-
sumed under the same kind of generalizing law that universal

gravitation had provided for mechanics; and his followers shared that hope. But for the time being that hope remained an article of faith, and the experimental sciences retained their grossly empirical form, not inspiring the kind of optimism engendered by gravitational mechanics.

The mathematical physicists similarly dissociated themselves from the kind of hypothesis-building that often characterized both pre- and post-Newtonian mechanical philosophies. Although Newton himself had probably wanted to construct a natural philosophy not unlike the mechanical philosophies of the seventeenth century (the Queries to the *Opticks* point the way to his scheme),[25] neither he nor his mathematical followers granted mechanical or ethereal speculations the same status as the demonstrated results of mathematical mechanics.

The optimistic attitude of the physicists toward rational mechanics harked back to two seventeenth-century assumptions. One was the realism of astronomical—and hence physical—theory. The other was the mechanical philosophy of nature which postulated certain primary qualities as the subject-matter for mechanics, thus providing philosophical warrant for claiming that mechanics deals with the real nature of things.

Although the ideas of Locke and Hume also emerged from the framework of the mechanical philosophy, they saw a different world from that of the physicists. Encouraged in their scepticism by the theological and philosophical currents from which their thought emerged, they stressed a different aspect of the mechanical philosophy and thus espoused far more limited goals for scientific knowledge. Viewed from different standpoints, the same mechanical philosophy could yield markedly divergent philosophies of science. Where the physicists sought a science known with certainty, the philosophers saw at best the possibility of probable knowledge.

II

The probabilism of the seventeenth- and eighteenth-century philosophers of science had its roots in the sceptical crisis that convulsed European thought in the wake of the Reformation.[26]

Faced with Luther's challenge to the authority of the Catholic church, European philosophers and theologians found themselves in the midst of a debate about the so-called "rule of faith." Protestant thinkers, having rejected the church's claim to authority, argued that the only authority in questions of religion was the word of God as revealed in Scripture. Catholics argued that such a view would lead to religious anarchy. To counter this danger, they claimed that an authority was needed to determine a universal rule of faith, an authority which, they argued, had been vested in the Roman Catholic church. The question of who or what is the proper authority in religious matters led to the further question of the proper criterion for judging among rival claims to authority, and, further, how one decides which of several conflicting criteria is adequate. Coupled with the concurrent revival of the ancient sceptical writers—particularly Sextus Empiricus—this debate over the rule of faith led to the sceptical crisis which left no realm of knowledge unaffected. The ramifications of this debate for the foundations of scientific knowledge were profound.

For some thinkers, the stakes were extremely high. Either the truth of one's views was known with absolute certainty, or one would suffer eternal damnation.[27] Some Protestant writers, particularly in England, took a more moderate position. According to them, the alternative to dogmatism—the position that we can achieve certainty in our knowledge about theological or other matters—is not scepticism, but rather a kind of mitigated certainty or reasonableness wherein our degree of belief is proportioned to the quality and quantity of evidence at hand.[28]

Arguing that the sceptical arguments destroy any hope for absolute certainty, they appealed to the methods of ordinary, common-sense experience as a proper way to deal with theological questions. "If we will disbelieve everything, because we cannot certainly know all things, we shall do much what as wisely as he who would not use his legs, but sit still and perish, because he had no wings to fly."[29] Just as in ordinary life we temper our degree of assent to the evidence we have, so too in theological matters we can measure our degree of belief by the amount and reliability of the evidence in its favor. A number of seventeenth-century thinkers argued that there are several levels of certainty, determined by the nature of the available evidence.[30]

In the context of discussions concerning degrees of certainty, questions about the probabilistic character of knowledge arose. The sceptical arguments had eliminated the possibility of the absolute certainty sought by Aristotle, Bacon, and Descartes. Knowledge was now identified with propositions we can assert as probable or true beyond any reasonable doubt.[31] Why were these thinkers so ready to believe that human knowledge is limited, that certainty is rare and that more often than not we must settle for moral certainty or mere probability? The answer derives in part from a changing view of the laws of nature that resulted from the Reformation. According to the Christianized Aristotelianism which was the currency of the natural realm in the late Middle Ages, the cosmos is a self-sustaining system which operates in accordance with certain reified "laws" or "natures" that govern its behavior. These natures are secondary causes, the primary cause being the Deity. As secondary causes, they possess ontological reality and an independent existence. Moreover they are intelligible, and so the inner workings of the natural world are open to human understanding. All this changed when the Reformation thinkers returned to the Bible and rebelled against the strictures of scholastic philosophy.[32] According to the Biblical account of nature, God created the natural world which is entirely dependent on Him for its existence. God's omnipotence renders all knowledge of nature utterly contingent, because He can intervene at any time at His will and disturb the order of things. The miracles of both the Old and New Testaments were considered examples of such divine interventions. Post–Reformation nature, especially, but not exclusively, in Protestant writers, possesses a contingency that represents a fundamental departure from the necessary and intelligible laws that had characterized the earlier Christian-Aristotelian philosophies of nature. If the order of nature is contingent, any generalizations we might make about nature cannot be known as necessary truths. The "laws" of nature depend on experience; they are all *a posteriori*. If nature depends immediately on God's will, if that fact implies that all knowledge of nature is contingent, and if contingency implies the fundamentally *empirical* nature of natural knowledge, what can we know of the natural world when the senses had been subject to such a scathing sceptical critique?

Pierre Gassendi gave one answer which proved to be quite influential. A contemporary of Descartes, Gassendi advocated a Christianized version of Epicurean atomism and, like Descartes, was one of the most influential sources of the mechanical philosophy which came to dominate natural philosophy during the seventeenth century. Elaborating an atomic theory of matter, which differed considerably from Descartes' plenum and infinitely divisible matter, Gassendi also advocated a more moderate solution to the sceptical difficulties. Reiterating the sceptical arguments in an early book, *Exercitationes paradoxicae adversus Aristoteleos* (1624), Gassendi concluded that although there is no possibility of certainty in scientific matters, probability is attainable if we pursue a "science of appearances." That is to say, although the sceptical arguments prove that our senses are unreliable sources of information about the inner reality of things, they nonetheless inform us about how things appear. By studying the appearances and discovering regularities among them, we can develop a science about them. Such a science lacks certainty and fails to penetrate into the real essences of things; but it will provide a knowledge useful for practical life, which itself is composed of appearances. This knowledge of appearances will possess some degree of probability. Science, for Gassendi, meant a science of secondary qualities.

Gassendi's probabilism found its way into the epistemology of many of the mechanical philosophers. The doctrine of primary and secondary qualities and Gassendi's probabilism, coupled with the theological discussions about certainty and probability, provided the components of the philosophy of science which was to dominate English thought well into the eighteenth century. The first fully articulated version of this philosophy was found in Locke's *Essay Concerning Human Understanding* (1690).[33]

Locke's *Essay* was a full-fledged philosophy of science incorporating the following elements: the mechanical philosophy of nature, an emphasis on experience as the basis for all knowledge, and the recognition that probability, not certainty, is the proper goal of scientific knowledge.[34] He was thus heir to the traditions we have examined—the post–Reformation debates over the "rule of faith," the discussion about the place of certainty and probability in human knowledge, and the mechanical philosophies of Descartes and Gassendi. He transformed his legacy into a coherent philosophy of science that spoke to the questions concerning his contemporaries. Why did Locke maintain that probability, not certainty, is the proper goal for science?

Locke wrote the *Essay* to provide foundations for human knowledge in an age that was deeply concerned with both religion and science. The *Essay* grew out of a discussion of the "principles of morality and revealed religion."[35] The difficulties issuing from the discussion led him to examine the foundations of human knowledge, which, by the time he published the *Essay*, came to revolve around the underpinnings of the science which had become such an important feature of the intellectual landscape.[36] Starting from the assumptions that genuine knowledge is equivalent to certainty and that the material world is composed of small particles of matter, Locke maintained that we have no genuine knowledge of the material world; at best our knowledge is probable. His entire discussion in Book IV of the *Essay* which is entitled "Of Knowledge and Probability" aimed at a clear understanding of what we can and cannot know with certainty. Among other things, Locke extended the earlier discussions of certainty and probability to the realm of natural philosophy, at which point he broke from the orthodox philosophies of science to maintain that empirical knowledge can never yield certain knowledge. Reinforcing his probabilism was the belief that empirical science is the science of secondary qualities. In this respect his conclusions were at odds with those of the mathematical physicists.

Locke began his discussion of knowledge with the statement that all our knowledge ultimately concerns the contents of our minds.[37] Such knowledge comes in two degrees, intuition and demonstration, determined by the kind of evidence available to us.[38]

These two, viz. intuition and demonstration, are the degrees of our *knowledge* whatever comes short of one of these, with what assurance soever embraced, is but *faith* or *opinion*, but not knowledge . . .[39]

One other category falls under the rubric of knowledge, *"the particular existence of finite beings about us,"* but this perception, although it goes "beyond bare probability," does not reach "perfectly to either of the foregoing degrees of certainty."[40]

Locke thus accepted the traditional equation between knowledge and certainty. But, if only the relations between ideas in our minds can be known with certainty, what is the status of natural philosophy, which concerns the relations among objects in the world? For Locke, the answer was clear: As important, interesting, and useful as such understanding may be, it is not knowledge, for it cannot be known with certainty.

The reason whereof is, that the simple ideas whereof our complex ideas of substances are made up are, for the most part, such as carry with them, in their own nature, no *visible necessary* connexion or inconsistency with any other simple ideas, whose co-existence with them we would inform ourselves about.[42]

Our ignorance of such necessary connections stems from the relation between primary and secondary qualities.[43] Although, for Locke, our ideas or primary qualities *resemble* the primary qualities themselves, they only do so in the sense that we know all bodies must possess some bulk, figure, mobility, etc.; of the primary qualities of the small particles which are the ultimate constituents of matter, we know only that the particles must possess them. We are ignorant of the specific primary qualities they actually possess, just as we are ignorant of any necessary connections between these primary qualities and the ideas they produce in our minds. Our knowledge of substances—the content of natural philosophy—is confined to the phenomenal properties of bodies, that is, the ideas they produce in our minds:

. . . our ideas of the species of substances . . . being nothing but certain collections of simple ideas united in one subject, and so co-existing together; v.g. our idea of flame is a body hot, luminous, moving upward; of gold a body heavy to a certain degree, yellow, malleable, and fusible:

for these or some such complex idea as these, in men's minds, do these two names of different substances, flame and gold, stand for. When we would know anything further concerning these, or any other sort of substances, what do we inquire, but what *other* qualities or powers these substances have or have not? Which is nothing else but to know what *other* simple ideas do or do not co-exist with those made up of this complex idea.[44]

This knowledge of secondary qualities leaves us in the dark about any necessary connections that may link primary and secondary qualities or any possible connections among the secondary qualities of a particular substance.[45] As a consequence of our ignorance—our "want of ideas," our "want of a discoverable connexion between the ideas we have," and a "want of tracing and discovering our ideas,"[46]—what we can know of the world with certainty is limited to tautologies and to demonstrative truths such as those of mathematics.[47]

It follows, for Locke, that natural philosophy, relying as it must on empirical methods, cannot give us certain knowledge of the world. Empirical knowledge, the science of appearances, is useful: It broadens and even deepens our knowledge of the properties of bodies. But in the end it cannot penetrate to their essences. And Locke concluded that for these reasons, *"natural philosophy is not capable of being made a science."*[48] Lack of certainty, however, did not cause Locke to relapse into sceptical despair. Much in the spirit of the earlier theologians who argued that moral certainty, though inferior to the absolute certainty which is the private reserve of the Deity, is an adequate basis for the decisions of both practical life and religious doctrine, Locke argued that in the absence of certainty, probable knowledge is adequate to our needs in this life. We can know enough to get along in the world, and natural philosophy is a worthwhile pursuit, both for utilitarian and morally uplifting reasons. But we must once and for all abandon hope of attaining a science of nature that will give us certainty.

Locke's probabilism was far more sceptical about the possible achievements of science than the methodological optimism of the physicists. Locke's sceptical ideas grew out of theological discussions about the rule of faith while the physicists' optimism developed from the realism of Copernicus and his followers. These differences emerged in their respective attitudes toward the mechanical philosophy. Both agreed that observational science lacks the certainty of deductive science. They differed in their choice of subject-matter—the physicists dealing with primary qualities and Locke concerning himself with the science of secondary qualities. A point of potentially more substantive disagreement between them never arose, namely the question of whether mechanics is really an *a priori* science or whether it, in the end, has empirical roots. That question was to be raised by a later age.

III

Claiming that probable knowledge is the best that scientific methods can attain is one thing; examining in depth the meanings of probability and justifying the methods of science are quite another. The attempt to justify inductive inference arose only later, in the philosophy of David Hume (1711-1776). Hume's stated goal was to penetrate beyond mere description of the processes and products of the human mind to "discover, at least in some degree, the secret springs and principles, by which the human mind is actuated in its operations." He compared himself to Newton in this regard, who had not been content to describe the phenomena of astronomy, but had sought out the "laws and forces, by which the revolutions of the planets are governed and directed."[49] In seeking the foundation of human knowledge, Hume developed the critical tools which enabled him to formulate questions about the justification of empirical methods and to examine the epistemological basis of the science of his day.

Hume moved the discussion forward on two fronts: he looked critically at the traditional distinction between primary and secondary qualities and found it inadequate as a basis for scientific knowledge; and he continued the discussion of probability and the logic of belief, shifting the grounds of the argument from a question of description—what are the origins of probable knowledge?—to one of justification—what kind of warrant can we give non-demonstrative inferences? By denying the validity of the distinction between primary and secondary qualities, Hume implied that all of the sciences—mechanics as well as the experimental sciences—share the same epistemological base. Then, by raising the problem of justifying inductive methods, he claimed that the truth of these sciences cannot be guaranteed.

Hume's views of the nature of scientific knowledge rested on the dual assumptions that all scientific knowledge depends on the empirical knowledge of cause and effect, and that all empirical knowledge is contingent since "Whatever *is* may *not be*. No negation of a fact can involve a contradiction. . . ."[50] These assumptions underlie both his criticism of the doctrine of primary and secondary qualities and his formulation of the problems of induction.

Traditionally, primary qualities had been distinguished from secondary qualities on the grounds that primary qualities are permanent, real attributes of bodies, while secondary qualities do not "exist in the objects themselves, but are perceptions of the mind, without any external archetype or model, which they represent."[51] Locke had said that the primary qualities are further distinguished by the fact that our ideas of primary qualities actually resemble the qualities in bodies.[52]

Hume denied that there is any real difference between the two kinds of qualities: If the secondary qualities are held to be only in the mind, the same must be said of primary qualities. He showed that we cannot form ideas of primary qualities without having recourse to secondary qualities; e.g., we have no idea of extension apart from color or other secondary qualities.[53] Thus, in the end, the primary qualities are just as much derived from the senses as the secondary.[54] Aside from the sensible qualities, there is nothing in the universe.[55] Furthermore, Locke's criterion of resemblance between primary qualities and our perceptions of them cannot be defended. Sensations are of a different order of existence from objects, and the two things cannot properly be said to resemble each other. Moreover, if we consider an example of an alleged primary quality, say solidity, it is clear that the quality in the body remains constantly the same whereas the impressions of touch vary markedly with the circumstances of touching.[56] Thus, it is not the case that primary qualities resemble our perceptions of them.

If there is not a viable epistomological distinction between primary and secondary qualities, what happens to the special status the science of mechanics was supposed to enjoy in contrast to the obviously empirical sciences? Clearly, one implication of Hume's argument is that all the sciences share the same epistemological status. The claim of a special status for mechanics had been grounded in the fact that its subject–matter was confined to the realm of primary qualities. With that ground eliminated, mechanics must share the same empirical basis as the other sciences.

How did Hume deal with epistemological foundations of the empirical sciences? His early work, the *Treatise of Human Nature: Being an Attempt to Introduce the Experimental Method of Reasoning into Moral Subjects* (1739), remained descriptive and empirical in approach. "... as the science of man is the only solid foundation for the other sciences, so the only foundation we can give this science itself must be laid on experience and observation."[57] At this point, Hume's empiricism was no more critical than Locke's in the sense that he saw no need to examine the logical or epistemological foundations of empirical methods; to describe them was sufficient.[58] This is notably true of his discussion of probability and knowledge which occupies over one hundred pages of the book. His concern was to show how different kinds and degrees of evidence support different degrees of probability and belief, and he did this entirely in terms of the relative intensity of the impressions produced in our minds by different varieties of evidence.

In the *Enquiry*, Hume went beyond the descriptive task of the *Treatise* to raise the question of how we can justify reasoning from past experience to the future, from the observed to the unobserved. He not only acknowledged that science had adopted a new theory of knowledge, he went beyond Locke's descriptive approach to ask what kinds of epistemological foundations such a science can have, and this question led him to the problem of induction. Hume's statement of the problem is well known. It begins with the assumption that all our knowledge of matters of fact is contingent, for "The contrary of every matter of fact is still possible; because it can never imply a contradiction, and is conceived by the mind with the same facility and distinctness, as if ever so conformable to reality."[59] If matters of fact are contingent, how can we reason from observed facts to those as yet unobserved? All our reasonings about matters of fact are based on the relation of cause and effect. A critical analysis of the causal relation, however, reveals that there is no necessary connection discernible between cause and effect; all we find is the habit of our minds, the product of observing the constant conjunction of similar kinds of events over long periods of time.[60] Our reasonings are confined to observations of constant conjunctions. Nothing more is possible. Thus, the causal relation is ultimately based on experience.[61] It is the justification of this inference from experience—the basis of the methods of empirical science—that Hume undertook to explore.

How then can we justify inductive reasoning? We cannot provide a demonstrative justification, because it is always logically possible that in the next instance the future will not resemble the past; that is to say, matters of fact are synthetic propositions, and are not tautological. On the other hand, appeal to experience will result in circular reasoning.[62]

Hume claimed that all we can say by way of resolution to this problem is that the constant conjunctions we experience create in us a sense of expectation that the next instance will be like the past. Consequently, all science, which is based on empirical knowledge, has a fundamentally different epistemological status from that of demonstrative, deductive knowledge. There can be no guarantees of its truth.

And this brings us back to our starting point, the apparently paradoxical fact that the philosophers of science of the eighteenth-century emphasized the probabilistic aspects of scientific knowledge in the face of the astonishing success and optimism of the mathematical physicists. Where the physicists saw an increasingly powerful tool for understanding and predicting the phenomena of nature, Hume perceived the fundamental uncertainty of all human knowledge.

It is confessed, that the utmost effort of human reason is to reduce the principles, productive of natural phenomena, to a greater simplicity, and to resolve the many particular effects into a few general causes, by means of reasonings from analogy, experience, and observation. But as to the causes of these general causes, we should in vain attempt their discovery, nor shall we ever be able to satisfy ourselves by any particular explication of them. These ultimate springs and principles are totally shut up from human curiosity and inquiry. Elasticity, gravity, cohesion of parts, communication of motion by impulse; these are probably the ultimate causes and principles which we shall ever discover in nature; and we may esteem ourselves sufficiently happy, if by accurate enquiry and reasoning we can trace up the particular phenomena to, or near to, these general principles. The most perfect philosophy of the natural kind only staves off our ignorance a little longer: as perhaps the most perfect philosophy of the moral or metaphysical kind serves only to discover larger portions of it. Thus the observation of human blindness and weakness is the result of all philosophy, and meets us at every turn, in spite of our endeavours to elude or avoid it.[63]

The fact is that for Hume a science based on appearances can never penetrate into the real essences of things and yield necessary laws of nature. The predictive successes of the empirical sciences could in no way affect the truth of this insight. Laplace might speculate about an all-knowing intelligence whose knowledge would range over the entire universe and all of history, but, if this intelligence had to rely on empirical evidence— and how else would he know positions and forces?—even he could not penetrate into the "secret springs and principles" producing these phenomena. Nor could he justify his claims to such knowledge until he could provide a solution to Hume's problem of induction.

The eighteenth-century witnessed the triumph of rational mechanics, but it also witnessed a rising interest in probability— both as a philosophy of knowledge and as a mathematical theory. Faced with the probabilistic character of scientific knowledge and the problematic status of its foundations, it is no wonder that the same Laplace who enunciated the classic statement of optimism about physics was the very man who undertook pioneering studies in the newly developing mathematical theory of probability. Writing once again about his all-knowing intelligence, Laplace compared the knowledge such an intelligence would have with the imperfect and uncertain state of human knowledge.

> Physical astronomy, that subject of all our understanding most worthy of the human spirit, offers us an idea, albeit imperfect, of what such an intelligence would be. The simplicity of the laws that make celestial bodies move, the relationship of their masses and their distances allow us to follow their motion through analysis, up to a certain point, and in order to determine the state of the system of these large bodies in past or future centuries, it is enough for the mathematician that observation provide him with their positions and speeds at any given instant. Man has this advantage because of the power of the instrument he uses and of the small number of relations he employs in his calculations; but the ignorance of the diverse causes that produce the events and their complication joined to the imperfection of analysis prevent him from making assertions with the same certitude on most phenomena. For him, therefore, there are many things that are uncertain, and some that are more or less probable. In view of the impossibility of really knowing them, he has tried to compensate for this by determining different degrees of appearance, so that we owe to the feebleness of the human spirit one of the most delicate and ingenious of mathematical theories, the science of chance or probability.[64]

The same Laplace who marvelled at the determinism of nature recognized the limits of human knowledge. "Strictly speaking it may even be said that *nearly all our knowledge* is problematical; and in the small number of things which we are able to know with certainty, even in the mathematical sciences themselves, the principal means for ascertaining truth—induction and analogy—are based on probabilities. . . ."[65]

That physics could achieve remarkable results is one thing; whether man can penetrate into the inmost secrets of nature is quite another. The critical tools developed by Hume, particularly his distinction between the *origins* of knowledge and its *justification*, allowed even Laplace to acknowledge that the most astonishing successes of mechanics could not transcend its fundamentally empirical foundations; and insofar as its foundations are empirical, to that extent certainty is elusive. Beginning, for historical reasons, by regarding the mechanical philosophy from opposing standpoints, the physicists and philosophers formulated opposing views of the kind of knowledge that science can achieve. The differences, however, turned out to be illusory, a fact which could only be recognized after sufficiently powerful analytical tools had been developed in philosophy. The same philosophy of nature which led men to boast of the depths to which science could penetrate ultimately led them to recognize the limits of knowledge.

Notes

1. The scope of this paper is limited to the study of a few examples. To take account of all the complexities would require a much longer study. Thus, among the physicists, one would need to sort out the Newtonian, Cartesian, and Leibnizian positions, their differences and interactions. Similarly, an adequate account of the various philosophical schools would involve not only an account of the British empiricists presented here—with the notable exception of Berkeley—but also an examination of the rationalist strands. Despite the inherent limitations of the examples considered in this paper, I think the basic thesis is sound with regard to the central role of the distinction between primary and secondary qualities in defining the two attitudes toward scientific knowledge. As support for this contention, consider the fact that the thesis applies to both MacLaurin and d'Alembert, despite the fact that their ideas developed from very different aspects of the traditions mentioned above.

2. For an interesting discussion of the varieties of seventeenth-century theories about primary and secondary qualities, see John J. MacIntosh, "Primary and Secondary Qualities," *Studia Leibnitiana*, 8 (1976), 88-104.

3. René Descartes, *Principles of Philosophy*, Part II, Propositions XLV-LII. *Oeuvres de Descartes*, edited by Charles Adam and Paul Tannery (Paris: Librairie Philosophique J. Vrin, 1964), Vol. IX, pp. 89-93.

4. Richard S. Westfall, *Force in Newton's Physics* (New York: American Elsevier, 1971), pp. 146-158.

5. This follows from Newton's deriving the laws of impact from his three "Laws of Motion" in which the basic physical parameters are motion and force (mass and change of motion). Isaac Newton, *Mathematical Principles of Natural Philosophy*, translated by Andrew Motte and revised by Florian Cajori (Berkeley: University of California Press, 1962), p. 13.

6. Colin MacLaurin, *An Account of Sir Isaac Newton's Philosophical Discoveries* (Hildesheim: Georg Olms, 1971). Original edition, 1748), p. 2.

7. Ibid., pp. 183-196.

8. Ibid., p. 100.

9. Ibid., p. 183.

10. Ibid., pp. 103-104.

11. Ibid., p. 98.

12. For a lucid discussion of the eighteenth-century substitution of the "esprit systematique" for the love of system for its own sake that had characterized seventeenth-century thought, see Ernst Cassirer, *The Philosophy of the Enlightenment*, translated by Fritz C. A. Koelln and James P. Pettegrove (Boston: Beacon Press, 1951), esp. Chapter I. See also Robert Kargon, "Newton, Barrow, and the Hypothetical Physics," *Centaurus*, 11 (1965), 46-56.

13. MacLaurin, op. cit., p. 9.

14. Ibid., pp. 9-10.

15. For a thorough analysis of d'Alembert's methods, goals, and achievements, see Thomas L. Hankins, *Jean d'Alembert: Science and the Enlightenment* (Oxford: Clarendon Press, 1970). Hankins discusses in detail the Cartesian and Newtonian aspects of d'Alembert's science. See esp. Chapters I, II, V, VII, and VIII.

16. Jean d'Alembert, *Preliminary Discourse to the Encyclopedia of Diderot*, translated by Richard N. Schwab and Walter Rex (Indianapolis: Bobbs-Merrill, 1963), pp. 24-26, 43-44; *Traité de dynamique* (Paris: 1743), pp. i-ii.

17. *Preliminary Discourse*, p. 29.

18. *Traité de dynamique*, p. iii.

19. Ibid., p. 3.

20. Ibid., pp. v-vi.

21. Ibid., pp. xiv-xv; Hankins, op. cit., p. 185.

22. *Traité de dynamique*, p. 25.

23. Ibid., pp. xi-xii.

24. Pierre Simon, Marquis de Laplace, *A Philosophical Essay on Probabilities*, translated from the 6th French edition by F. W. Truscott and F. L. Emory (New York: Dover Publications, 1951), p. 4.

25. Henry Guerlac, "Where the Statue Stood: Divergent Loyalties to Newton in the Eighteenth Century," in Earl R. Wasserman, editor, *As-*

pects of the Eighteenth Century (Baltimore: Johns Hopkins University Press, 1965), p. 333.

26. Richard H. Popkin, *The History of Scepticism from Erasmus to Descartes* (revised edition, New York: The Humanities Press, 1964), Chapter 1. Of course there were earlier traditions in philosophy that focused on the probabilistic character of scientific knowledge; but the thought of Locke and Hume seems to have been most directly influenced by the theological debates issuing from the Reformation. For some of the earlier probabilistic views, see: Pierre Duhem, *To Save the Phenomena: An Essay on the Idea of Physical Theory from Plato to Galileo*, translated by Edmund Doland and Chaninah Maschler (Chicago: University of Chicago Press, 1969; first published 1908); Edward Grant, "Hypotheses in Late Medieval and Early Modern Science," *Daedalus*, 91 (1962), 500-516.

27. E. G. Theodore Beza, Calvin's associate, maintained that one needed a sure and infallible sign; subjective certainty would not suffice: this sign is "ful perswasion, [which] doth separate the chosen children of God from the castawayes, and is the proper riches of the Saintes." *A Discourse of the True and Visible Markes of the Catholique Churche* (London: 1582), 44th page, unnumbered, as cited by Popkin, op. cit., p. 9. The alternatives were sharp and clear: salvation or damnation, certainty or scepticism. There was no middle road. Many Catholic defenders of the faith adopted a similar position, claiming that because our personal perceptions and reasonings are vulnerable to sceptical arguments, the only option we have is faith: faith in scripture as interpreted by the authority of the Church.

28. Sebastian Castellio, a Calvinist who defended Servetus, adopted this position in his book *De Haereticis* (Magdeburgh: 1554) and *De Arte Dubitandi* which was not published in his lifetime. See Popkin, op. cit., pp. 9ff.

29. John Locke, *An Essay Concerning Human Understanding*, edited by Alexander Campbell Fraser (New York: Dover Publications, 1959), Vol. I, p. 30. Locke was an immediate heir to these ideas.

30. This tradition is described in the very useful book by Henry G. Van Leeuwen, *The Problem of Certainty in English Thought: 1630-1660* (The Hague: Martinus Nijhoff, 1963). Van Leeuwen focuses his discussion on the writings of William Chillingworth (1602-1643), John Tillotson (1630-1694), John Wilkins (1614-1672), and Joseph Glanvill (1636-1680), as well as Boyle, Newton, and Locke. William Chillingworth, for example, agreed that although the Scriptures are the perfect rule of faith, there is no assurance that the rule has been properly applied when it is invoked to settle theological questions. The possibility of error in application means that we can never know for sure whether our knowledge is absolutely certain. Chillingworth believed that all knowledge has some

measure of certainty; and he described these degrees of certainty as follows:
1. Absolute infallible certainty: this is the kind of certainty Descartes
sought in the *Meditations,* a certainty which excludes every possibility
of doubt. Such knowledge is the preserve of God alone and cannot be
attained by mortal man.
2. Conditionally infallible certainty, or mathematical certainty: although not the absolute certainty enjoyed by the Deity, this is the
highest degree of certainty available to man and characterizes mathematics and other demonstrative knowledge. This is characteristic of knowing, in contrast to belief or opinion; assent to such knowledge is compelled rather than voluntary.
3. Moral certainty: this characterizes belief as opposed to knowledge.
Error is possible, but any sane, reasonable person, having considered all
the evidence for and against a proposition, knows its truth with a moral
certainty in proportion to the kind and amount of evidence in its favor.
It is with moral certainty that we accept or reject courses of action in daily
life; and it is with similar assurance that we can decide the questions of religion. Lack of absolute certainty is no more grounds for religious scepticism than it is grounds for inaction in daily life. Van Leeuwen, pp. 20–31.

31. The ideas of these writers were influential on legal philosophy as
well as the philosophy of science. See Theodore Waldman, "Origins of the
Legal Doctrine of Reasonable Doubt," *Journal of the History of Ideas,* 20
(1959), 299–316; and Barbara J. Shapiro, "Law and Science in Seventeenth-
Century England," *Stanford Law Review,* 21(1969), 727–766.

32. R. Hooykaas, *Religion and the Rise of Modern Science* (Grand
Rapids, Michigan: William Erdmans Publishing Company, 1972), fully
articulates this argument. Francis Oakley, "Christian Theology and the
Newtonian Science: The Rise of the Concept of the Laws of Nature,"
Church History, 30(1961), 433–457, traces these voluntarist ideas back
to the Nominalist philosophers of the fourteenth century. Also pertinent is
Laurens Laudan, "The Clock Metaphor and Probabilism: The Impact of
Descartes on English Methodological Thought, 1650–1665," *Annals of
Science,* 22(1966), 73–104.

33. I have argued elsewhere that Locke's *Essay* can, from one standpoint, be regarded as a philosophical analysis of seventeenth-century
science. *John Locke and Some Philosophical Problems in the Science of
Boyle and Newton,* unpublished dissertation (Bloomington, Indiana:
1968).

34. For Locke and certainty, see my article, "John Locke and the
Changing Ideal of Scientific Knowledge," *Journal of the History of Ideas,*
31(1970), 3–16.

35. "Were it fit to trouble thee with the history of this *Essay*, I should tell thee, that five or six friends, meeting at my chamber, and discoursing on a subject very remote from this, found themselves quickly at a stand, by the differences that arose on every side." *Essay*, Vol. I, p. 9.

36. Ibid., p. 14.

37. Ibid., Vol. II, pp. 167–168.

38. Ibid., Vol. II, pp. 176–178.

39. Ibid., Vol. II, p. 185.

40. Ibid., Vol. II, p. 185.

41. ". . . with me, to know and to be certain, is the same thing; what I know, that I am certain of; and what I am certain of, that I know. What reaches to knowledge, I think may be called certainty; and what comes short of certainty, I think cannot be called knowledge." Letter to Stillingfleet, June 29, 1697. *The Works of John Locke* (10th edition, London: 1801), Vol. IV, p. 145.

42. John Locke, *Essay*, Vol. II, p. 200.

43. Ibid., Book II, Chapter 8 contains Locke's full discussion of primary and secondary qualities.

44. Ibid., Vol. II, pp. 199–200.

45. Ibid., Vol. II, p. 205.

46. Ibid., Vol. II, p. 213.

47. Locke also believed that the principles of morality could be deduced from axioms in the manner of mathematics. "Upon this ground it is that I am bold to think that morality is capable of demonstration, as well as mathematics: since the precise real essence of the things moral words stand for may be perfectly known, and so the congruity and incongruity of the things themselves be certainly discovered; in which consists perfect knowledge," Ibid., Vol. II, pp. 156–157.

48. Ibid., Vol. II, p. 350.

49. David Hume, *Enquiries Concerning the Human Understanding and Concerning the Principles of Morals*, reprinted from the posthumous edition of 1777, edited etc., by Selby Bigge (2nd edition, Oxford: The Clarendon Press, 1961), p. 14.

50. Ibid., pp. 163–164.

51. Ibid., p. 154.

52. John Locke, *Essay*, Vol. I, pp. 179-181.

53. David Hume, *A Treatise of Human Nature* (London: 1739), pp. 228-230.

54. Hume, *Enquiry*, p. 154.

55. Hume, *Treatise*, p. 231.

56. Ibid., p. 231.

57. Ibid., p. xx.

58. Ibid., p. xx. Keith Michael Baker discusses this point in depth. See his important book, *Condorcet: From Natural Philosophy to Social Mathematics* (Chicago: University of Chicago Press, 1975), especially the section entitled "Positivism and Probabilities." James Noxon, *Hume's Philosophical Development: A Study of His Methods* (Oxford: Clarendon Press, 1973), details Hume's changing approach. Noxon also provides some useful background on Hume's knowledge of Newton's writings and their impact on his philosophical development.

59. Hume, *Enquiry*, p. 25.

60. Ibid., Chapter VII. Despite his extensive critique of the concept of cause and his denial that there is any evidence for the existence of necessary connections in nature, Hume maintained a deterministic view of nature itself, a view which he shared with the scientists. "It is universally allowed that nothing exists without a cause of its existence, and that chance, when strictly examined, is a mere negative word, and means not any real power which has any where a being in nature." *Enquiry*, p. 95. He makes a similar assertion in the *Treatise*, p. 132.

61. Hume, *Enquiry*, p. 32.

62. Ibid., pp. 35-36.

63. Ibid., pp. 30-31.

64. Pierre Simon, Marquis de Laplace, "Researches on the integration of differential equations of finite differences, and on their use in the theory of chances," quoted and translated by Roger Hahn, "Laplace as a Newtonian Scientist," (Los Angeles: William Andrews Clark Memorial Library, 1967), p. 16.

65. Laplace, *A Philosophical Essay on Probabilities*, p. 1. My italics.

The Odds Against Friday: Defoe, Bayes, and Inverse Probability

Paul K. Alkon

The footprint terrifies Crusoe. During a sleepless night following its discovery, he wonders if it might be supernatural: "Sometimes I fancy'd it must be the Devil; and Reason joyn'd in with me upon this Supposition: For how should any other Thing in human shape come into the Place? Where was the Vessel that brought them? What marks was there of any other Footsteps? And how was it possible a Man should come there?"[1] The seeming impossibility of any person leaving a *single* footprint provides rational as well as fanciful ("I fancy'd . . . Reason joyn'd") grounds for Crusoe's first hypothesis. By an event which intuitively appears impossible, Defoe arouses every reader's curiosity to the maximum degree, thus quickening the narrative pace by directing attention forward to the solution of a mystery. Less mystery, and therefore also less suspense and a slower acceleration of pace would have resulted from an event—say, two footprints, or a trail of footprints—that merely seemed improbable, or else probable in some degree that could be specified. In a book whose title-page promises a story filled with "Strange Surprising Adventures," the footprint is the most surprising. *Ad-*

venture meant "chance, accidental encounter, hazard; also an extraordinary or surprizing Enterprise."[2] The footprint is both extraordinary and surprising. But while it is regarded as something not "possible a Man should come there" to leave, there is no ready way to decide whether Crusoe's encounter with it is the result of chance or design.

Defoe builds this episode upon a distinction between what is possible and thus admits degrees of probability, and what is impossible and therefore does not. But no degrees of probability are estimated in Crusoe's next speculation: "Then to think that *Satan* should take human Shape upon him in such a Place where there could be no manner of Occasion for it, but to leave the Print of his Foot behind him, and that even for no Purpose too, for he could not be sure I should see it; this was an Amusement the other Way; I consider'd that the Devil might have found out abundance of other ways to have terrify'd me than this of the single Print of a Foot" (154–155). Crusoe assumes that frightening him is proper work for the Devil. Unlike Captain Singleton's group marching across Africa unable to suppose that Satan might have business with *their* souls, or find it worthwhile to visit such a thinly populated region, Crusoe understands that even one soul might justify Satan's journey to some out-of-the-way place.[3] The idea is not improbable. There were grounds for Crusoe's belief.[4] And even after the idea of a diabolical visitation has been rejected, Crusoe's terror efficiently performs Satan's work: "Thus my Fear banish'd all my religious Hope; all that former Confidence in God which was founded upon such wonderful Experience as I had had of his Goodness, now vanished" (156). Crusoe's fear of the unlikely (or impossible) footprint leads to the interval of despair which is a major turning-point of *Robinson Crusoe*.

What enables Crusoe to rule out Satanic presence in only the thought that leaving one footprint would be pointless because "he could not be sure I should see it." The implication is clear. If Satan could have been sure, he might have adopted the strategy. Crusoe does not reject his initial hypotheses by directly stating the likelihood that Satan left the footprint. Instead, matters are considered from the Devil's point of view. To follow Crusoe's argument, readers must go backward in time to imagine how likely his *discovery* of the footprint would have seemed before it occurred. We see that the prior probability was not high. But our confidence in that estimate may be rattled by awareness that Crusoe does discover the footprint. Yet Defoe leaves no doubt that Satan would have governed himself by estimating the likelihood that Crusoe would pass near the footprint during his random walk.

Crusoe's next statement shifts from the vocabulary of intuitive or quasi-philosophical probability discussions to the language of numerical calculations associated first with games of chance, and then more closely with mathematical theories of probability: "As I liv'd quite on the other Side of the Island, he would never have been so simple to leave a Mark in a Place where 'twas Ten Thousand to one whether I should ever see it or not, and in the Sand too, which the first Surge of the Sea upon a high Wind would have defac'd entirely: All this seem's inconsistent with the Thing it self, and with all the Notions we usually entertain of the Subtilty of the Devil" (155). Details about the footprint's precarious location incline readers to accept these odds. Nor does anything ever call them in question. Yet Crusoe not only discovers the footprint: It is still there five days later when he goes back for another look. Defoe makes the low probability of its discovery and survival appear valid, while also building into the narrative a reminder that even the most accurate odds do not predict particular cases. These odds are given in a context that underscores their dubious utility. But Defoe takes for granted that such doubts would not have troubled Satan.

Crusoe assumes that Satan will calculate the odds, that he can do so, and that he will act accordingly. Thus for him, to borrow a phrase that Bishop Butler might not wish to lend, probability is the very guide of life. The arch probabilist is Satan. A willingness to be guided by working out the probabilities is part of his notorious "Subtilty." Probabilistic thinking—and acting—is thus in his case a character trait associated with his worst flaws. The universe would be a better place without Satanic varieties of subtlety, perhaps including an inclination to work out the odds beforehand as a basis for conduct.

If this proposition is debatable, the issues involved are at least dealt with by Defoe in ways that vanish from the more comfortable assumptions underlying the work of such mathematical probabilists as Laplace. He opens his *Philosophical Essay on Probabilities* as well as the 1812 dedication (to Napoleon) of his *Théorie Analytique Des Probabilités* with assurances that "the most important questions of life" are "indeed for the most part only problems of probability."[5] But what if they are not? The twentieth century has reconsidered that possibility. Our attempts to deal with the moral issues related to probabilistic reasoning are conveniently symbolized by Einstein's reluctance to admit that God plays at dice with the universe. But instead of providing a refutation of quantum mechanics, Einstein left only an aphorism suggesting that God and Satan differ morally yet must now be supposed to think alike: "God is subtle, but he is not malicious." Butler argued that God would have no use for the subtleties of probabilistic reasoning: "For nothing which is the possible object of knowledge, whether past, present, or future, can be probable to an infinite Intelligence; since it cannot but be discerned absolutely as it is in itself."[6]

Here Butler speaks for the main stream of Western thought up to the moment when quantum mechanics displaced previous paradigms. It is hard to find many philosophers in the lonely tradition of Rabbi Levi Ben Gershon, who deviated from *all* fourteenth-century orthodoxies by maintaining that in some areas God's knowledge is only probable.[7] Now, however, even an Oxford don is not joining any lost cause when he argues that "Perfect information may be unattainable even in principle; indeed quantum mechanics seems to demand just this, and we may be compelled to believe that objective probabilities do exist, and cannot be accounted for simply in terms of our subjective lack of perfect information. . . . And if we . . . maintain that they do, we must be prepared to pay a considerable price in the alterations we shall have to make to our view of the world."[8] Part of that price is abandonment of the idea that, because time is conceptually reversible, retrodiction may be as valid as prediction. To illustrate the moral consequences of this loss, I will explore Defoe's resort to the language of probability.

Explicit Probability

Defoe's brilliant adventure of the single footprint shows that if Satan had worked out the odds and then acted accordingly, he would have missed a perfect opportunity. Although Crusoe's despair reminds us that modern man will do Satan's work for him, the footprint's discovery against long odds nevertheless underscores the unreliability of probability as a guide to the future. So, by their very unpredictability, do many of Crusoe's other adventures. But this point would be lost on Satan—or anyone in the Satanic predicament of being cut off from God and left to rely only on the calculation of probabilities as a basis for conduct. In *The History of the Devil*, Defoe explains that "the Devil has no knowledge of events, or any insight into futurity; nay . . . he has not so much as a second sight, or knows today what his Maker intends to do tomorrow."[9] The Devil is "blind, short-sighted . . . perfectly in the dark, and unaquainted with futurity."[10] So are people: Thus far also Bishop Butler in explaining why our knowledge (like Satan's, though Butler avoids the comparison) must be only probable. But, unlike Satan, people may trust in God. He may be on their side, but will not help Satan, who is thus left to his own mathematical devices.

These differences are illustrated by Crusoe's encounter with Friday. Well before the event, Crusoe decides (mistakenly) that his only hope of leaving the island is to acquire a cooperative native: "my only Way to go about an Attempt for an Escape, was, if possible, to get a Savage into my Possession" (199). What prompts this conclusion is a dream (prophetic, as it turns out) of rescuing a native. The dream comes just after an intensification of Crusoe's longing for "some-body to speak to, and to learn some Knowledge from of the Place where I was, and of the probable Means of my Deliverance" (198). Unable without more geographical information to form any probable plan of escape, Crusoe finds that he cannot even figure out some probable way—much less calculate the odds—of capturing a native: "I resolv'd, if possible, to get one of those Savages into my Hands, cost what it would. My next Thing then was to contrive how to do it, and this indeed was very difficult to resolve on: But as I could pitch upon no probable Means for it, so I resolv'd to put my self upon the Watch, to see them when they came on Shore, and leave the rest to the Event, taking such Measures as the Opportunity should present, let be what would be" (200). Crusoe puts matters into the hands of Providence by leaving things "to the Event." While rescuing Friday, Crusoe assumes (correctly) that he "was call'd plainly by Providence to save this poor Creature's Life" (202). Before the rescue, Crusoe's measures are rational, but explicitly distinguished from a plan whose chance of success can be estimated in advance. There are "no probable Means" available, and therefore no ways of calculating the odds. Unless one infers that the probability of getting Friday was zero, which is belied by what happens, his rescue can only be described as an event for which there were no available odds either way. More to Defoe's point, Crusoe never speculates on the odds against Friday.

But he might have. In his first trading voyage, before being stranded on his island in 1659, Crusoe "got a competent Knowledge of the Mathematicks" (17). If this includes any smattering of the doctrine of chances, then Crusoe's mathematical education is another of Defoe's many anachronisms. They are not a problem that concerns this discussion. But the text is vague on the exact nature of what Crusoe studied. Wherever he acquired the ability, however, he is able to consider the odds, and does so twice on his own behalf as well as once from Satan's point of view.

Thus after Crusoe has settled down to a comfortable life, thanks to material salvaged from the wreck, he meditates on his situation: "Then it occur'd to me again, how well I was furnish'd for my Subsistence, and what would have been my Case, if it had not happen'd, *Which was an Hundred Thousand to one*, that the Ship floated from the Place where she first struck and was driven so near to the Shore that I had time to get all these Things out of her" (63). Later Crusoe mentions that during his third year on the island he often thought of escaping to the South American mainland where he "might find some Way or other to convey my self farther, and perhaps at last find some means of Escape" (124). But he did not sufficiently consider the odds against survival: "All this while I made no Allowance for the Dangers of such a Condition, and how I might fall into the Hands of Savages . . . That if I once came into their Power, I should run a Hazard more than a thousand to one of being kill'd, and perhaps of being eaten. . . . All these Things, I say, which I ought to have consider'd well of, and did cast up in my Thoughts afterwards, yet took up none of my Apprehensions at first, but my Head run mightily upon the Thought of getting over to the Shore" (124). These rash plans are of a piece with the impulsiveness that causes so many of Crusoe's problems.

But on the island he works hard and is protected by that Providence which he gradually comes to understand. In the context of his spiritual growth, Crusoe's lack of calculation appears harmless or even beneficial. There was no point in figuring the odds for the ship's reappearance before it happened. Nor did Crusoe think of computing the chances of that possibility. He merely assumed (mistakenly) that everything on board was lost. Yet that miscalculation—or noncalculation—does not prevent energetic steps to salvage what does turn up. Nor does it matter that he neglected to "cast up" the odds when trying to formulate a plan for going to the mainland. Circumstances keep him safely on the island. What does matter is Crusoe's ability to look back upon events and figure out probabilities: the greater than thousand-to-one odds are "cast up in my Thoughts afterwards;" he later realizes exactly how unlikely it was that the ship would be driven close to the shore. Appreciation of these odds enhances Crusoe's awareness that despite initial appearances, things worked out better than he had any (mathematical) right to expect. The Providential pattern of Crusoe's life is also more visible to readers in proportion to their understanding of the odds against his survival.

It is almost as if Defoe were dramatizing one point that Abraham de Moivre wished to make in the previous year when he published *The Doctrine of Chances.* In his dedication to Isaac Newton, de Moivre hopes that by giving "certain rules, for estimating how far some sort of Events may rather be owing to Design than Chance," the book might encourage readers to pursue "these Studies" and also learn from Newton's philosophy "how to collect, by a just Calculation, the Evidences of exquisite Wisdom and Design, which appear in the *Phenomena* of Nature throughout the Universe." This interest in bolstering arguments from design is directed at the establishment of natural laws, of course, rather than toward the appreciation of unlikely events in individual lives. Nor is there any such personal application suggested in de Moivre's example of two piquet decks with "from Top to Bottom, the same Disposition of the Cards in both Packs." Whether the disposition "ought to be attributed to Chance, or to the Maker's Design" is decided in favor of design by the "Doctrine of Combination," which shows that "there are the Odds of above 26313083 Millions of Millions of Millions of Millions to One, that the Cards were designedly set in the Order in which they were found."[11]

The rhetorical impact of these odds is clear enough. Nor would de Moivre's point be much strengthened for non-mathematicians by including the calculations behind his odds. Like Crusoe, de Moivre here omits computations, perhaps because they would only distract from his philosophical argument about the more general applications of probability theory. Nor does de Moivre state the exact odds; he only gives a minimum figure and suggests that the odds are in fact even greater. De Moivre's next sentence is confusing in its mention of increasing probabilities, though otherwise easy: "From this last Consideration we may learn, in many Cases, how to distinguish the Events which are the effect of Chance, from those which are produc'd by Design: The very Doctrine that finds chance where it really is, being able to prove by a gradual Increase of Probability, till it arrives at Demonstration, that where Uniformity, Order and Constancy reside, there also reside Choice and Design."[12] De

Moivre considers the small sample of two card decks. Crusoe reflects on the wider possibilities of human life. Defoe states odds for and against events, but provides a narrative context which allows readers to infer design. De Moivre explicitly calculates the odds favoring design. He is concerned with sequential events. Defoe suggests the odds on single events that do not (at first) appear connected. Crusoe never applies the doctrine of combinations, although it might help Defoe's readers.

De Moivre's example of the two piquet decks is the final gambit of an argument against superstitious belief in luck. The most general point illustrated by the huge odds in favor of the decks being designedly stacked is that "the same Arguments which explode the Notion of Luck, may, on the other side, be useful in some Cases to establish a due comparison between Chance and Design: We may imagine Chance and Design to be as it were in Competition with each other, for the production of some sorts of Events, and may calculate what Probability there is, that those Events should be rather owing to one than to the other.[13] Here it is useful to juxtapose a remark of John Calvin's that has been accepted as serving equally to express Defoe's rejection of superstitious belief in luck: "Fortune and Chance are heathen terms. . . . For if all success is blessing from God, and calamity and adversity are his curse, there is no place left in human affairs for "Fortune and Chance."[14] De Moivre's dismissal of luck is the prelude for exploration of the doctrine of chances. It is also a consequence of that doctrine. But Calvin's dismissal of fortune and chance," with their implications of a random universe, does not preclude a worthy role for the mathematical doctrine of chances. Nor were non-Calvinistic branches of Christian thought hostile to mathematical theories of probability. Eighteenth-century optimism on this point is typified by de Moivre's persuasion that his and similar work would strengthen arguments from design. Where the Christian tradition makes a profound difference is in the temporal orientation of probabilistic reasoning.

The secular doctrine of chances mostly deals with the future. Attention is focused on what may happen. Benjamin Gal-Or states our twentieth-century conviction that "one can calculate the probability that something physical will happen but not the probability that something did happen."[15] Satosi Watanabe explains that "nature is predictable but irretrodictable. . . . This means that when we guess the past on the ground of the present, we are relying on something else than a (probabilistic) natural law. . . . [This] may seem to contradict our daily experience in which the future is uncertain and unpredictable while the past is fixed and recorded. This apparent paradox reflects precisely the point I am making. In the case of guessing the future, we are relying on the probability given by nature, while in the case of deciphering the past record, we are invoking knowledge of an entirely different kind. The former may be represented by a broad probability distribution, the latter by a narrow one. Mathematically speaking, this latter is based on the so-called inverse probability in the sense of Baysian process of hypothesis evaluation which involves 'prior credibilities' expressing *our* extra-evidential evaluation."[16] Thomas Bayes's *Essay Toward Solving a Problem In The Doctrine of Chances* was not published until 1763.[17]

By that time, Bayes lay buried with Defoe, Bunyan and other Nonconformists in Bunhill Fields. I do not mean to suggest that Defoe influenced Bayes. But it is reasonable to conjecture that their common religious tradition played some role in attracting Bayes to the problem of inverse probability. Although he (like Defoe) was educated for the Presbyterian ministry and (unlike Defoe) ordained, it may be—and this is what I do mean to suggest —that a strong Christian background as much as any specifically Dissenting beliefs provided a framework within which inverse probabilities would seem more attractive than they now do. We cannot get along without all the books of Bayesian statistical decision theory. But inverse probability grates on modern sensibilities.

J. R. Lucas points to one consequence of our discomfort with the indispensable contribution of Bayes: "Probable propositional functions, unlike true conditional propositions, are one-way-only in the inferences they license, because they are essentially in subject-predicate form and one cannot negate the subject in the way one can negate the predicate. The inverse argument by contraposition and exhaustion, which is available for functional dependences, is not available for probabilistic ones. They are not symmetrical, either as regards inferences, or, therefore, as regards time. And so we cannot expect to have time-reversibility when we are dealing with probabilistic concepts."[18] Involved here is our departure from Newtonian physics, where time is reversible to the extent that ($-t$) works in all equations just as well as ($+t$), with the result that retrodiction and predictions are considered equally valid. In the Newtonian universe, time's arrow is reversible.[19] Modern physics has postulated, and recently confirmed experimentally, the irreversibility of time's arrow.[20] Nothing in the twentieth-century world-view strongly encourages retrodictive probability statements.

This increasingly future-oriented concern with probability is reflected to some extent in the controversies over inverse probability, and is also illustrated in the eighteenth-century by differences between Locke and Hume. Neither deals with mathematical doctrines of chance. Both consider epistemological questions like those which (to do him some justice) also occupied Butler when he coined the aphorism that I have put to a use only warranted by hindsight. Locke mostly discusses ways of determining the probability that particular propositions are true. How, in the famous example, would the King of Siam decide what to make of an assertion that in Europe during the winter it is possible to walk on (frozen) water? Such problems are static insofar as they deal with propositions about what does exist or what did exist or even what can (at any given moment) be the case. Locke is mainly interested in matters of fact "and such things as are capable of observation and testimony."[21] What can be observed and testified to either does exist or has existed. In the eighteenth century, only Swift's mad speaker in *A Tale of A Tub* gave ontological primacy to the future:

"If we consider that the debate merely lies between things past and things conceived . . . the question is only this—whether things that have place in the imagination, may not as properly be said to exist, as those that are seated in memory, which may be justly held in the affirmative, and very much to the advantage of the former, since this is acknowledged to be the womb of things, and the other allowed to be no more than the grave."[22]

Hume's discussion assumes dynamic situations in which events occur through spans of time. He considers more explicitly than Locke what is involved in estimating the probability of future events. Hume explains how assumptions about the past are mobilized in every prediction: "all our reasonings concerning the probability of causes are founded on the transferring of past to future."[23] This transfer depends on the assumption that the future will resemble the past. Hume stresses temporal continuities, and his entire discussion displays more awareness of time as well as greater concern with questions about how the present relates to possible futures. Hume also considers the imaginative aspect of all reasoning, including predictive estimates of probability. He argues that probabilities work on the imagination "by producing a stronger and more lively view of" objects.[24] He explains why imagination is necessary: "if the transference of the past to the future were founded merely on a conclusion of the understanding, it could never occasion any belief of assurance. . . . Belief arises not merely from the transference of past to future, but from some operation of the fancy conjoined with it. This may lead us to conceive the manner in which that faculty enters into all our reasonings."[25] Hume's attention to the imaginative side of probabilistic reasoning points to issues that did not concern mathematicians. But the rhetoric of probability cannot be ignored in considering the literary applications *and backgrounds* of both mathematical and philosophical probability theories.

The numbers chosen by Defoe, for example, differ for imaginative purposes of rhetorical impact rather than for any reasons that are made to seem grounded on explicit—or even possible—mathematical calculations. We never learn how Crusoe decides that it is ten thousand to one against the footprint being discovered, more than a thousand to one against survival on the mainland, and an hundred thousand to one against the wreck floating close enough for salvage. These differing figures are appeals to every reader's intuitive scales of likelihood. Their impact depends upon what might now be called mathematically incoherent but nevertheless persuasive subjective probabilities.

Readers are inclined to accept these figures as valid statements of Crusoe's beliefs about the likelihood of each event. These beliefs—subjective probabilities—are then accepted (or at least not disputed) as valid statements about the probabilities actually involved in his—shall we say hypothetical or imaginary?—adventures. Defoe expects readers to accept Crusoe's estimates as the equivalent of objective probability statements.

Acceptance depends as much on the fact that the figures differ as upon the exact figures given. Other odds would surely seem equally plausible. Had the odds been the same for each event, however, readers would dismiss the statements as unconvincing attempts to insinuate a religious thesis. Because the figures differ, readers are encouraged to match their subjective sense of different likelihoods against Crusoe's evaluation and then decide that his odds, though not mathematically verifiable, make sense. Dissent is also discouraged because Defoe supplies a uniform scale by making the figures differ in multiples of one thousand. The highest odds given, because they are applied to the most crucial event, upon which Crusoe's survival depended, underscore the impression (created in many other ways as well) that his island adventure reveals the working of Providence, not chance.

In *Captain Singleton*, where there is only one calculation of the odds, Defoe chooses a much larger figure. Of the Londoner rescued in the middle of Africa, Singleton reports that "the first Surprise of his seeing us was over before we came, but any one may conceive of it, by the brief Account he gave us afterwards of his very unhappy Circumstances; and of so unexpected a Deliverance, such as perhaps never happened to any Man in the World; for it was a Million to one odds, that ever he could have been relieved; nothing but an Adventure that never was heard or read of before, could have suited his Case, unless Heaven by some Miracle that never was to be expected, had acted for him."[26] Here again is a retrospective estimate of probability. During his captivity, the Londoner never bothered to calculate his chances. He does so afterwards. The ambiguous hint that his rescue is miraculous may be Singleton's indirect reporting of what the

Londoner said, or it may be Singleton's own comment. Either way, Defoe encourages readers to look on the incident as Providential, since the laws of chance could not lead anyone to expect an event of such low probability. Singleton also reports that the Londoner "would have it always as an Answer to himself, that to be sure wherever we were a-going, we came from Heaven, and were sent on purpose to save him from the most wretched Condition that ever Man was reduced to."[27] But this belief in miraculous intervention "to save him," with its punning suggestion of saving him physically and also saving his soul, is followed only by renewed efforts to strike it rich. The Londoner gets a fortune in gold and ivory. Then after losing it all he "died there of Grief."[28] If he had more fortitude, or acquired it by turning to God for consolation at the loss of worldly goods, he might have reached England alive. But obsession with money ruins his prospects for any kind of salvation. Even in a secular sense, the Londoner does not take proper advantage of his unexpected, highly improbable (and thus all the more merciful on God's part) last chance.

Defoe avoids the language of probability altogether in another book where he tells the real-life story on which he based the episode in *Captain Singleton*. In his *Atlas Maritimus & Commercialis*, Defoe merely reports that on seeing for the first time the rescue-party, Freeman, "As he was so inexpressibly supriz'd with the Sight, he was not able to speak for some time, but spread out his Hands by way of Admiration, as if questioning whether they really were Men, or whether it was a vision."[29] Far from figuring the odds and deciding that a miracle has occurred, Freeman only wonders whether he is seeing things. His response is only a reminder that Africa is a hot place where people must worry about sun-stroke and hallucinations. In the *Atlas*, Freeman's death is attributed to Providence in a routine phrase, but presented only as the premature loss of another potential contributor to an improved commercial atlas: "How accurate a Description both of the Country and of the People could this Person have given, had he lived to come to *England*. But Providence disposed otherwise for him; for . . . after he had guided them, and they guarded him to one of the *Portuguese* Settlements, he died there." No specific cause is given for Freeman's death.

Defoe's varied handling of this episode in *Captain Singleton* and the *Atlas* deserves to become the classic illustration of Forster's distinction between a story displaying only sequence (the queen died, then the king died), and a plot exemplifying causal connections. By changing "died there of Grief" to "he died there," Defoe transformed a novel's subplot into a story suitable for another genre. Because no religious moral is drawn in the *Atlas*, retrospective calculation of the odds would not much enhance Freeman's story. At most, a pointless irony would be stressed, and the very pointlessness would call God's Providence in doubt. Therefore Defoe eliminated the language of probability along with that of psychological analysis. Attention is deflected from situational ironies and moral flaws to the lesson in economic geography which Defoe teaches by Freeman's history in the *Atlas:* "This is enough to show, how both the Gold and the Ivory are found in this Country, and how inexhaustible a Store there is of both."[30]

The pattern of retrospective calculation of probabilities persists later in the eighteenth-century even in works that do not share the theological bent of *Robinson Crusoe*. Thus in his *Autobiography*, Gibbon looks back over his life and remarks: "When I contemplate the common lot of mortality, I must acknowledge that I have drawn a high prize in the lottery of life. The far greater part of the globe is overspread with barbarism or slavery; in the civilized world the most numerous class is condemned to ignorance and poverty; and the double fortune of my birth in a free and enlightened country, in an honorable and wealthy family, is the lucky chance of a unit against millions. The general probability is about three to one that a newborn infant will not live to complete his fiftieth year. I have passed that age. . . ."[31] It is no surprise that Gibbon flaunts the heathen terms *fortune* and *chance*. As usual throughout the *Autobiography*, he adopts a rhetorical stretegy of clearly implying without explicitly declaring the pagan outlook which he finds most appropriate for a civilized man. Gibbon is so anxious here to disclaim any Providential interpretation of his life that he not only speaks of his *double fortune*, but slips into the prescientific vocabulary which attributes favorable events to some *lucky* chance.

But the strategies which reveal Gibbon's ethical stance do not imply serious belief in a universe governed by luck instead of causal laws. Where a specific figure cannot be given, Gibbon resorts to a persuasive guess: "a unit against millions." Where mortality tables allow a more accurate statement, Gibbon provides it: "The general probability is about three to one." What links his passage to the conventions of Christian introspection is Gibbon's attempt to show how likely the main events of his life were, and then use such estimates to derive consolation. I cannot yet tell when this application of mathematics starts or stops in English literature. But examples so diverse as Defoe and Gibbon imply a significant tradition of the consolations of probability.

Gibbon's role as a transitional figure is suggested by his rejection of Providential interpretations even while he uses retrodictive probabilities to discover and explain the meaning of his life. He shares the view that only in retrospect can events be fully evaluated, and estimates probabilities for that purpose. Yet Gibbon also applies probabilistic reasoning to predict the future: "The present is a fleeting moment; the past is no more; and our prospect of futurity is dark and doubtful. This day may *possibly* be my last, but the laws of probability, so true in general, so fallacious in particular, still allow me about fifteen years, and I shall soon enter into the period which, as the most agreeable of his long life, was selected by the judgement and experience of the sage Fontenelle."[32] But Gibbon makes even this estimate of future probabilities serve for the traditional purpose of providing present comfort. No decision, no action depends on the calculation. All that may change is Gibbon's attitude. Where the future is concerned, however, probabilities are inherently less comforting, because they only apply statistically and cannot predict the individual case. The greatest consolation must always be provided by retrodictive probabilities.

Not, however, that even retrodictive estimates are always consoling. Sterne suggests this, although without so clearly illustrating the shift from past to future orientation that is one of the major turning-points of Western thought during the eighteenth century. *Tristram Shandy* pursues lost time. But its universe is a comic prophecy of that random existence so often assumed in the twentieth century: Why me? Why anybody? Walter Shandy explains his predicament in a way that defies further comment: "Take pen and ink in hand, and calculate it fairly, brother *Toby*, said my father, and it will turn out a million to one, that of all the parts of the body, the edge of the forceps should have the ill luck to fall upon and break down that one part, which should break down the fortunes of our house with it."[33]

Implied Probability

In *Robinson Crusoe*, Defoe uses non-mathematical statements about probability to show how seldom probability is the best guide to future conduct. Not that probabilistic reasoning is the worst guide. Crusoe's decision to run off to sea is not reasoned at all. Nor is it exactly located in time, as probability estimates must be. After storms that should have been taken as God's warnings against a maritime career, Crusoe goes to London "and there as well as on the Road, had many Struggles with my self, what Course of Life I should take, and whether I should go Home, or go to Sea" (15). There is no weighing of probabilities, nor any precise statement of how long or on what basis Crusoe wavered: "In this State of Life . . . I remained some time, uncertain what Measures to take, and what Life to lead" (16). What finally decides him is forgetfullness, the symptom of a hardening conscience: "As I stay'd a while, the Remembrance of the Distress I had been in wore off; and as that abated, the little Motion I had in my Desires to Return wore off with it, till at last I quite lay'd aside the Thoughts of it, and lookt out for a Voyage" (16). Only after his first captivity begins does Crusoe start considering probabilities. But they are no help. Enslaved by Moorish pirates in Sallee "I meditated nothing but my Escape; and what Method I might take to effect it, but found no Way that had the least Probability in it: Nothing presented to make the supposition of it rational" (19). Yet Crusoe does escape.

Defoe here inaugurates a pattern of explicit references to probability that calls attention to sequences of events that are individually improbable and, taken together in combination, even more unlikely than they seem one by one. His other novels are also filled with improbable episodes, of which Moll's incestuous marriage is only the most unlikely. But no where else does Defoe take so many pains as in *Robinson Crusoe* to remark improbababilities. Even its title page stresses how strange and surprising his adventures are. But we merely hear of THE LIFE, ADVENTURES AND PYRACIES, OF THE FAMOUS CAPTAIN SINGLETON; THE FORTUNES AND MISFORTUNES OF THE FAMOUS MOLL FLANDERS; THE MOST REMARKABLE OCCURRENCES of the plague year; THE HISTORY AND REMARKABLE LIFE OF THE TRULY HONOURABLE COL. JACQUES; and of THE FORTUNATE MISTRESS, OR A HISTORY OF THE VAST VARIETY OF FORTUNES OF . . . THE LADY ROXANA. *Remarkable* means memorable, not improbable. These title pages, whatever their other deficiencies as clues to Defoe's intentions, do accurately prepare readers for books which do not share *Robinson Crusoe's* attention to Providence. There is not so much emphasis on the sheer improbability of what happens to Moll, Singleton, Jack, and Roxana. In their tales, Defoe certainly exploits the interest aroused by unlikely encounters. But neither the vocabulary of mathematical probability nor that of ordinary statements about probability figures among major rhetorical devices. Defoe stresses sensational and usually shocking rather than conspicuously improbable adventures. Thus Roxana's life is characterized by "vast variety" rather than strange surprises, and we learn further into Moll's title-page that being married "once to her own Brother" merely contributed to "a Life of continu'd Variety."

When the "odd Circumstance" of an available boat "presented itself," no thanks to planning on his part, Crusoe escapes from Sallee. But there is no plan: "I prepar'd to furnish my self, not for a fishing Business but for a Voyage; tho' I knew not, neither did I so much as consider wither I should steer, for any where to get out of that Place was my Way. . . . My Resolutions were, blow which way it would, I would be gone from that horrid Place where I was, and leave the rest to Fate" (21-22). Crusoe then steers the least likely course, in order to elude pursuit: "For who would ha' suppos'd we were saild southward to the truly *Barbarian* Coast, where whole Nations of Negroes were sure to surround us with their Canoes, and destroy us." (23). Here, as in the episode of the footprint, Crusoe expects that others—villainous others—will work out probabilities and govern themselves accordingly. Crusoe imagines what the pirates would consider as a certainty: that on the southern coast savages "were sure to . . . destroy us." The key word is *sure*. The pirates will be sure. They will take the probability of death on a southern escape as one hundred per cent. Defoe encourages readers to notice that Crusoe's escape is against all the odds as they would appear if calculated beforehand. All the implied probabilities are against him. But Crusoe heads south, and lives.

Crusoe eventually forms a plan. But it is vague, and in describing it he neither talks about what is *sure*, nor calculates his odds in advance: "My Design in this way to make the River *Gambia* or *Sennegall*, that is to say, any where about the *Cape de Verd*, where I was in hopes to meet with some European Ship, and if I did not, I knew not what Course I had to take, but to seek out for the *Islands*. . . . I knew that all the Ships from Europe, which sail'd either to the Coast of *Guiney*, or to *Brasil*, or to the East-Indies, made this *Cape* or those *Islands;* and in a word, I put the whole of my Fortune upon this single Point, either that I must meet with some Ship, or must perish" (29). The metaphor of gaming, like earlier references to fate not Providence, matches Crusoe's spiritual blindness during this part of his life. Crusoe thought of his escape as depending on chance. He did not think of himself as trusting in God. But his gamble succeeds.

By encouraging readers to think of it initially as a gamble (before completing the book and seeing the episode differently), Defoe's metaphor creates implied odds. There is no encourage-

ment to state them mathematically here. Yet the idea of everything ("the whole of my Fortune") depending on a binary situation ("either . . . meet with some Ship, or . . . perish") in a
unique case ("this single Point") strongly suggests long odds.
Defoe's statement even creates the impression of longer odds,
and thus a greater gamble, than the situation warrants. If "all
the Ships from Europe" sail past, the likelihood of encountering
one seems strong. But even readers armed with de Moivre's *Doctrine of Chances* could not calculate the odds unless told how
many ships sailed from Europe each year. Defoe withholds any
hint of this crucial figure. He winds up the passage with language that implies only one chance ("this single Point") rather
than many chances. Defoe thus leaves the impression that Crusoe's rescue by the charitable captain was even more highly improbable than it need be considered. Defoe here manipulates
the reader's sense of subjective probabilities so that in retrospect
(after finishing *Robinson Crusoe*) this escape will most easily fit
into the pattern of Providential deliverances. At issue here is not
the establishment of that pattern, which Defoe mostly creates
later in the book by means that have been well described, but
the role of probabilistic statements in heightening awareness of
Robinson Crusoe's religious theme.

Defoe complicates matters by showing Crusoe's progress
from an almost totally thoughtless state through awareness that
rational planning based on probabilities does have its limited
uses. It might have enabled him to avoid many of his troubles.
He remarks that if he had been content to remain on his Brazilian plantation living something like the life recommended by his
father, "I had in all Probability been exceeding prosperous and
rich" (35). But at the end of the novel he winds up rich anyway.
Defoe's manipulation of implied probabilities is in fact a major
clue to the meaning of Crusoe's wealth.

There is no reason to doubt Crusoe's retrodiction of the financial probabilities involved in that alternate unlived past which
he rejected in favor of a future that he did not in any way predict. Yet readers will nevertheless see that there is not much
purely financial difference between the alternate lives. By this

irony among others, Defoe introduces the paradox of the fortunate fall. It is the unforeseen solitary life which makes possible
Crusoe's salvation as well as the prosperity which is associated
with it. Crusoe's retrodiction of the likelihood of his having been
"exceeding . . . rich" is part of his recognition of "how just" he
must acknowledge his "lot" to have been. The older Crusoe
who looks back on his life as he narrates it correctly blames
himself while admitting God's justice: "all these Miscarriages
were procured by my apparent obstinate adhering to my foolish
inclination of wandring abroad and pursuing that Inclination, in
contradiction to the clearest Views of doing my self good in a
fair and plain pursuit of those Prospects and those measures of
Life, which Nature and Providence concurred to present me
with, and to make my Duty" (38). Defoe's vocabulary here
stresses Crusoe's disobedience and willfulness as the causes of
his "miscarriages." The explicit language of probability is avoided
in this remark. Crusoe does not exactly say that he should have
followed the most probable (as it then would have seemed) path
to riches.

If he had done so, he might indeed have been rich, but might
not have discovered his proper relationship to God. If his motive for staying had been obedience to Providence, well and
good. But if he had stayed out of pure self-interest, that would
have been (as it is) another story. Crusoe would in either case
not have gone through the afflictions which make his story as
Defoe tells it in *Robinson Crusoe* parallel *The Book of Job*. Nor
in that case would Crusoe's prosperity have seemed deserved in
the same way that Job's final wealth does. The money which
Crusoe does in fact acquire thus has a very different meaning
from that fortune which might have been amassed by following
the least hazardous and most probable path to riches: staying
on the plantation. By making Crusoe speak of *clearest* and *most
probable* "Views of doing my self good," Defoe shifts this passage away from advocacy of probability as the best guide to life.
He only suggests ironically that in this case there may have been
some coincidence between what seemed best (because most
probable) and what was best in fact. The passage is phrased to

avoid explicit recommendation of probability as a basis for decision, while not denying that sometimes thinking about probabilities may do no harm. What the passage enforces is the novel's message that obedience is a necessary virtue.

After this preparation, Defoe includes an explicit reference to probability when the same decision to leave the plantation is evaluated four pages later: "I took all possible Caution to preserve my Effects, and keep up my Plantation; had I used half as much Prudence to have look'd into my own Interest, and have made a Judgement of what I ought to have done, and not to have done, I had certainly never gone away from so prosperous an Undertaking, leaving all the probable Views of a thriving Circumstance, and gone upon a Voyage to Sea, attended with all its common Hazards; to say nothing of the Reasons I had to expect particular Misfortunes to my self. But I was hurried on, and obey'd blindly the Dictates of my Fancy rather than my Reason" (40). Here Crusoe laments his lack of prudence, and associates with prudence an ability to act according to "all the probable views" that "reason" would suggest. This passage, like the entire novel, recommends prudence. But as in all ironic works, key passages like this one acquire a different meaning when they are considered in the light of the story's final outcome.

First time through *Robinson Crusoe*, the passage seems to recommend prudent behavior while also defining it as consideration of "probable views" as a basis for planning future conduct. In retrospect, however, or on the second reading which any ironic work invites, Crusoe's departure from probable views of his best future course turns out to have been after all the best—because in fact the actual—means to his conversion. Because readers wind up with an overwhelming impression that Crusoe's conversion depended on the improbable chain of events leading to isolation on what he misnames the Island of Despair, there remains an equally strong impression that without that adversity Crusoe would have become merely rich without any spiritual improvement. On the island he learns that sin is worse than affliction, which applies for readers the converse lesson that

Godliness not prosperity is the best goal. And this moral calls in question even Crusoe's occasional worldly reflections that he might have been wealthy (which he is anyway) or wealthier yet, had he guided himself by probable views. Readers will also remember that despite his fine speech, Crusoe takes the money from the wreck. His conversion does not turn Crusoe into a saint. Nor does he ever lose what the novel portrays as an almost excessive interest in portable property. When he thinks about how rich he might have been, we may smile as we do when he keeps taking useless money from shipwrecks. However, subsequent episodes narrating his discovery of God do not call in question Crusoe's observation that it would have been better to obey his father even to the belated extent of staying in the middle station of life afforded by the Brazilian plantation.

The strategies by which Defoe emphasizes that Crusoe's escape from Sallee was highly improbable also intensify awareness that his establishment on a Brazilian plantation was unlikely. Crusoe's neglect of that chance in turn heightens our sense that yet another opportunity to live according to God's will is highly improbable. Defoe's inclusion of the Sallee episode has been a minor puzzle. To the reasons that have been given for this lengthy prelude to Crusoe's arrival on his island, another can be added: Defoe uses the episode as an appeal to every reader's intuitive sense that a sequence of unlikely events becomes more improbable than even the most unlikely single event. The subjective probabilities formalized by de Moivre's application of the doctrine of combinations are mobilized through a sequence of improbable events accompanied by language calling attention to their improbability. This intensifies appreciation of God's mercy in saving Crusoe: first from the wreck, then from a life of sin, and perhaps from an eternity in Hell. In this context the hundred-thousand-to-one odds against salvaging the ship become only a part of what, as a whole, seems an even less probable situation. But no figure is ever given, as in *Captain Singleton*, to sum up *all* the odds involved. Rhetorically it is more effective to imply without specifying the very high odds against what happens to Crusoe during the entire island adventure. One reason why it is more effective is that, with the publication of de Moivre's *Doctrine of Chances* the year before *Robinson Crusoe,* readers had available as never before—although there were some previous discussions—a lucid explanation of how odds may be scientifically calculated. And it requires little mathematical sophistication to notice that life is not like a card-game, a lottery, or even two stacked decks.

At the point where mathematical theories of probability begin to assume their distinctively modern character of scientific rigor, they also diverge from ready application to the ordinary events of life. Insofar as readers become more aware of mathematical concepts, their elusiveness also becomes apparent. Therefore to say, as Defoe does in *Captain Singleton,* that it is a million to one odds against rescue, is effective only at first glance. Sooner or later—and much sooner if they have actually read de Moivre's *Doctrine of Chances*—readers will ask how, for that total situation of an Englishman stranded in Africa, it was possible to arrive at any precise odds. Why not two million, or ten million? Even de Moivre's (presumably) correct figures for the two piquet decks elude imaginative comprehension, as all large numbers do. In his statement of the odds, as in so many other matters, Defoe was most adroit in *Robinson Crusoe:* he kept his figures small enough to retain meaning, and avoided any attempt to pin down the probability that Crusoe would live his strange surprising life. Implied probability is best.

Beyond Probability
Prudence concerns the future. According to Bailey's *Dictionarium Britannicum,* "Prudence is defined to be a Habit of the Mind, whereby a Man judges and determines truly how he should act and proceed; what he should do or avoid in all Things relatting to his Advantage, temporal or eternal, so as to render himself happy both here and hereafter." In *Robinson Crusoe* prudence is gradually dissociated from prior estimation of the odds, or any variety of explicitly probabilistic reasoning. Crusoe pro-

gresses from total lack of prudence, which the novel condemns, through prudence based entirely on rational grounds, to prudence based on faith which supplements reason. Crusoe learns to act rationally but leave the outcome to God. He also learns to ground his prudence on listening to the voice of Providence. Crusoe advances toward the Christian prudence which Defoe illustrates most vividly at the outset of *A Journal of the Plague Year.*

H. F. cannot decide whether to stay in London or leave to escape the plague. Instead of estimating his chances of survival by trying to compute the odds, or even by considering the probabilities, he "endeavored to resolve first, what was my Duty to do, and I stated the Arguments with which my Brother had press'd me to go into the Country, and I set against them the strong Impressions which I had on my Mind for staying; the visible Call I seem'd to have from the particular Circumstance of my Calling, and the Care due from me for the Preservation of my Effects, which were, as I might say, my Estate; also the Intimations which I thought I had from Heaven, that to me signify'd a kind of Direction to venture, and it occurr'd to me, that if I had what I might call a Direction to stay, I ought to suppose it contain'd a Promise of being preserved, if I obey'd."[34] Probabilities *follow from* correct appreciation of Divine will. If God wishes H. F. to stay, it follows that the probability of his survival will approach certainty. If H. F. stays in furtherance of his own will, there is no way for him to estimate his chances.

To decide, he resorts to the traditional *sortes sanctorum:* "Turning over the Bible, which lay before me ... I cry'd out, WELL, *I know not what to do, Lord direct me!* and the like; and at that Juncture I happen'd to stop turning over the Book at the *91st Psalm.* ... I scarce need tell the Reader, that from that moment I resolv'd that I would stay in the Town, and casting my self entirely upon the Goodness and Protection of the Almighty, would not seek any further Shelter whatever; and that ... if he did not think fit to deliver me, still I was in his Hands, and it was meet he should do with me as should seem good to him" (12–13). For anyone who will trust God, probabilities no longer matter.

H. F. uses metaphors taken from gaming, but divorces them from prior estimation of probabilities. God sends hunches that tell where "to venture." After coming upon the Biblical passage that settles his decision, H. F. mentions "casting" himself on God's protection. This is a gamble and no gamble. Crusoe's metaphor of putting his whole fortune upon a single point invokes only the gaming table and the long odds against him. It is Defoe's invitation for readers to start noticing a developing combination of probabilities as episodes unfold. After completing the novel, Crusoe's metaphor also becomes an invitation to see that at that stage of his life, he lacked the highest kind of prudence, which is grounded on interpretation of God's will not calculation of chances. In *A Journal of the Plague Year* Defoe is not concerned to build a narrative whose episodes combine to enhance our awareness that H. F.'s survival is unlikely and therefore Providential. The point is made early and assumed throughout the book. There is no portrayal of spiritual growth.

Crusoe also turns to the Bible during a spiritual crisis, and discovers an appropriate passage which he interprets as a message from God. Later he sees the prophetic dream of rescuing a native as one more indication that it was his duty to do so, not just a probable means of aiding his escape. The encounter with mutineers that does lead to his deliverance from the island was unforeseen and is another in the chain of events that are made to seem even more improbable taken together than considered separately. When Crusoe does start behaving in a prudent manner with respect to his temporal situation—the prelude to prudent consideration of his eternal prospects—there is no explicit mention of probabilities: "I considered from the beginning how I would provide for the Accidents that might happen, and for the time that was to come, not only after my Ammunition should be spent, but even after my Health or Strength should decay"(63). This remark is in the same paragraph where Crusoe estimates the hundred-thousand-to-one odds against having salvaged anything from the wreck, and is part of his general explanation of how he took advantage of that improbable event by acquiring material that would help him live after his gunpowder was gone. This aside about how he "considered" ways of coping with his island future departs from the language of probability—a departure all the more conspicuous for appearing in the same passage where the retrospective odds are stated.

After the beginning of his repentence ("Now I look'd back upon my past Life with such Horrour"), Crusoe's first major decision about his temporal future is whether to keep living in his cave or move inland. He reasons that by the shore "It was at least possible that something might happen to my Advantage . . . the same ill Fate that brought me hither, might bring some other unhappy Wretches to the same Place; and tho' it was scarce probable that any such Thing should ever happen; yet to enclose my self among the Hills and Woods, in the Center of the Island, was to anticipate my Bondage, and to render such an Affair not only Improbable, but Impossible; and that therefore I ought not by any Means to remove" (101). This statement that arrival of any one else on the island is "scarce probable" again encourages readers to appreciate the surprising turn of Crusoe's final adventures with the mutineers. Their arrival is later described as "A strange and unforseen Accident . . . of which the like has not perhaps been heard of in History" (249). Crusoe's decision to stay by the shore is based on a weighing of probabilities. But there is no mathematical calculation. Crusoe simply balances a possibility against an impossibility and grimly decides in favor of guiding himself by what may happen even though it is "scarce probable." The vocabulary of probabilistic reasoning here underscores the desperate nature of his predicament.

Crusoe's decision is rational, although it hardly indicates much advance over his former thoughtlessness. In his situation, it requires little foresight to distinguish possibility from impossibility and then decide against the plan whose probability of success is zero. Yet even this logically inescapable decision proves unsatisfactory. When cannibals start arriving on the shore for their feasts, Crusoe regrets living by the seaside. In *Robinson Crusoe*, events never fully ratify even the most unobjectionable probabilistic reasoning.

Crucial decisions are made on better grounds. What finally discourages Crusoe from going alone to the mainland is not estimation of the probability that, as he later realizes, there would have been more than a thousand-to-one chance of being killed. He discards the plan because he lacked the foresight to build a sufficiently large canoe: "The Smallness of my Boat assisted to put an End to that Design, and now I thought no more of it" (136). Measures to improve his fortifications prove useful, although not undertaken as a result of any specific prediction of later events: "I foresaw nothing at that Time, more than my meer Fear suggested to me" (162). For saving his goats, Crusoe picks "the most rational Design," but does not describe it as the plan with the highest probability of success (162). For him rational planning is not synonymous with probabilistic reasoning. That is applied most usefully in retrospect to appreciate God's Providence or else, at the level of secondary causes, to understand more fully what has already happened. When Crusoe finds nothing on the Spanish wreck but a live dog and two drowned men, he "concluded, as is indeed probable, that when the Ship struck, it being in a Storm, the Sea broke so high, and so continually over her, that the men were not able to bear it, and were strangled with the constant rushing in of the Water, as much as if they had been under water" (191). Speculating on why he had never seen cannibals before discovering the footprint, although they must have landed more than once, Crusoe concludes "that if at any Time they should be driven here, it was probable they went away again as soon as ever they could, seeing they had never thought fit to fix there upon any Occasion, to this Time" (160).

When Crusoe takes prior frequencies as the basis for a prediction about the cannibals, his probabilistic logic is again impeccable: "I knew I had been here now almost eighteen Years, and never saw the least Foot-steps of Humane Creature there before; and I might be here eighteen more, as entirely conceal'd as I was now, if I did not discover my self to them"(166). But Crusoe does not remain concealed for another eighteen years. Events render his logic irrelevant. Finally, the outcome of Crusoe's meditation on the lawfulness and prudence of killing cannibals leads him to transcend probability: "Upon these, and many like Reflections, I afterwards made it a certain Rule with me, that whenever I found those secret Hints, or pressings of my Mind, to doing, or not doing any Thing that presented; or to going this Way, or that Way, I never fail'd to obey the secret Dictate; though I knew no other Reason for it, than that such a Pressure, or such a Hint hung upon my Mind: I could give many Examples of the Success of this Conduct in the Course of my Life; but more especially in the latter Part of my inhabiting this unhappy Island" (175). Crusoe does not reject reason in favor of enthusiasm. Nor does he discard prudence: he works rationally to cultivate his land, protect his livestock and strengthen his fortifications. He avoids rash exposure when others arrive. Crusoe learns to supplement reason by leaving to heaven the measure *and* the choice. Defoe thus distinguishes Christian prudence from Satanic self-sufficiency. Crusoe does not renounce reason, but achieves prudence grounded on faith that allows him to go beyond reliance on probability as a guide of life.

My title mentions Bayes to stress an affinity. Strictly speaking, however, Defoe provides neither inverse probabilities nor what a physicist would call retrodiction. Watanabe explains that "if the probability of a final state (of an isolated system) as a function of the initial state is given by a natural law and not affected by other factors, we say that the phenomenon is predictable. If the probability of an initial state as a function of the final state is given by a natural law and not affected by other factors, we say that the phenomenon is retrodictable."[35] This rigorous definition, like those provided for inverse probability by Bayes and his followers, renders my use of parallel terms metaphoric. Far from denying this, I wish to insist on the difference and make it explicit. Spiritual retrodiction may be a useful metaphor, but only if it is recognized *as* a metaphor, like aesthetic distance and many other critical concepts. Otherwise, discussions like this one will merely become bad mathematics. But intuitive areas of the mind may provide metaphors which form the basis for conceptual models which are later formalized in rigorous ways that conceal relationships to their irrational (but not therefore useless) origins. There will of course always be rational origins that are more available for discussion and perhaps more significant. Surely de Moivre's mathematical formulas were a necessary condition for the later work of Bayes. And no doubt if Bayes had not developed inverse probability theorems another mathematician would have. But it was Bayes, not some one else, who provided that important legacy from the eighteenth century to the twentieth. His theological and literary environment is therefore relevant to both cultures.

Where I do claim more than metaphoric affinities is in suggesting the distinction between probabilities as a guide to the future. This distinction cuts across disciplinary boundaries. It is part of the more general question of the historical development of the concept of time. But that issue, especially as it concerns literature, can only be dealt with by further attention to such particulars as I have discussed here. More investigation is certainly needed. Swift hints at a long tradition of explicit statements of the odds when he makes the speaker of *A Tale of A Tub* remark that "there have been several famous pieces lately published both in verse and prose, wherein, if the writers had not been pleased, out of their great humanity and affection to the public, to give us a nice detail of the sublime and the admirable they contain, it is a thousand to one whether we should ever have discovered one grain of either." We need to locate other statements mentioning the odds before deciding what relationship they have to mathematical discussions of probability.

Defoe's awareness of mathematics is another question I hope can be pursued. In *Essays Upon Several Projects* he mentions William Petty's *Political Arithmetic*, and also discussed an insurance scheme. But payments by those taking out policies are to be sealed up or down each year according to actual deaths, not according to probabilistic projections. Nor, even much later, in the novels, does Defoe use the terms *risk* and *expectation* in their mathematical senses. I do not know whether Defoe read de Moivre's *Doctrine of Chances*. But his early interest in its topic is suggested not only by the *Essays Upon Projects*, but by an explanation in the *Review* of December 9, 1704: remarking on his political forecasts, Defoe explains that "This way of Writing is something like Judicial Astrology, where tho' all seems to be mere Guess, yet the Calculation of Probabilities may yet give a Man an insight farther into an Affair, and its Consequences, than every one may think possible; and when what was rationally deduc'd comes to pass, the Man is taken for a Conjurer, with some that know nothing of the Matter, when in Truth, every man may Conjure as well as he, if he would study the Reasons, and Natural Consequences of the thing," Perhaps it will be possible to explore Defoe's relationship to the intense activity of the period between 1690 and the publication of *Robinson Crusoe*. Before de Moivre there appeared Pierre-Rémond de Montmort's *Essai d'Analyse sur les Jeux de Hasard* (1708); James Bernoulli's *Ars Conjectandi* (1713); Nicholas Struyck's *Calcul des Chances* (1713); and the two English translations of Christianus Huygens's *De Rationciniis in Aleae Ludo:* anonymously in 1692 as *Of the Laws of Chance*, and again in 1714 by W. Browne as *The Value of All Chances in Games of Fortune, Cards, Dice Wagers, Lotteries, etc. Mathematically Demonstrated.*

Notes

1. Daniel Defoe, *Robinson Crusoe*, ed. J. Donald Crowley (London: Oxford University Press, 1972), p. 154. Subsequent references to this edition appear in my text.

2. Nathan Bailey, *Dictionarium Britannicum* (London, 1730).

3. Daniel Defoe, *Captain Singleton*, ed. Shiv K. Kumar (London: Oxford University Press, 1973), p. 105.

4. *Genesis:* 3; John Milton, *Paradise Lost.*

5. Pierre Simon, Marquis de Laplace, *Théorie Analytique Des Probabilités* (Paris, 1812); *A Philosophical Essay on Probabilities*, trans. F. W. Truscott and F. L. Emory (1902; rpt. New York: Dover, 1951), p. 1.

6. Joseph Butler, *The Analogy of Religion* (New York: Frederick Ungar, 1961), p. 2.

7. Nachum L. Rabinovitch, *Probability and Statistical Inference in Ancient and Medieval Jewish Literature* (Toronto and Buffalo: University of Toronto Press, 1973), p. 77.

8. J. R. Lucas, *The Concept of Probability* (Oxford: Clarendon Press, 1970), p. 20.

9. Daniel Defoe, *The History of the Devil*, in *The Works of Daniel Defoe* (London, 1843), III, 44-45.

10. Ibid.

11. Abraham de Moivre, *The Doctrine of Chances: or A Method of Calculating the Probability of Events in Play* (London, 1718), p. vi.

12. Ibid.

13. Ibid., p. v.

14. John Calvin, *Institutes of the Christian Religion*, trans. Henry Beveridge (1953), I. 179. Cited in Maximillian E. Novak, *Defoe and the Nature of Man* (Oxford: Oxford University Press, 1963), p. 7.

15. Benjamin Gal-Or, "The Crisis about the Origin of Irreversibility and Time Anisotropy," *Science*, 1976, No. 4030 (1972), 11-17.

16. Satosi Watanabe, "Time and the Probabilistic View of the World," in *The Voices of Time*, ed. J. T. Fraser (New York: George Braziller, 1966), pp. 527-563.

17. Thomas Bayes, "An Essay Towards Solving a Problem in the Doctrine of Chances," *Philosophical Transactions* (Royal Society of London), 53 (1763), 370-418. Available edited with a biographical note by G. A. Bernard & reprinted from *Biometrika* 45 (1958), 293-315.

18. Lucas, p. 198.

19. Norbert Wiener, "Newtonian and Bergsonian Time," *Cybernetics*, 2nd ed. (Cambridge, Mass.: M.I.T. Press, 1961), pp. 30-44.

20. Robert G. Sachs, "Time Reversal," *Science*, 176, No. 4035 (1972), 587-597.

21. John Locke, *An Essay Concerning Human Understanding*, ed. A. C. Fraser (New York: Dover, 1959), II, 379.

22. Jonathan Swift, *Gulliver's Travels and Other Writings*, ed. Louis A. Landa (Cambridge, Mass.: Riverside Press, 1960), p. 332.

23. David Hume, *A Treatise of Human Nature*, ed. Ernest C. Mossner (Baltimore: Penguin Books, 1969), p. 188.

24. Hume, p. 187.

25. Hume, p. 190.

26. Defoe, *Captain Singleton*, p. 121.

27. Ibid., p. 122.

28. Ibid., p. 137.

29. [Daniel Defoe] *Atlas Maritimus & Commercialis* (London, 1728), p. 252.

30. *Atlas*, p. 253.

31. *The Autobiography of Edward Gibbon*, ed. Dero A. Saunders (New York: Meridian Books, 1961), p. 204.

32. Gibbon, p. 206.

33. Laurence Sterne, *The Life and Opinions of Tristam Shandy, Gentleman*, ed. Ian Watt (Boston: Houghton Mifflin, 1965), p. 210.

34. Daniel Defoe, *A Journal of the Plague Year*, ed. Louis Landa (London: Oxford University Press, 1969), p. 12.

35. Watanabe, op. cit.

Probability and Character in the Eighteenth Century

Paul J. Korshin

The probability of character concerned few people before the eighteenth century. As Bernouilli observes in his *Ars Conjectandi* (1713), "probability is a degree of certainty, and differs from absolute certainty as a part differs from the whole."[1] In the centuries before the art of conjecturing, the concept of probability, the laws of chance, and the law of large numbers were understood, characters—whether those in literature or those in historical reality—were seldom thought to vary widely from absolute certainty or (to use Archbishop Tillotson's phrase) "moral certainty." The imaginary characters that appeared in literature were, to seventeenth-century English and French thinkers, absolutely certain renditions of real people, drawn according to an elaborate code or series of character types. This code was widely available to all in collections of maxims, books of characters, and numerous homilies on human behavior.[2] The seventeenth-century literary character, no matter how unlikely such a personage may seem to us today, seemed appropriate to the contemporary audience. Hence the exaggerated heroes and heroines of English and French drama, the malevolently crafty villains of tragedy and comedy, the pure creations of romance sacred and profane, were thought highly probable. Or, to express the same thought in negative terms, literary theorists and educated readers found no *improbability* in them. If they questioned the presentation of a fictional character as somehow *unreal*, arguments were ready at hand to prove that the heroic play or the prose romance might distort reality by compressing and intensifying circumstances, but not by perverting human nature.[3]

When we turn to the trustworthiness or probability of living characters, the best vehicle we have for judging their evaluation is the criminal code. In legal trials, the prevalent seventeenth-century practice was to accept a witness's testimony as true, without checking on circumstantial evidence or employing cross-examination. Thus the witness (or "real character") was, in the eyes of seventeenth-century jurisprudence, taken to represent a moral certainty, a probability of 999/1000, which is all but absolute certainty. The gradual shrinking of a witness's natural credibility or moral certainty during the next hundred years of jurisprudence is mainly a topic in the history of evidence and criminology.[4] This process is related to the nature of probability, since probability theory is closely associated with conjecture and with circumstantial evidence. Both of these concepts will enter into the nature of literary character in the eighteenth century, completely transforming the seventeenth-century notion of character to something close to our twentieth-century treatment of human personality.

We do not conjecture about the probability of a character as we do about the probability of a given roll of the dice, the chances of a given hand at cards, or the results of a game. Yet recent literary theory, especially game theory and semiology, has suggested that literature may be regarded as a game.[5] If so, we may consider it to fall within the realm of probability as much as the ordinary doings of life. Bernouilli knew that conjecturing could be applied to everyday affairs: "The *art of conjecturing* or the *stochastic art* is defined by us as the art of measuring as exactly as possible the probabilities of things with this end in mind: that in our decisions or actions we may be able always to choose or to follow what has been perceived as being superior, more advantageous, safer, or better considered; in this alone lies all the wisdom of the philosopher and all the discretion of the statesman."[6] Probability theory, then, for everyday life, consists of making conjectural predictions of the future or regarding future actions based on accumulated evidence ("experience").

As this prolegomenon may indicate, the term "probability" as I use it in my title and text has several possible meanings. First, it may mean "degree of verisimilitude or closeness to truth" (cf. "improbable"); in this sense, a *probable character* is a likely one, a fictional personage whose closeness to reality is very great. Second, "probability" may refer to the *predictability of a fictional character.* By this I mean that a probable character could be one whose behavior, attitudes, qualities, etc. conform so closely to an accepted mold that an audience, on making its acquaintance, would be able to predict how this person would act. This kind of probable character is the figure we know as the *character type;* such creations, in seventeenth-century character books and a good number of eighteenth-century novels, function typologically, or predictively. We might think them limited characters today, but their comfortable probability (amounting to an absolute certainty) must have been a *desideratum* for the contemporary reader, as their frequency demonstrates. Third, "probability" may be understood in mathematical terms to describe a *degree of certainty*, the likelihood of a certain set of odds being operative in a given situation. Likelihood is itself an aspect of probability theory, now regarded as part of statistics. However, since it deals with the frequency of events, and the calculation of their possibilities, I shall not discuss it further in relation to literary character.[7]

Let me now turn to the question of "character." Here, too, we are confronted with a variety of meanings. Seventeenth-century writers often observe (following the derivation from the Greek) that character signifies *engraving*, something permanent, like a medal, an emblem, or an iconographic figure. Through its derivative, "characteristic," we come to something like *general quality:* "Know well each ANCIENT'S proper *Character.*"[8] A character can be a "type" sketch, often with predictive overtones and, finally, it can be a fictional representation of a person believable enough to be actual or, in other words, a person who impresses the reader as *probable.* In dealing with this last variety of character, the creator or novelist will wish to maximize the probability of a given character since, strategically, the wisest course for a verisimilitudinous writer is to come as close as possible to absolute certainty in imitating nature.[9] The kinds of character most important for the probabilist are *character types* and the fictional sketches which attempt to be credible. At first glance, they may appear to be alike. In fact, however, they are substantially different; an understanding of how and why they differ may help us grasp the influence of concepts of mathematical probability on eighteenth-century literature.

Characters begin as early as the sixteenth century. The early editions of Theophrastus (1527 et seq.), especially that made by Isaac Casaubon (1592), were influential throughout Europe. The Theophrastan character joined with the virtues-and-vices characters from medieval drama and the *commedia dell'arte* and the "humours" characters of Elizabethan drama to enrich seventeenth-century prose narrative. These early characters did not become known as "types" until the mid-nineteenth century; so far as I have been able to determine, this term is akin in meaning to "stereotype," a stock, repetitive character. There were scores of them in Renaissance drama. I have introduced the word "types" to describe them in an entirely different sense, for the evidence of seventeenth-century theoretical texts suggests that these one-sided representations of virtues and vices were also intended to be "types" in the theological sense. In the same way that a biblical type was understood to foreshadow or predict an antitype, the characters of Renaissance drama and the early character books were also predictive. A reader familiar with the standard representation of the wise man, the fool, the pedant, the honest man, the traitor, the faithful man or woman, the rake, the innocent young woman, the enthusiast, and dozens of others could be expected to predict (in the act of reading) the behavior of that literary creation. Variety is introduced from time to time by creating sub-groups within one character type. The character of the good magistrate, for example, might be varied by making him subject to lasciviousness, pederasty, gluttony, or some other vice or peccadillo which does not obliterate the basic quality of the character but does vary the experience of the reader. The consistency and probability of these characters were assumed to be very high. Bishop Hall, in a crisp "Premonition" to his *Characters of Vertues and Vices* (1608), assured his audience that the ancients, in making engraved characters on medals, "bestowed their time in drawing out the true lineaments of every vertue and vice, so lively, that who saw the medals, might know the face."[10] Hall evidently had no qualms that someone might look at a character and come to the wrong conclusion about what or whom it was meant to represent. Later authors of character books were equally confident in the predictive skills of their readers. If Sir Thomas Overbury (1622) or John Earle (1650) were the least bit dubious about the moral certainty of their characters, they allowed no hint of it to creep into their works.[11] There was also a rich tradition of character writing in seventeenth-century sermons which runs from Thomas Adams to John Tillotson. Like its secular counterpart, it is based on the belief that a literary representation, however one-sided (and all were very much so), was an entirely accurate view of the real world. When writers deal so confidently in absolute certainties, perhaps it is wrong to say that they have any awareness of probability at all, for probability is only a fraction of certainty.

Who first muddied the crystal spring of the certain character? It was La Bruyère, whose *Characters, or the Manners of the Age ... with the Characters of Theophrastus* appeared in an English translation in 1699. La Bruyère's characters are not stock figures or engravings at all; they are rather collections of notes and gossip on a number of kinds of human behavior. They demonstrate that the varieties of human behavior are so numerous that it is impossible to expect a single real person or fictional character to be consistent in any one way. The 1690s was a decade of heightened awareness, both in England and France, of the application of mathematics to literature; Arbuthnot's "Essay on the Usefulness of Mathematical Learning" (1700) shows how widespread the interest was.[12] La Bruyère argues that the monolithic, stock, or "typed" character was unsatisfactory, if not impossible:

> What probability is there to please all the so different tastes of Men, by one single tract of Morality? Some search for Definitions, Divisions, Tables and Method, these are desirous to have explained to 'em, what Vertue is in general, and then every Vertue in particular, what difference there is between Valour, Fortitude and Magnanimity; the extream Vices, either in defect or excess, between whom each Vertue is placed; and of which of these two extreams it most participates: other sort of Doctrine does not at all please them. Others are satisfied to have manners reduced to the Passions, and that these be explain'd by the motion of the Blood, by the Fibres and Arteries, they'll excuse an Author all the rest.[13]

"Probability" in this passage appears to be a mathematical usage: La Bruyère is calculating the chance of drawing the virtues and vices *"in particular"* and finds it remote, perhaps impossible. The difficulty with La Bruyère's method is that it is *unmethodical* and unselective. He does not see the character sketch or the fictional character as a moral vehicle: He is more the historian, nay, the journalist, than the moralist.

He was far ahead of his time and he would soon be criticized for this dangerous departure from strict didacticism. Henry Gally, an early eighteenth-century translator of Theophrastus, added "A Critical Essay on Characteristic-Writings" to his edition. This is a rare theoretical statement on the theory of character. Gally regarded the character book as serious business: "For the Learned *Isaac Casaubon* has observ'd that *Characteristic-Writing* is, as it were, a Medium between Moral Philosophy and Poetry."[14] His definitions have a certain authority to them:

> The original Design of Characteristic-Writings is to give us the real Images of Life. An exact Imitation of Nature is the chief Art which is to be us'd. The Imagination, I own, may be allow'd to work in Pieces of this Kind, provided it keeps within Degrees of Probability: but Mr. *de la*

Bruyère gives us Characters of Men, who are not to be found in Nature; and, out of a false Affectation of the Wonderful, he carries almost every thing to Excess; represents the Irregularities of Life as downright Madness, and by his false Colours converts Men into Monsters.[15]

Later Gally explains that inconsistency in a character is abhorrent, and that different qualities must not be mingled in one portrait (p. 73). We observe, I think, the strain between the two kinds of characters I have singled out for discussion here. The old character type was comfortably predictable, with a probability of one; it was ideally suited to the purposes of moral writing, *"provided it keeps within Degress of Probability"* (a mathematical description). That in 1725 this method should have been thought of as capable of presenting "the real Images of Life" shows how deeply ingrained a literary habit it must have been.

From Gally's definition, we can extract the central question that would face novelists and theorists of fictional character for the next sixty years. What method of character drawing had the highest degree of certainty (or probability)—the one-sided type or the multivalent blend of character? The first echoes the character books and stresses one kind of probability, that which is induced by deliberately suppressing some evidence about a character because it may be inconsistent with a larger moral purpose. The second echoes La Bruyère and stresses another kind of probability, that which permits a probability judgment about a character based on all available information, or a great amount of detail, concerning the person in question. This second method of character drawing owes much to Bernouilli's Theorem, sometimes known as the Law of Large Numbers. Bernouilli's Theorem, mathematicians and philosophers observe, does not provide a probability of one; it can only furnish an approximation of the probability that a certain event will take place.[16] As de Moivre, translating Bernouilli's *Ars Conjectandi*, would put it, in calculating the probability of an event's happening or failing to happen, "the greater the number of Experiments has been, so much nearer the Truth will the conjectures be that are derived from them."[17] According to the second method, we will have to

know a great deal about a character before we can make a judgment relating to his or her probability but, equally important,
what we know about the figure will not be one-sided or directed
toward a single tendency. Instead, it will be varied, including a
mixture of traits, sometimes opposing each other.

The multivalent character evolves slowly. Defoe, whose
knowledge of mathematical writings seems to have been respectable, sometimes draws characters so varied and contradictory
that they transcend the monolithic old types, as in *Robinson
Crusoe*, *Moll Flanders* and *Roxana* (these novels also abound
with traditional character types). Yet he was also criticized for
his inconsistencies, improbabilities, and even impossibilities.[18]
Richardson crowds his novels with traditional, though finely
drawn, character types; he, too, would later be censured for
their one-sidedness and hence their improbability.[19] The much-
quoted remarks of Johnson on fictional characters, in *Rambler*
4, reveal one of the central problems in creating the multivalent
character:

> In narratives, where historical veracity has no place, I cannot discover
> why there should not be exhibited the most perfect idea of virtue; of
> virtue not angelical, nor above probability, for what we cannot credit
> we shall never imitate, but the highest and purest that humanity can
> reach, which, when exercised in such trials as the various revolutions of
> things shall bring upon it, may, by conquering some calamities, and en-
> during others, teach us what we may hope, and what we can perform.
> Vice, for vice is necessary to be shewn, should always disgust; nor
> should the graces of gaiety, or the dignity of courage, be so united with
> it, as to reconcile it to the mind. Wherever it appears, it should raise
> hatred by the malignity of its practices, and contempt by the meanness
> of its stratagems; for while it is supported by either parts or spirit, it
> will be seldom heartily abhorred.[20]

Johnson would prefer not to violate probability, of whose mathematical senses he was well aware; thus he recognizes the mathematical impossibility of perfect characters. Unfortunately, he
is traditional enough, susceptible enough to the old morality
and its character types, to insist that evil characters ought always to disgust, even though a completely repugnant evil person
is just as improbable in the real world as a completely perfect

good person. In the *Dictionary*, he would define "Probability" as "Likelihood; appearance of truth: *evidence arising from the preponderation of argument:* it is less than moral certainty" (italics added). His central clause implies an awareness of Bernouilli's Theorem, for preponderation of evidence is important to valid probability judgments. So in Johnson we see a step toward the new character, but only a small one. His treatment of probability and character will mature later, in his Shakespeare criticism.

The *Rambler* comment on character and the *Dictionary* definition of probability show that Johnson is unable to resolve the conflicting demands of the didactic character type and the natural "probable" character. Probability, in the mathematical sense, may indeed be obtained by weighing a preponderation of evidence relating to the occurrence of an event. But in the drawing of a literary character, probability is not necessarily achieved by presenting massive amounts of evidence about a person. The evidence could all be very one-sided: mere *length* or *richness of description* does not automatically make a character highly probable. The *Characters* of Samuel Butler, for instance, notable for their length and scurrilous detail, are perhaps the most elaborate types ever constructed.[21] Those of Smollett, also unusually rich in detail for the eighteenth-century novel, are almost always types; they are readily *predictable*, in the typological manner, but their *probability* is dubious.[22] The solution to the problem of this kind of character lies elsewhere than in length. At this point, let me refer to Fielding.

Fielding thought more about the nature of character than any other eighteenth-century writer. From "An Essay on the Knowledge of the Characters of Men" to his last novel, the probability of character concerned him.[23] The concept of the ruling passion or "the true Characteristic" of people was especially popular in the first half of the eighteenth century. It would have been easy for Fielding to subscribe to it in his novels, as he does in his early "Essay." In the preface to *Joseph Andrews*, however, he is careful to steer a middle course between the two genres, romance and burlesque, which produce character types most readily. Not that personages with names like Abraham Adams and Joseph Andrews are without their typed qualities. But in introducing them Fielding says, "And here I solemnly protest, I have not Intention to vilify or asperse any one: for tho' every thing is copied from the Book of Nature, and scarce a Character or Action produced which I have not taken from my own Observations and Experience, yet I have used utmost Care to obscure the persons."[24] This is the author's argument for accuracy, backed up by sound empirical methodology. Two years later, in his preface to Sarah Fielding's *The Adventures of David Simple*, Fielding continues to develop his theory of character:

> As to the Characters here described, I shall repeat the Saying of one of the greatest Men of this Age, *That they are as wonderfully drawn by the Writer, as they were by* Nature *herself.* There are many strokes in *Orgeuil*, *Spatter*, *Varnish*, *Le-vif*, the *Balancer*, and some others, which would have shined in the Pages of *Theophrastus*, *Horace*, or *La Bruyere*. Nay, there are some Touches, which I will venture to say might have done honour to the Pencil of the immortal *Shakespear* himself.[25]

The names of Sarah Fielding's characters make them sound as if they were traditional types, but this is deceptive. They are actually multivalent characters; only David Simple is a genuine type.

Fielding's emphasis on drawing directly from Nature and experience rather than from books is significant, but so far he makes no perceptible link to probability theory. The link appears in *Tom Jones*, VIII.1, the longest of that novel's prefatory chapters. Here Fielding proposes that "we must keep . . . within the rules of probability" in describing human nature, or character. The novelist cannot imitate the historian, for the writer of fiction has "no public notoriety, no concurrent testimony, no records to support or corroborate" what he delivers. How to convince an audience that a fictional character is probable? Clearly, the authority of the author as an accurate witness must be established, something Fielding is careful to do at this point by reporting on two historical characters from contemporary England, the evil Henry Fisher and the good Ralph Allen, in such a way that his readers could validate his trustworthiness. Here it may be helpful to refer to a maxim in eighteenth-century evidentiary proceedings: "All men have an equal right to be believed, unless the contrary has been established from elsewhere."[26] Once Fielding has established his veracity (other novelists might do the same thing through various narrative devices), we can accept his statement that "every good author will confine himself within the bounds of probability." But what kind of characters will an audience find most probable? Here, too, Fielding is ready with an answer:

> In the last place, the actions should be such as may not only be within the compass of human agency, and which human agents may probably be supposed to do; but they should be likely for the very actors and characters themselves to have performed; for what may be only wonderful and surprising in one man, may become improbable, or indeed impossible, when related of another.[27]

Fielding's argument for the probability of character, then, is based on a mathematics which reduces the possibility of failure (or improbability) by limiting a given character's behavior to a human scale. *"Within the compass of human agency"* suggests that romance is unacceptable to a high degree of probability. Probability of character can then be achieved not by copiousness of descriptive detail but by a reputation for honesty and credibility: the witness becomes more important than the evidence. Fielding was not above creating old-fashioned character types like Squire Western or his disputatious parson and philosopher. But the central characters in *Tom Jones*, Bliful and Tom, are highly believable, mixed, multivalent people, mainly because their qualities are confined to human dimensions.

About a decade after *Tom Jones*, Bishop Hurd writes about the decline of romance. It weakened, he suggests, because it was superhuman; the characters were incredible. "Men of sense were doubly disgusted to find a representation of things *unlike* to what they observed in real life, and *beyond* what it was ever possible should have existed."[28] Beyond what was ever possible—too low on the scale of probability to qualify as credible: We have started to move away from Bernouilli's Theorem as it may apply to literature. The *quantity* of evidence has become less important than the *quality* of the presentation. Perhaps the point is made best by Johnson in the "Preface" to his edition of Shakespeare's *Works* (1765). In a famous passage, he ridicules the improbability of many characters in the theatre: "For this, probability is violated, life is misrepresented, and language is depraved." His observations on character recall those of Fielding cited above:

> Other dramatists can only gain attention by the hyperbolical or aggra- vated characters, by fabulous and unexampled excellence of depravity, as the writers of barbarous romances invigorated the reader by a giant and a dwarf; and he that should form his expectations of human affairs from the play, or from the tale, would be equally deceived. Shakespeare has no heroes; his scenes are occupied only by men, who act and speak as the reader thinks he should himself have spoken or acted on the same occasion: Even where the agency is supernatural the dialogue is level with life.[29]

The probable character is one whom we have no difficulty in comprehending because he or she falls within the common ex- perience of everyday life. A moment later Johnson tells us the praise of Shakespeare is "that his drama is the mirrour of life . . . by scenes from which a hermit may *estimate* the transactions of the world, and a confessor *predict* the progress of the pas- sions."[30] It is no accident that Johnson illustrates the under- standing of a Shakespearean play by employing mathematical terms, one from statistics, the other from probability theory. The purpose of probability judgments is to make the most ac- curate conjecture possible about the future, based on the limited evidence available to us. Johnson suggests that with Shakes- peare's characters we may make certain predictions, with a probability of one.

A few rules, now, as a guide to the probability of character. We have moved from character types, whose probability is en- forced by an unnatural arrangement of behavioral traits, to the beginnings of the modern character, where probability is com- pelled (*if* it is compelled) by attention to the rules of evidence. Both the credibility of the author and the competence of his or her evidence are supreme desiderata.[31] Above all, we must keep to a human scale, one the reader can credit. *Shakespeare has no heroes.* Could Thackeray have had this dictum in mind as a guide to his characters in *Vanity Fair* when he subtitled it "A Novel without a Hero"?

Notes

1. *Ars Conjectandi*, IV.i, in *Translations from James Bernouilli*, trans. Bing Sung (Cambridge, Mass.: Harvard University, Department of Statistics, 1966), p. 8.

2. I have in mind collections of maxims like those of La Rochefoucauld, books of characters like those of Joseph Hall, Overbury, and Earle, the *Characters* of La Bruyère, and the homiletic tradition of character writing, included in sermons.

3. Dryden's argument in favor of improbability in "Of Heroic Plays: An Essay" is an example of this kind of defense. See *Of Dramatic Poesy and Other Critical Essays*, ed. George Watson, 2 vols. (London: Dent, 1962), I, 156-166.

4. A good view on the development of sureties for validating a witness' testimony may be obtained from Jeremy Bentham's *The Rationale of Judicial Evidence*, written early in the nineteenth century and published by Bentham's executor after his death. See *The Works of Jeremy Bentham*, ed. John Bowring, 11 vols. (Edinburgh, 1838-1843), VI, 17-28.

5. For example, see Martin Price, "The Fictional Contract," in *Literary Theory and Structure*, ed. Frank Brady, John Palmer, and Martin Price (New Haven: Yale University Press, 1973), pp. 151-178, esp. pp. 152-158. Price discusses characters (pp. 161-162), but without suggesting what might seem obvious in such an essay, that their probabilistic qualities may help to involve the reader in the experience of a novel.

6. *Ars Conjectandi*, ed. cit., p. 13.

7. See A. W. F. Edwards, *Likelihood: An account of the statistical concept of "likelihood" and its application to scientific inference* (Cambridge: Cambridge University Press, 1972), pp. xv, 1-7.

8. *An Essay on Criticism*, 119.

9. There are limiting factors to this statement, such as those dictated by genre requirements, or those caused by historical or narrative errors. Cf. David Hackett Fischer, *Historians' Fallacies: Toward a Logic of Historical Thought* (New York: Harper & Row, 1970), pp. 131-163.

10. *Characters of Vertues and Vices in two Bookes* (London, 1608), Sig. A5^r.

11. See Sir Thomas Overbury, *His Wife. With Additions of New Characters . . .* , 11th ed. (London, 1622), Sig. Q4^{r-v}, "What a Character Is," and John Earle, *Micro-Cosmographie. Or, A Piece of the World Characteriz'd* (London, 1650). Earle makes no attempt at a theoretical statement, but his characters are extremely one-sided.

12. See *The Life and Works of John Arbuthnot*, ed. George A. Aitken (Oxford: Clarendon Press, 1892,), pp. 409-435, esp. 422 (on the application of concepts of probability). Arbuthnot also wrote *Of the Laws of Chance* (London, 1692). On probabilistic thought in the 1690's, see I. Todhunter, *A History of the Mathematical Theory of Probability* (London, 1865), pp. 44-55.

13. *The Characters, or the Manners of the Age* (London, 1699), "Prefatory Discourse" to *The Moral Characters of Theophrastus* (included with La Bruyère), Sig. Gg4^{r-v}.

14. *The Moral Characters of Theophrastus* (London, 1725), p. 7.

15. Ibid., pp. 66-67.

16. See J. R. Lucas, *The Concept of Probability* (Oxford, Clarendon Press, 1970), pp. 83-85; cf. p. 73.

17. Abraham de Moivre, *The Doctrine of Chances*, 3rd ed. (London, 1756), p. 242.

18. See Charles Gildon, *The Life and Strange Surprizing Adventures of Mr. D— De F—, of London, Hosier*, 2nd ed. (London, 1719), pp. 1-2, and passim. Gildon's "improbabilities" are curious. He had Friday confront his author and complain of the improbability that he had been shown to speak pidgin English after only a few months, but that he showed no further improvement in the next seven years.

19. James Beattie, "On Fable and Romance," in *Dissertations Moral and Critical*, 2 vols. (Dublin, 1783), II, 312-314, makes a sound early critique of Richardson's improbabilities of character.

20. Johnson, *Works*, Yale Edition (New Haven, 1954-   ), III, 24.

21. None of Butler's characters appeared before 1759, but they were written in the 1660s. They are numerous (nearly 200), and deal with the extremes of human behavior. See the *Characters*, ed. Charles W. Daves (Cleveland: The Press of Case Western Reserve University, 1970), pp. 12-27.

22. Beattie, "On Fable and Romance," *Dissertations Moral and Criti-*

cal, II, 316, mentions the improbability of many of Smollett's humorous characters.

23. The "Essay" appeared in the *Miscellanies*, Volume I (1742), but had clearly been much influenced by Pope's theory of characters presented in the *Moral Essays* seven years earlier. See. H. K. Miller, *Essays on Fielding's Miscellanies* (Princeton: Princeton University Press, 1961), pp. 189–228; and Sean Shesgreen, *Literary Portraits in the Novels of Henry Fielding* (DeKalb, Ill.: Northern Illinois University Press, 1972), pp. 15-21 only.

24. *The History of the Adventures of Joseph Andrews*, 2 vols. (London, 1742), I, xviii.

25. *The Adventures of David Simple*, 2nd ed., 2 vols. (London, 1744), I, xi.

26. This is cited as an hypothesis by John Craig in his *Theologiae Christianae Principia Mathematica* (Mathematical Principles of Christian Theology) (1699), an attempt to prove the basic truths of Christianity by mathematical methods, including probability theory. A translation appears as *Craig's Rules of Historical Evidence, 1699*, in *History and Theory*, Beiheft 4 (1964); see. p. 7.

27. *Tom Jones*, Modern Library ed. (New York, 1950), p. 337, cf. pp. 332-339.

28. *Letters on Chivalry and Romance* (London, 1762), p. 105.

29. *Works*, VII, 63-64.

30. *Works*, VII, 65; italics added.

31. See Charles T. McCormick's helpful chapter on "The Competency of Witnesses," in *Handbook of the Law of Evidence* (St. Paul, Minn.: West Publishing Co., 1954), pp. 139-150.

White of Selborne: The Ethos of Probabilism

Hoyt Trowbridge

I

Having previously discussed Dr. Johnson's *Preface to Shakespeare* as an example of probable reasoning in humanistic thought,[1] I should like here to examine another example, taken from a quite different area of inquiry: Gilbert White's *The Natural History and Antiquities of Selborne* (1789), a work on the botany, zoology, topography, and climatology of a small rural district—actually, a single parish in Hampshire.

Probable reasoning can legitimately and profitably be considered from a purely technical point of view, as a kind of logic or method of proof, with its own special rules of evidence, types of argument, and criteria of validation. White makes only a few generalizations about method in his book; he is not writing a technical treatise, and he seems to have assumed that the standards for valid biological inference and proof could be taken for granted, as well established by previous naturalists and generally understood by intelligent readers. The criteria governing his own reasoning, however, are quite clearly discernible in his arguments on particular questions, as well as in a number of brief statements and asides. Using a binomial system of classification, as he himself habitually does in identifying plants and animals, we may describe his kind of thinking as Baconian empiricism in genus, Lockeian probabilism in species. His relation to both of those great predecessors will be discussed below. But probabilism, as conceived and practiced by many eighteenth-century English writers, has a further, non-technical dimension, a matrix of religious and ethical concepts and attitudes, as much imaginative and emotional as they are intellectual. In discussing White's *Natural History*, I will begin with the technical aspect, moving at the end of the essay to the extralogical framework, the ethos which suffuses the technical procedures with larger meanings and values.

II

Gilbert White (1720–1793) was an Anglican country parson, classically educated at Basingstoke Grammar School and Oriel College, Oxford (B.A. '43, elected fellow '44, M.A. '46), who was interested from boyhood in the flora and fauna of his native Hampshire. He early developed habits of close and systematic observation of natural phenomena, recorded first in a Garden Kalendar day by day, later in the Journal which became the basis of the *Natural History*, his one published book.[2]

The work is composed in the form of three series of letters. The first two, totaling a hundred and ten letters between them, are concerned with natural history; the third, on the antiquities of Selborne, will be disregarded here. The first forty-four letters are addressed, under dates ranging from 1767 to 1780, to Thomas Pennant, author of *British Zoology*, a very popular book published by White's brother Benjamin, a London bookseller, who also published *Selborne* itself. The second series, sixty-six letters dated between 1769 and 1787, is addressed to the Hon. Daines Barrington, a lawyer, antiquarian, and gentleman naturalist (and incidentally, a member of Dr. Johnson's Club).

The tone and style of the letters are in keeping with the epistolary form and the character of the addressees. Both Pennant

and Barrington were well-educated men, fully participating in
the Christian-classical culture of the period; White writes as a
member of the same culture who shares with them a special
interest in natural history. He speaks throughout in the first
person, and one of the chief sources of the much-celebrated
charm of the letters is the omnipresence of White's highly individual, yet unmistakably eighteenth-century, mind and voice.
He freely quotes passages in Greek or Latin, usually without
translating, and he refers to the works of other naturalists as to
writings already familiar to his correspondents. He is also fond
of quoting from the poets, especially Milton, Thomson, and
Virgil; one of his pleasantest letters speculates on the particular
species of *hirundo* Virgil had in mind in a passage of the Geor-
gics, concluding from several details that it was probably one of
the swallows.[3]

All the letters are short, ranging in the first and most later
editions from a single page to a maximum of four or five. Some
are extremely miscellaneous, but a number of letters assemble
observations, made over a long period of time, on a single subject. Among such "monographies," as White calls them, are the
series of four letters on the chief English species of *hirundines*
(DB 16, 18, 20, 21)[4] and the remarkable letter on earthworms,
scarcely a page long, which anticipates many of the findings in
Darwin's classic treatment of the subject (DB 35).[5] Many subjects are returned to again and again; White reaches a definite
conclusion on some of the questions raised, but several of the
most important of them are left open.

White in the Baconian Tradition

Anything like a full account of Bacon's program for the reform
of philosophy and the sciences would obviously be out of place
here, but a few of the most basic planks in his platform may be
briefly summarized in order to bring out the Baconian strain in
White's thought.

A fact that is not much stressed by some students of Bacon,
though it seems to me fundamental, is his forceful rejection of
both dogmatists and sceptics. After a few cursory observations,

he says, the former "lay down the law of nature as a thing already searched out and understood," while the latter "have taken a contrary course, and asserted that absolutely nothing can be known."[6] The attitude of mind that Bacon advocates is not the Acatalepsis of the Greek Sceptics, but Eucatalepsis—"not denial of the capacity to understand but provision for understanding truly, for I do not take away authority from the senses, but supply them with helps; I do not slight the understanding, but govern it" (*New Organon*, Aph. cxxvi; cf. Aph. xxxvii; Sp. VIII, 158, 75). Truth is attainable, but only if it is pursued with a humble submission of mind to the facts of nature, and by means of the proper method, rigorously applied.

Bacon envisioned a New Philosophy to be developed in two distinct stages. The first, the compilation of an encyclopaedic natural history, was an immense task, requiring the collaborative effort of many workers over a considerable, though not infinite, period of time—perhaps several generations. Its purpose was to record the results of comprehensive observations and experiments and to draw from them the first tentative, relatively low-level generalizations or axioms which they directly warranted. Bacon came to believe that the natural history, as the basis, starting point, and "true nursing mother" of philosophy, was even more essential than the methodology which he had hoped to develop in the *Novum Organum*:

> ... my Organum, even if it were completed, would not without the Natural History, much advance the Instauration of the Sciences, whereas the Natural History without the Organum would advance it not a little. (*De historia naturali et experimentali monitum*, Sp. V, 133–134).

It was only in the second phase, nevertheless, that the great Instauration would be brought to fruition. This phase, the Interpretation of Nature, would build on the foundation of the natural history a complete philosophy, a pyramidal theoretical structure of principles and laws in natural philosophy, physic, and metaphysic (*De Augumentis*, Bk. III, Ch. iv; Sp. VII, 507). Bacon believed that the work of the first phase could be done by men of moderate mental capacity, but that the second phase required a higher kind of talent. He would have dearly loved to reserve the whole Interpretation of Nature for himself, if only the natural history had been in existence to build it on.[7]

In both stages, the method was to be inductive. Bacon's theory of induction—with its interlocking doctrines of designed rather than random observations, inclusions and exclusions through comparison of positive and negative instances, tables for selecting and sorting the mass of historical data, and so on— is far too complex and debatable to be treated adequately here. For present purposes, it is perhaps sufficient to illustrate Bacon's most basic methodological conviction by citing a well-known passage in the *Magna Instauratio:*

> . . . in dealing with the nature of things I use induction throughout, and that in the minor propositions as well as the major. For I consider induction to be that form of demonstration which upholds the sense, and closes with nature, and comes to the very brink of operation, if it does not actually deal with it. . . . Now my plan is to proceed regularly and gradually from one axiom to another, so that the most general are not reached till the last, but when you do come to them, you find them to be not empty notions but well defined, and such as nature would really recognize as her first principles, and such as lie at the heart and marrow of things. ("The Arguments of the several Parts," *M.I.*, Sp. VIII, 42).

Bacon's many warnings against trust in authority are in part a consequence of his conception of the state of learning in his age. Since he believed that the truths of nature could be discovered only by making a totally new start, using a different method, all previous philosophy and commonly received opinions fell under suspicion; they might be good for something, but not for the New Philosophy. The Idols of the Theatre—the phantasms implanted in the mind by dogmas, systems, and wrong laws of demonstration—are given that name because all those principles, axioms, and rules are "but so many stage-plays, representing worlds of their own creation after an unreal and scenic fashion" and received by men through tradition, credulity, and negligence (*N.O.*, Aph. xliv; Sp. VIII, 78). But there is a more permanent and philosophical reason for rejecting arguments from authority, for even if the Baconian natural history now existed, the truth of its axioms would depend not on the prestige of its authors but on the observations and experiments from which their generalizations were derived. In the search for truth, we must go not to books but to nature, to the things themselves; if we aspire not to guess and divine, but to discover and know, we must "go to facts themselves for everything" (*M.I.*, Sp. VIII, 46).

Two other precepts, though less basic, are important as anticipating certain aspects of the new inductive sciences soon to be developed on Baconian principles. One is that the things observed should, wherever possible, be "numbered, weighed, measured, defined." The value of careful measurements is partly utilitarian, because "practical working comes of the due combination of physics and mathematics," but they are also needed in many cases to guarantee the accuracy and dependability of the naturalist's generalizations. The other rule is that no aspect of nature—however ordinary or seemingly trivial, however "mean, illiberal, filthy"—should be neglected by the new philosophy; since the observations to be set forth in the natural history are not collected on their own account, their importance is to be measured not by what the things observed are worth in themselves, but "according to their indirect bearing upon other things, and the influence they may have upon philosophy" (*Parasceve*, Aphs. vi, vii; Sp. VIII, 365).

Finally, there is Bacon's deeply rooted conviction that scientific knowledge would be "operative to relieve the inconveniences of man's estate" (*De Aug.*, Bk. II, Ch. ii; Sp. VII, 415). He distinguishes between experiments of "light" and experiments of "fruit," repeatedly asserting that the aim of the new philosophy is to bring light through axioms concerning the natures and causes of things (*N.O.*, Aph. xcix; Sp. VIII, 135). He warns against over-eagerness in the pursuit of immediate practical benefits:

> . . . I wait for harvest-time, and do not attempt to mow the moss or to reap the corn. For I well know that axioms once rightly discovered will

carry whole troops of works along with them, and produce them, not here and there but in clusters. And that unseasonable and puerile hurry to snatch by way of earnest at the first works which come within reach, I utterly condemn and reject, as an Atalanta's apple that hinders the race. (*M.I.*, Sp. VIII, 48).

Bacon is not an utilitarian or a pragmatist, since use is not for him a sign or test of truth, but the usefulness of scientific knowledge in improving man's condition is a great argument for its value.

In comparing White with Bacon, we must remember that a century and a half had intervened between the posthumous publication of Bacon's last work, *The New Atlantis* (1627), and the publication of White's *Natural History*. It was the same period in which America grew from the Mayflower Compact to the Constitution, and progress in the world of science was similarly spectacular. The main outlines of Bacon's program for science had been adopted and institutionalized by the founding of the Royal Society (incorporated by royal charter in 1662), which Joseph Glanvill saw as the fulfillment of Bacon's "Prophetick Scheam" of Salomon's House.[8] Its official journal, the *Philosophical Transactions*, had appeared continuously for more than a century when White wrote. By his generation, men were at work on scientific studies all over Europe, and a network of learned societies, books and journals, collections, museums, and botanic gardens had been built up, providing naturalists with much accumulated knowledge and many aids and models.

White was by no means isolated from the main currents of life and thought in his time. Though he lived in a small village, not easily accessible, he had responsibilities in London and Oxford which took him regularly to both centers. He was familiar with the major works of seventeenth- and eighteenth-century biology, both English and Continental. In identifying species, and for other purposes as well, he habitually cites John Ray (1627-1705), the first great English naturalist, and the later *Systema Naturae* of the Swede Linnaeus (1707-1778). He also refers to the writings of Ray's associates, Francis Willughby and

William Derham, and to Edward Stillingfleet and Stephen Hales among British natural philosophers, and to such European biologists as Brisson, Réaumur, and Buffon, all Frenchmen, and Swammerdam, Kramer, and Scopoli, who were Dutch, Austrian, and Italian respectively. White's greatest debt is to men like these, rather than directly to Bacon, but they were all Baconian in working by inductive methods toward a universal natural history.

White describes himself as an "out-door naturalist," one who seeks to achieve the relatively humble aim of observing closely and recording accurately the "natural productions and occurrences" of a single topographical area ("Advertisement," p. 13; cf. DB 1). His most comprehensive biological generalization is the obvious, almost undisputable one that animal behavior is motivated by two instinctual drives, self-preservation and the propagation of the species (DB 8, 11), and his few original discoveries are all of a low order of generalization, very close to the observed phenomena.[9] Bacon would surely have judged him to be a commendable worker in the vineyard of natural history, a man of moderate talent doing essential, though unspectacular, tasks.

But White does not distinguish, as Bacon does, between two stages in the development of the new science. He thought of himself as a "thinking man" (a phrase he uses several times). Though not aspiring to resolve fundamental problems having broad theoretical implications, he did wish to study the world around him philosophically—to connect one observed phenomenon with others, to go beyond description to discover causes and mechanisms, to learn wherever possible not only the fact but the reason for the fact (DB 4, 66). He believed that systematic taxonomy is necessary, for without it nature would be a pathless wilderness, but that the botanist should not be content with a list of names:

> ... he should study plants philosophically, should investigate the laws of vegetation, should examine the powers and virtues of efficacious herbs, should promote their cultivation. ... System should be subservient to, not the main object of, pursuit. (DB 40)

White was not satisfied to be a collector and classifier; he hoped in some measure to be not merely an observer, but an Interpreter of Nature.

White's commitment to Baconian induction is everywhere apparent. The very notion of "parochial history" is Baconian, since it rests on the assumption that conclusions must always be grounded on close observation of particulars. As he repeatedly says, generalizations about nature can be asserted with confidence only after "many years of exact observation" (DB 16, 21). It is for this reason that he puts such a high value on "monographies," studies of limited scope dealing either with a single species or genus of animals, like his paper on earthworms, or with a variety of species inhabiting a particular district, like *Selborne* as a whole. Speaking of Scopoli's book on the flora and fauna of the Tyrol, he says:

> Monographers, come from whence they may, have, I think, fair pretence to challenge some regard and approbation from the lovers of natural history; for, as no man can alone investigate all the works of nature, these partial writers may, each in their department, be more accurate in their discoveries, and freer from errors, than more general writers; and so by degrees may pave the way to an universal correct natural history. (TP 31; cf. DB 7, 10, 16).

White's attitude toward authority is less polemical than Bacon's, but as a good empiricist he "takes his observations from the subject itself, and not from the writings of others" (DB 1). He does need additional observations, to extend his data beyond those he has been able to observe himself; and he kept urging his relatives, friends, and correspondents to observe regularly in their own neighborhoods, to keep records and send him reports, and to send or bring specimens for first-hand study. He is always cautious and discriminating, however, in accepting the testimony not only of lay correspondents but of men like Réaumur, Linnaeus, Ray, and other naturalists. Some of his informants are "nice" or "very exact" observers, but others are less worthy of credit because they are not naturalists, lack ornithological knowledge, report facts at second hand, or observe too carelessly (TP 10, 44; DB 4, 14, 23, 24). White does not give implicit trust even to the fellow-scientists whom he respects most, but maintains his independence of judgment and tests their findings against his own observations. Linnaeus's theory that swallows hibernate under water seems to him incredible; and Scopoli, though generally a good naturalist, falls into errors by comparing one animal with another by memory, without specimens before him (TP 32). Even Ray sometimes errs; after procuring and studying several specimens, both alive and dead, of a bird described by Ray, White concludes that it was "so strangely classed" by his much admired predecessor, who ranged it under a quite impossible order (TP 25). For White, as for Bacon, the ultimate authority can only be nature itself, the objective phenomena, the facts.

White is also Baconian in his belief that no aspect of nature is unworthy of study. He is never squeamish; and many of the subjects he discusses might be considered "mean, illiberal, filthy" by some fastidious people, such as the burrowing habits of field-crickets, the mysterious mechanisms of generation in toads and eels, the copulation of swifts while on the wing, the food of hedgehogs as indicated by their dung, the means by which young birds in the nest are saved from poisoning by their own excreta (TP 17, 27, 40; DB 21). He was well aware, too, that most things in nature are subject to quantitative variation, and that many phenomena can be accurately described only after careful counts or measurements, carried out over a long period of time. Speaking of mean rainfall, an obvious example, White gives figures for total annual rainfall in Selborne during the years 1779–1787, which vary from 27 to 39 inches, but he declines even to estimate the average amount: "As my experience in measuring the water is but of short date, I am not qualified to give the mean quantity" (TP 5). He does give dates for the arrival and departure of migratory birds, and also the dates on which various species of birds begin and cease to sing; but he is careful to state that the figures can only be approximate, since the timing varies from year to year (DB 1–3). He remembers, too, that individuals within the same species may vary widely in size, weight, and other features, and that allowance must always be made for sex, age, and other variables. In reporting his most heroic effort of this kind, when he measured the putrefying carcass of a female moose, he apologizes because the stench made a closer and more detailed examination insupportable (TP 28).

On the usefulness of natural knowledge, as on the dangers of trusting to authority, White is more moderate than Bacon but holds an essentially similar view. He thinks, for example, that a full history of noxious insects "would be allowed by the public to be a most useful and important work," and regrets that such knowledge lies scattered, needing to be collected (TP 34). In a similar vein he reports on the raising and harvesting of hops, a principal Selborne crop, and gives an exact account of the process of manufacturing rush-lights, as a much cheaper substitute for candles (TP 1; DB 26). He wishes that some future faunist would make a field expedition to Ireland, a country little known to naturalists, because a "person of a thinking turn of mind" would surely draw many just remarks and useful reflections from such a survey (TP 42). White believes that the kind of knowledge presented by a natural historian could be of great practical benefit, and he does not hesitate to point out possible applications of his own observations, but his primary aim in studying nature is simply to know and understand it. Light comes first, though fruits will surely follow.

III

Locke, of course, is another member of the Baconian genus. His theory of human understanding is an autonomous philosophy, with its own internal structural relations, its own vocabulary of concepts and terms; it incorporates many principles and distinctions not to be found in Bacon, and a number of Bacon's most cherished ideas (such as the Tables of Discovery for ordering observed data) have no place in Lockeian epistemology. Locke does subscribe, nevertheless, to several basic planks in Bacon's platform, adapting and restating them in his own terms.

The parallel is particularly close on the attainability of truth. Bacon offers a middle way between the dogmatists and the sceptics. In different words but to the same effect, Locke speaks scornfully of both the Pyrrhonists, who "question everything, and disclaim all knowledge, because some things are not to be understood," and at the opposite extreme those over-confident reasoners who presume that "the whole vast ocean of being is the natural and undoubted possession of our understandings."[10] Truth in many things is not beyond men's grasp, if they will only use properly the powers of understanding which have been given to them.

Because of his view that all reasoning consists in the comparison of ideas to determine their agreement or disagreement, Locke does not speak of induction and deduction; but he is as emphatic as Bacon in asserting that all knowledge begins in particulars, as perceived through observation and experience: "For in *particulars* our knowledge begins, and so spreads itself, by degrees, to *generals*" (IV, vii, 11). His attack on the syllogism as useless for the discovery of truth, good only for overcoming an opponent in debate, is as vigorous and eloquent as any of Bacon's many disquisitions on that subject.[11] His attitude toward authority is the same as Bacon's: It is utter folly for anyone who wishes to comprehend truth to regulate his assent by the opinion of others, because the only arguments that give true instruction are those which bring to the question "light arising from the nature of things themselves" (IV, xvii, 19–22; cf. xx, 17). Though he has little to say about the need for exact quantitative measurements, his understanding of the role of mathematics in science—thanks partly to Newton, born more than a generation too late to be known to Bacon—is actually much better than Bacon's.

One of the differences between Bacon and Locke is on the usefulness of natural knowledge. While Locke agrees that important material benefits may be expected to flow from inductive science, he does not press that point in defending his revolutionary approach to philosophy; when he speaks of the uses of understanding, he is much more inclined to think of its ethical value, as providing guidance in the pursuit of happiness and the conduct of our moral lives ("Introduction," Fraser, I, 30).

Like White, he also differs from Bacon in conceiving science and philosophy as a single continuous process, thus collapsing the Baconian distinction between the first and second phases, the natural history and the interpretation of nature.

But the most fundamental difference between Bacon and Locke, at least in the present context, is their sharply divergent attitudes toward probable reasoning. Bacon believed that induction, correctly used, could arrive at clear and certain truth, eventually revealing the natures or forms, the inner causal principles explaining all the things and processes of the world and of man. He was familiar with probable reasoning, which had been discussed at length by Aristotle, Cicero, and other ancients; but he associated it with rhetoric and the wrangling of the schools. He says that the probabilism of the New Academy, allowing "some things to be followed as probable, though of none to be maintained as true," is merely a diluted form of Pyrrhonism, which carries men round in a whirl of arguments and disheartens them for the severe but constructive discipline of inductive investigation (*N.O.*, Aph. lxvii; Sp. VIII, 98). The end of the new philosophy is to invent arts, principles, and works, not arguments and probable reasons. Its aim is to comprehend nature in action: "to seek, not pretty and probable conjectures, but certain and demonstrable knowledge" ("Preface, " *Magna Instauratio;* "Plan of the Work," *M.I.;* "Preface," *N.O.;* Sp. VIII, 30–31, 40–41, 63–64).

While agreeing that truth is attainable in many things and that Pyrrhonism is mere nihilism and despair, Locke recognizes two paths toward human comprehension, not one alone. The first, which he calls "knowledge," is far superior because it leads to clear and certain truths: the existence of God and the necessity of obeying his commandments, the existence of external things and of ourselves as individuals, the axioms and conclusions of pure mathematics (IV, i–xiii). But Locke denies that our minds are capable of certain and demonstrable knowledge in any aspect of nature. What Bacon calls the forms or natures of things—in Locke's vocabulary, their "real essences"—are concealed from us. Since we can understand the species of natural substances only through an "imperfect collection of those apparent qualities our senses can discover," we cannot know the "precise bounds and extent" of any such species, nor grasp the causal relationships among their observable attributes and powers. To comprehend nature, therefore, we must fall back to the second path—from the bright sunshine of knowledge to the twilight of probability, a method leading to "*belief, assent,* or *opinion,* which is the admitting or receiving any proposition for true, upon arguments or proofs that are found to persuade us to receive it as true, without certain knowledge that it is so" (II, xxiii; III, vi, 9; IV, vi, 4-15; xv, 4).

For Locke, then, probable reasoning is a legitimate and fruitful method of inquiry, providing a rational basis for accepting or rejecting many propositions of great theoretical and practical importance. Though admittedly second-best, because it can never attain certainty, it is all we have to guide us both in the inductive sciences and in the ordinary affairs of human life.

The *Essay Concerning Human Understanding* is, of course, a theoretical treatise on epistemology, not a handbook of practical logic. In the seven chapters devoted to probable reasoning in the fourth Book, nevertheless, Locke does establish the distinctive "grounds and measures" governing such reasoning and develops a number of specific concepts or principles concerning its use for discovery and proof. Since they were summarized at some length in my earlier paper, these ideas will not be reviewed again here. Instead, four of them will be briefly restated below, followed in each case by examples from the *Natural History*, in which White invokes the same principle or rule in reaching conclusions on the various biological problems that he considers.

White As Probabilist
1. How testimonies should be weighed
According to Locke, the second of two general "Grounds of Probability" is the testimony of others, vouching their observation and experience. In weighing testimonies, he says, we should apply six criteria: the number of witnesses; their integrity; their skill; the author's design, if the testimony is cited from a book;

and contrary testimonies (IV, xv, 4). In judging the degree of credence to be given to the reports of lay correspondents and the findings of other naturalists, as we have seen above, White does not give implicit trust to the factual observations, still less to the opinions, of any authority. But the naturalists as a group are more reliable, because of their greater skill and integrity, though some of them are more rigorous than others; Ray is more dependable than Scopoli, but Ray too can err. Among the laymen, some are almost as intelligent, veracious, and exact as the best of the professionals, while others are careless, have too little knowledge, depend on hearsay, fail to mention the circumstances under which observations were made, or claim as fact what other observers have repeatedly denied. White's attitude toward authority is Baconian, but the specific criteria by which he weighs testimonies are those which Locke lays down.

2. Reasoning from analogy

The first, and more basic, ground of probability is the principle of analogy, the agreement or conformity of any proposition with *"common observation in like cases"* (xvi, 9). Since Locke contends that in "most parts of the works of nature" all that we perceive is the sensible effects, we can only guess and conjecture concerning the "ways or means how they are produced," judging alleged causes to be probable or improbable "as they more or less agree to truths that are established in our minds, and as they hold proportion to other parts of our knowledge and observation. *Analogy* in these matters is the only help we have, and it is from that alone we draw all our grounds of probability." Locke recognizes that analogies can be false and deceptive, but he believes that a "wary" reasoning from analogy can often lead us to "the discovery of truths and useful productions, which would otherwise lie concealed" (xvi, 12).[12]

White frequently reasons from analogy, but he is extremely wary of its possible dangers. His ambiguous attitude is apparent in one of the letters to Pennant, in which he says that a problem which had long puzzled him, the reasons for the early departure of the swifts, might be resolved by analogy with a large species of bat:

> Though I delight very little in analogous reasoning, knowing how falla-
> cious it is with respect to natural history; yet in the following instance,
> I cannot help being inclined to think it may conduce towards the expla-
> nation of a difficulty that I have mentioned before, with respect to the
> invariable early retreat of the *hirundo apus*, or swift, so many weeks be-
> fore it's congeners.

Both the birds and the bats fly higher in feeding and emigrate
earlier than related species; these are the observed phenomena,
the "sensible effects" that Locke speaks of. White conjectures
that in both cases the unknown cause is the kind of food available at those high altitudes, "some sorts of high-flying gnats,
scarabs, of *phalaenae*, that are of short continuance; and that
the short stay of these strangers is regulated by the defect of
their food" (TP 26).

In spite of his qualms, White reasons from analogy on dozens
of questions. He confesses—"not without some degree of shame"
—that in believing that ousels and fieldfares migrate to Selborne
from the north he had reasoned only from analogy with other
autumnal birds (TP 25). He confirms observations about the behavior of stone-curlews by parallels with the manners of bus-
tards, who also resemble the curlews in aspect and make, and in
the structure of their feet (TP 33). He speculates that the relatively rare large bats may not be a separate species from the
commoner small variety, but only males of the same species; the
discrepancy in numbers might be explained by the ability of
one male to serve many females, as among sheep and other
quadrupeds (TP 36). He also draws inferences about the fatten-
ing of long-billed birds during moderate frosts from observations on rabbits and hogs; about the coloration of young birds
by analogy with the lack of sexual differentiation in the young
of quadrupeds and men; about a skeletal structure in fallow deer
from an apparently similar one in men, and about the physiological function of that structure from facts about asses and
horses (DB 5, 6; TP 14).

The dangers of analogous reasoning in natural history are well
illustrated by the last of these instances, for modern biologists
have shown quite conclusively that the resemblance between

the spiracula of the fallow deer and the *puncta lachrymalia* in the human head is superficial and misleading, and that the spiracula are not secondary breathing-places, as White supposed, but outlets for a glandular secretion.[13] But in many of the works of nature, as Locke observes, analogy is "the only help we have, and it is from that alone we draw all our grounds of probability." White does not violate Locke's principles in comparing the spiracula with the *puncta lachrymalia*, since he claims no more than that they are "*probably* analogous" (italics mine).

3. Hypothesis in biological reasoning

In explaining any phenomena of nature, Locke says, it is not improper to "make use of any probable hypothesis whatsoever: Hypotheses, if they are well made, are at least great helps to the memory, and often direct us to new discoveries." He warns, however, that hypotheses can easily lead us astray. Unless they are grounded on well-examined particulars, take account of negative instances, and are advanced tentatively rather than dogmatically, they can impose upon us by "making us receive that for an unquestionable truth, which is really at best but a very doubtful conjecture; such as are most (I had almost said all) of the hypotheses in natural philosophy" (IV, xii, 13; I, iii, vii; IV, vii).

A striking example of White's way of reasoning is his refutation of an hypothesis advanced by Herissant, a French anatomist. The problem is an old one, on which many naturalists had speculated: The causes which prevent cuckoos from hatching their own eggs. Herissant hypothesizes that the placement of the cuckoo's crop, behind the sternum and immediately over the bowels, makes the process of incubation very uncomfortable, if not impossible. Having first confirmed the anatomical observation by making his own dissection of a specimen cuckoo, White then goes on to procure and dissect two other kinds of bird, the fern-owl and ring-tail hawk, both of which are known to hatch their eggs. Since it turns out that the crops of both birds lie in the same situation as the cuckoo's, Herissant's conjecture falls to the ground, leaving the problem still unsolved (DB 30). White's experiment neatly illustrates Bacon's method

of positive and negative instances, as well as Locke's rule that
hypotheses, though legitimate and necessary, should always be
tested against observed data.

Faced with a problem which "baffles our searches" (DB 21),
as naturalists so frequently are, a thinking man can only "hazard a supposition" (DB 23). In his search for the reason behind
the fact, for the unknown causes of visible effects, White offers
such conjectures on many occasions. Why should frequently
flooded lands be poor? (DB 35). Why has leprosy almost totally
disappeared in England? (DB 32). Why do house-martins often
reappear for a single day in November, after apparently departing, to a bird, early in October? (DB 36). How might we account for the fact that many kinds of birds, unsocial during
most of the year, gather in great flocks during harsh winter
weather? (DB 10). What motives could explain why "so cruel
and sanguinary a beast as a cat" should adopt and foster a baby
rabbit, usually its natural prey? (DB 34). To these and other
queries, White sometimes offers a single possible solution, sometimes several alternative hypotheses. Whether singular or plural,
these conjectures are legitimate, in a Lockeian logic of probability, because White never mistakes them for unquestionable
truths. They are always advanced tentatively, almost diffidently,
and often with a wish for additional information or an invitation for others to refute or support his proposals with further
evidence.

4. The degrees of assent

According to Locke, "the principal act of ratiocination is *the
finding the agreement or disagreement of two ideas one with
another, by the intervention of a third.*" This is the process
both in demonstrative arguments, which can lead to certain
knowledge, and in probable reasoning, which cannot; the difference is that in demonstration the agreement of the inter-
mediary idea with the two extremes is clear and certain, while
in judgments of probability it is only a "*usual* or *likely* one,"
a connexion which is not constant and immutable, but "is, or
appears for the most part to be so." Since the usual and the
likely admit degrees of frequency—as "for the most part" also

implies—a sound judge of probability must "take a true estimate of the force and weight of each probability; and then casting them up all right together, choose that side which has the over-balance." The degree of assent that we give to any probable proposition should be proportional to the extent of the overbalance favoring the more probable side. As the latter may vary "from the very neighborhood of certainty and demonstration, quite down to improbability and unlikeliness, even to the confines of impossibility," so the former should range from "full assurance and confidence, quite down to conjecture, doubt, and distrust" (IV, xv, 1, 2; xvii, 16, 18).

The conception that all thought consists in the comparison of ideas is an essential element in Locke's epistemology, but it arises from philosophical issues which need not concern a working naturalist. White does not speak of the agreement or disagreement of ideas; while always remembering that he knows his plants and animals only through observation and experiment, he assumes in commonsense fashion that he is comparing things with things, facts with facts. He is entirely in accord with Locke, however, in recognizing that biological propositions can never be certain, and that the degree of our confidence in them should be proportioned to the force and weight of the evidence in each case, which varies over a very wide range.

Since White, like Locke himself, has no statistical techniques for quantifying such judgments, he is forced to express the varying shades of assurance by a collection of graduated verbal distinctions. At one end of the scale, propositions so strongly supported that they almost reach the neighborhood of certainty may be described as "very near the truth" or even as "past all doubt," though such endorsements are often qualified by a "seems" or "appears" (TP 21, 22; DB 8, 21). At the opposite extreme are questions which are "too puzzling to answer," on which we are "very much in the dark" (TP 17, 34, 40). In between lies a spectrum from the very probable or more probable to the probable, the improbable, and the very improbable. Some generalizations are "true on the whole," and on some problems we can be "pretty sure," "pronounce with some certainty," or believe with "sufficient show of reason" (TP 17; DB 7, 17, 42). In some cases the evidence "seems to be a full proof" or constitutes "a strong proof to the contrary," but in others we may "have some doubt" or be "ready to doubt" (DB 1, 3, 8, 16). This vocabulary, almost identical with the one Dr. Johnson uses for the same purpose in the *Preface to Shakespeare*, was the only language available for making such discriminations in a pre-statistical age. Though imprecise, it expresses very well the shadings appropriate to the second-best method, to the twilight world of probable reasoning.

IV

The "ethos" of probabilism, as I have rather vaguely called it, is grounded on a set of mutually coherent concepts in morality and divinity, "those parts of knowledge that men are most concerned to be clear in" (Locke, ed. Fraser, I, 16), but it is not wholly intellectual; associated with the ideas is an interlocking complex of imaginative and emotional responses or attitudes toward God, nature, and man. Both aspects of this *Weltanschauung* are manifested in ideas and feelings expressed by Locke, by John Ray, the English naturalist so much admired by White, and by White himself.

Locke and the Ethos of Probabilism

Locke's *Essay* is a secular work on a specialized subject. It is based not on revealed truth but on arguments and evidence available to natural reason, and its epistemological conclusions describe human understanding as it operates on this earth and is comprehended by us through observation, experience, and ratiocination. But Locke was a deeply religious man who saw nature and mankind in a theological perspective. Without violating his empirical methodology or overstepping the boundaries of his specialized concerns, he indicates in many places that the powers and limits of the human mind may be set into a wider context of religious and philosophical truths.

Locke believed that the existence and attributes of God

could be proved with demonstrative certainty; his argument is an inference from an intuitively known effect, our own existence as thinking beings, to its cause, the prior existence of *"an eternal, most powerful, and most knowing Being"* (IV, x, 1-6). He also believed, but does not attempt to prove, that from the ideas of a supreme Being and of ourselves as corporeal rational creatures "a great part of morality might be made out with that clearness, that could leave, to a considering man, no more reason to doubt, than he could have to doubt of the truth of propositions in mathematics, which have been demonstrated to him." Since he does not prove this proposition, but merely asserts it as a possibility, he is careful to describe it as a "conjecture" which he has "suggested" (III, xi, 16; IV, iii, 18; iv, 7; xii, 8).

The wise and almighty Being is the creator not only of man but of all existing things. If there are spiritual creatures higher than man in the scale of being—a fact which natural reason can only conjecture from a probable argument by analogy, but which may be certainly known from revelation—there must remain an infinite gap between the highest of such creatures and the Supreme Being (xvi, 12). As for sublunary things, inanimate or animate, they are all dependent, imperfect, subject to change and dissolution. By the goodness of the Maker, nevertheless, each kind has been given the qualities and powers which fit it for the specific conditions and state of being which have been assigned to it in the divine scheme of the whole (II, ix, 11-14; xxiii, 12-13).

Man is the only corporeal creature endowed with understanding—"an intelligent, but frail and weak being, made by and depending on another" (IV, xiii, 4). His mixed, imperfect nature is suited to the conditions of his life, a "fleeting state of action and blindness," and his understanding, capable of certain knowledge in a few things but for the most part given only the flickering light of probability, is appropriate to that "state of mediocrity and probationership he has been pleased to place us in here." The business of our lives, as intended by God, is to "spend the days of this our pilgrimage with industry and care, in the search and following of that way which might lead us to a state of greater perfection" (xiv, 2; xvi, 4).[14]

In spite of our weakness and frailty, God has given us powers which are sufficient, if we will only use them rightly, to comprehend "whatsoever is necessary for the conveniences of life and information of virtue" ("Introduction," Fraser, I, 29). The bright sunshine of knowledge is a marvellous gift, though its extent is very short and scanty. Where it fails, we must fall back upon probable reasoning; though it will always leave us in twilight, it is a power we are meant to use actively to understand ourselves, nature and our place in it, and our duties toward God and our fellow man. In Lockeian ethics, intellectual sloth is one of the worst of sins, because it shows an impious ingratitude toward our maker.

This view of God, nature, and man has obvious emotional correlatives, which Locke expresses at several points. Toward the Creator, if we sincerely believe in him, the natural and proper feelings are love, reverence, and humble gratitude. In spite of Locke's belief that *"the proper science and business of mankind in general"* is morality, he does not disesteem the study of nature nor dissuade men from it, because nature is God's creation and "the contemplation of his works gives us occasion to admire, revere, and glorify their Author" (xii, 11–12). Toward man and human understanding, the right attitude is a mixture of humility for our weakness, an uncomplaining acceptance of the limits of our powers, gratitude for the capacities which we have been given, pleasure and pride in their active use, and an untiring love of truth:

> For though the comprehension of our understandings comes exceeding short of the vast extent of things, yet we shall have cause enough to magnify the bountiful Author of our being, for that proportion and degree of knowledge he has bestowed on us, so far above the rest of the inhabitants of this our mansion. ("Introduction," I, 29; cf. IV, xii, 12; xix, 1).

By such ideas and feelings, Locke places the logic of probability in a religious and ethical context, which animates the technical procedures with larger meanings and values.

John Ray and the Physico-theologists

John Ray presents the ethos of probabilism in a form that is somewhat different from Locke's, but is fully consistent with it. He was a contemporary of Locke, Newton, and Boyle, a fellow of the Royal Society from 1667 until his death in 1705, and a devout Anglican who gave up his Cambridge fellowship and the priesthood because he could not bring himself to subscribe to the Act of Uniformity. In addition to works on ornithology, quadrupeds, plants, fishes, and insects, Ray published near the end of his life a book, *The Wisdom of God manifested in the Works of the Creation* (1691), which uses a wide-ranging knowledge of astronomy, zoology, and botany to provide *a posteriori* proofs of the existence and attributes of an Almighty Power, creator of the universe and all things in it. The book, which took its original inspiration from Henry More's *Antidote against Atheism* (1652), belongs to a tradition known to intellectual historians as "physico-theology." In his Preface, Ray mentions More, Ralph Cudworth, Edward Stillingfleet, and Robert Boyle as earlier writers on the same subject; he incorporates ideas, arguments, and examples from all of them along with much additional material from other sources and from his own investigations.

As a scientist, Ray was a Baconian and a probabilist of the same kind as White. Like Bacon, he expresses great scorn for natural philosophers who "endeavour to give an Account of any of the Works of Nature, by preconceiv'd Principles of their own." His example is Descartes, whose theories of the pulse of the heart and the transference of motion from one body to another are "grossly mistaken, and confuted by Experience."[15] Like Locke, he distinguishes between demonstrative and probable proofs (25–26, 44), argues warily from analogy (71), recognizes that all hypotheses are open to question, but that some are far more probable than others (36), and regulates the degree of his assent to any proposition in proportion to the force and weight of the evidence for and against it (72, 76, 121-122, 217). White needed no other instructor and model for sound biological reasoning, for all the elements of his method are already clearly present and powerfully operative in Ray.

The common element in the writing of all the physico-theologists is an elaborate, scientifically sophisticated version of the argument from design. Ray's text, quoted at the beginning of Part I of his book, is a passage from the Psalms: "How manifold are thy Works, O Lord! In Wisdom hast thou made them all" (25; *Ps.* civ. 24). We may "trace the Footsteps of his Wisdom" in the composition, order, harmony, and uses of the visible creation, offering "Proofs, taken from Effects and Operations, expos'd to every Man's View, not to be deny'd or question'd by any" (Preface). In Part I he first reviews the heavenly bodies, then turns to terrestrial inanimate bodies—fire, air, water, including the sea, its tides, and freshwater springs and rivers—and finally to the structures, parts, and behavior of living things. Part II discusses in a similar manner the shape and motion of the earth and the anatomy and physiology of man. Ray believes, again in opposition to Descartes, that final causes can be discovered in organic life, though not with certainty (42, 182), and that mechanical principles cannot explain the actions of living creatures, which require as their efficient cause some kind of "*plastick Nature*, or vital Principle" (49-51, 74, 93-94, 243). Since animals and men are not machines or automata, the God to be inferred from them cannot be a mere clockmaker. This rejection of the teaching of "*mechanick Theists,*" like Descartes, is perhaps the most distinctive feature of physico-theological thought (45).

Ray's religious view of nature, as bearing everywhere the "Signatures of the Divine Art and Wisdom" (46), has far-reaching moral implications. Bacon had said that nothing in nature is unworthy of study, because axioms contributing to the primary history can be drawn even from things which in themselves seem mean, illiberal, and filthy. Ray gives a different reason for the same conclusion. When the Psalmist calls upon all creatures to praise God, it is as much as to say:

> Ye Sons of Men, neglect none of his Works, those which seem most vile and contemptible: There is Praise belongs to him for them. Think not that any Thing he hath vouchsafed to create, is unworthy thy Cognizance, to be slighted by thee. It is Pride and Arrogance, or Ignorance and Folly, in thee so to think. There is a greater Depth of Art and Skill in the Structure of the Meannest Insect, than thou art able for to fathom, or comprehend. (156)

It would be pride and folly for such a being as man to admire himself or seek his own glory, for he is, no less than the plants and animals, "a Dependent Creature, and hath nothing but what he hath received; and not only dependent but imperfect; yea, weak and impotent" (159–160). But the Creator in his goodness has endowed man, alone among his creatures, with the capacity for knowing and understanding his works, and it is our bounden duty to use those powers in his service:

> And therefore those who have Leisure, Opportunity, and Abilities, to contemplate and consider any of these Creatures, if they do it not, do as it were rob God of some Part of his Glory, in neglecting or slighting so eminent a Subject of it, and wherein they might have discovered so much Art, Wisdom and Contrivance. (156)

For Ray, the study of nature is a form of worship, to be pursued with *"Admiration, Humility, and Gratitude"* (Preface)— admiration for the splendor of all God's works, humility for our own weakness, and gratitude for the boundless gifts of a wise and merciful Creator. The greatest of these gifts is the human understanding, imperfect though it is, which is given to us not only so that we can plant and build for our greater comfort, but in order that we may comprehend God's creation and repay him with thanks and praise.

White as Physico-theologist

There is only one explicit reference to physico-theology in White's *Natural History*, but it is a very appealing one. He des-

cribes the playful sporting and diving of rooks on an autumn
evening, which is accompanied by a continual cawing, softened
by the air to "a pleasing murmur, very engaging to the imagination," until they finally retire to the woods for the night. White
then comments:

> We remember a little girl who, as she was going to bed, used to remark
> on such an occurrence, in the true spirit of *physico-theology*, that the
> rooks were saying their prayers; and yet this child was much too young
> to be aware that the scriptures have said of the Deity—that 'he feedeth
> the ravens who call upon him.' (DB 59)

There is also only one reference to Ray's *Wisdom of God* (TP
17), but White must have known the book well, for many pieces
of information scattered through the letters can also be found
in Ray's book, from which we may presume they were taken.[16]
In his biography of Ray, Charles Raven mentions White, along
with Bishop Butler and John Wesley, as eighteenth-century
Christians who followed Ray in their reverence for nature and
in defending its study not only as compatible with religion but
as filled with religious meaning and value.[17]

White does not write as a parson, though he was one, and his
religious views are not obtruded upon the reader. It is obvious,
however, that he shares Ray's belief that the effects and operations of nature reveal an admirable wisdom and contrivance,
which White ascribes in his mild, unpreachy manner to Providence. Speaking of the transformations of the frog, from the
fishlike tadpole to the tailless but footed adult, he exclaims:
"How wonderful is the oeconomy of Providence" in adapting
the animal first to an aquatic and then to a terrestrial life (TP
17). Speculating on a suggestion of Barrington's that cuckoos
appear to be selective in choosing nursing mothers for their eggs
and young, White says that, if the observation is true, it "would
be adding wonder to wonder, and instancing, in a fresh manner,
that the methods of Providence are not subject to any mode or
rule, but astonish us in new lights, and in various and changeable appearances" (DB 4). He finds it curious, too, in comparing
the nest-building of the sand-martin with that of the house-
martin and swallow, "to observe with what different degrees of

architectonic skill Providence has endowed birds of the same genus, and so nearly correspondent in their general modes of life!" (DB 20). The times of blooming of the vernal and autumnal crocuses, which the best botanists have been unable to distinguish by any other attribute, also seem to him strange and wonderful: "This circumstance is one of the wonders of the creation, little noticed, because a common occurrence: yet ought not to be overlooked on account of it's being familiar, since it would be as difficult to be explained as the most stupendous phenomenon in nature" (DB 41). White even wrote a short poem on the crocuses; he asks what impels or retards their blooming, and then answers:

> The *God* of *Seasons!* whose pervading power/ Controls the sun, or sheds the fleecy shower;/ *He* bids each flower his quick'ning word obey,/ Or to each lingering bloom enjoins delay. (World's Classics ed., p. 9)

White's reasoning on biological problems is rational and objective, using an empirical and probabilistic method, but his response to nature is far from being purely intellectual. As he frequently remarks, natural phenomena appeal strongly to the imagination. In recommending that some future faunist should pay a visit to Ireland, he predicts that such an expedition would produce not only just conclusions and useful remarks but also great aesthetic pleasure from the "picturesque lakes and waterfalls, and the lofty stupendous mountains, so little known, and so engaging to the imagination when described and exhibited in a lively manner" (TP 42). He feels that way himself whenever he sees the majestic sweep of the Sussex downs; though he had known them for thirty years, he still finds new beauties and feels fresh admiration whenever he visits them. Echoes from the wooded hill back of Selborne have a fine effect on the imagination, especially when they cease and then resume, "like the pauses in music"; and the grotesque shapes into which snow was driven during a prodigious storm in 1776 were "so striking to the imagination as not to be seen without wonder and pleasure" (DB 17, 60, 62). Feeling, too, enters strongly into his response to nature, especially toward all kinds of animals. He speaks with great affection of the busy field-crickets and curious hedgehogs; of Timothy the tortoise, who lived for many years in the garden of an aunt of White's and was moved after her death to his own; and, above all, of his beloved *hirundines*, those "amusive" swallows, martins, and swifts which he observed with so much attention and pleasure almost all his life (TP 10, 23, 27; DB 6, 13, 46, and passim).

Though of course highly personal, White's imaginative and emotional reactions to nature have an intellectual basis and justification in his conviction that Creation everywhere manifests an order, design, purposiveness, and inexhaustible bounty reflecting its divine Maker. His outlook can perhaps be summed up by a final quotation. As so often in White, it is the swallows and martins which call forth his deepest reflections:

> I could not help being touched with a secret delight, mixed with some degree of mortification: with delight, to observe with how much ardour and punctuality those poor little birds obeyed the strong impulse towards migration, or hiding, imprinted on their minds by their great Creator; and with some degree of mortification, when I reflected that, after all our pains and inquiries, we are yet not quite certain to what regions they do migrate; and are still further embarrassed to find that some do not actually migrate at all. (TP 23)

Whether these birds migrate or hibernate is one of the questions to which he returns again and again throughout the letters, but which remains unresolved because the evidence for and against both possibilities is so evenly balanced that a conscientious probabilist can make no decision. Though it is mortifying to reach that conclusion after so many pains and inquiries, it is not at all surprising: In the twilight world of probable reasoning, our searches must often be baffled. But whatever the solution to this problem may be, White does not doubt that the cause will finally turn out to be an impulse planted in the minds of his creatures by the great Creator, still another manifestation of his power, wisdom, and goodness, and that is what makes the behavior of those poor little birds so delightful.

To be clear about the thesis of this essay, I should add that I do not mean to argue that there is any necessary connection between a commitment to probable reasoning, in biology or in any other field of inquiry, and the complex of religious and moral ideas and attitudes which I have been sketching. There have been many thinkers in several ages who have accepted probability as the best—even the only possible—method of discovery and proof, but who have not been willing to subscribe to the *Weltanschauung* within which that method was so intimately integrated by Locke, Ray, White, and Johnson. The obvious exceptions in the same period are Gibbon and Hume, both probabilists though neither was an orthodox Christian, and of course there have been many others in different countries and ages who have divorced the logic of probability from its theological and ethical context. All I want to claim is that for many British thinkers of the seventeenth and eighteenth centuries, the technical procedures of probable reasoning were suffused with religious meaning, and that we cannot fully understand their writings unless we recognize that fundamental fact.

Notes

1. Hoyt Trowbridge, "Scattered Atoms of Probability," *Eighteenth-Century Studies*, V (1971), 1-38.

2. The standard biography is by Rashleigh Holt-White, *Life and Letters of Gilbert White of Selborne* (London, 1901), 2 vols. Selections from the "Naturalist's Journal" have been edited by Walter Johnson, *Gilbert White's Journals* (New York: Taplinger, 1970).

3. *The Natural History and Antiquities of Selborne*, Letter 19 to Barrington. The text I have followed is that of the World's Classics edition (London: Oxford University Press, 1902). References will be given within parentheses in the text; the letters to Pennant will be identified as TP, with the number of the letter in Arabic, and those to Barrington as DB 7, etc. Since the letters are so short, page numbers will not be given.

4. The substance of these letters had previously been published in the Royal Society's *Philosophical Transactions*, but White makes several corrections and additions in preparing them for inclusion in the *Natural History*.

5. See *Darwin on Humus and the Earthworm*, ed. Howard (London: Faber & Faber, 1966); the study was originally published in 1881.

6. "Preface" to *The New Organon, The Works of Francis Bacon*, ed. Spedding, Ellis, and Heath (Boston, 1861 and following years), VIII, 59; hereafter cited as Sp., with volume and page numbers within parentheses in the text.

7. In the Utopian fictional image of this scheme in the *New Atlantis*, it is striking that only three of the thirty-six fellows in Salomon's House are Interpreters of Nature, who "raise the former discoveries by experiments into greater observations, axioms, and aphorisms," all the rest being engaged in various tasks of the natural history.

8. Joseph Glanvill, *Scepsis Scientifica*, ed. John Owen (London, 1885), p. lxv; first published in 1665. Cf. Thomas Spratt, *History of the Royal Society*, ed. Cope and Jones (St. Louis: Washington University Press 1958), pp. 35-36.

9. White's most important contributions were the identification of two new species, the harvest mouse and the noctule owl; the separation of willow-wrens into three distinct species; and the conclusions from a variety of evidence that the ring-ousel is migratory and that the genetic ancestor of the domestic pigeon was the blue rock-dove (TP 12, 16, 19, 24, 44).

10. Locke, *Essay concerning Human Understanding*, ed. Fraser (Oxford, 1894), I, 30-32. All references and quotations will be from Fraser's ed., giving Book numbers in Roman capitals, chapter numbers in lower-case Roman, and section number in Arabic, within parentheses in the text. Where no Book number is given, the reference is to Book IV.

11. For Bacon's attack on syllogistic reasoning see, e.g., *De Aug.*, Bk. V, ch. ii; Sp. IX, 69-70. Cf. Locke, *Essay*, IV, xvii, 4-8.

12. Cf. Locke's *Conduct of the Understanding*, ed. Thomas Fowler, 5th ed. (Oxford, 1901), sec. 40.

13. Cf. *Natural History of Selborne*, ed. Grant Allen (New York: Dodd, Mead, 1923), p. 63n.

14. Cf. the entry on "Theology" in *Conduct of the Understanding*, sec. 23.

15. *The Wisdom of God in Creation*, 11th ed. (Glasgow, 1744), pp. 48-49; page numbers will be given within parentheses in the text. The best biography of Ray is Charles E. Raven, *John Ray, Naturalist: His Life and Works* (Cambridge: The University Press, 1942).

16. A particularly striking example is the discussion of maternal instinct, or *storge*, by Ray, pp. 109-110, and by White (DB 4, 14). White also refers (TP 34) to William Derham's Boyle Lectures, *Physico-Theology:*

or a Demonstration of the Being and Attributes of God from his Works of Creation (1712).

17. Raven, pp. 452, 447–478.

II. TIME

World Enough, and Time

Lewis White Beck

Mr. Shandy, in the act of begetting Tristram, terminates his
carnal intercourse with his wife in order to wind the clock.
Rousseau, expecting death, sells his clock, exulting, "I shall
never have to know the time again." These two *beaux gestes*
symbolize two extreme attitudes towards time in the eighteenth
century.

When Plato defined time as "the moving image of eternity,"
he set a perennial problem for philosophy. It was a special, and
an especially difficult, formulation of the wider problem of the
relation of appearance to reality. While no philosopher can entirely avoid this problem and probably none can solve it, the
urgency of the problem can be reduced by directing the attention to one or the other of the two polar opposites and forget-
ting, or at least neglecting, the other. The history of the philosophy of time shows alterations in where the focus of attention
falls, either in eternity as ontologically real and basic, or in time
as empirically experienced and quantified appearance. It does
not solve the problem of their relation to attend to only one of
them, but where the attention rests emphasizes the relative

tractableness and importance of one or the other of the two. Philosophical weight is given to what one sees as the proper vehicle or receptacle of knowledge and aspiration. Seeing things under the aspect of eternity and seeing them under the aspect of time are usually symptoms of an other-worldly and a this-worldly orientation respectively. Finding *this* world quite enough is a characteristic trend of the Enlightenment, which nurtured the growth of time at the expense of eternity. This essay will attempt to chronicle this development in a few representative philosophers of the century.

There are few genuinely new ideas in the philosophy of time in the eighteenth century. Many of the ideas which the student of the history of ideas identifies as "Newtonian", "Lockeian", "Leibnizian", and "Kantian" are named after only their most prominent eighteenth-century proponents; but most of the component ideas (though not the complex ideas made up of them) can be found in earlier philosophers such as Plotinus, St. Augustine, Nicholas of Cusa, Telesio, Bruno, Galileo, Descartes, and Gassendi. But for the purposes of this brief essay on the eighteenth century, may I be allowed to write, for the most part, as if the eighteenth century got its ideas of time from Newton, Leibniz, and Locke?

I. Newton

Aristotle had defined time as the number, or measure, of motion, by which he understood any kind of change. He recognized that rapid and slow motions may occupy, and be measures of, the same amount of time,[1] and hence that motions are measures of time but not time itself, in which the motions occur. In this he was followed by Descartes, for whom time was only "a mode of thinking" adding nothing to what is being thought about, which he calls duration.[2] This duration is a distant descendant of Plato's eternity and an almost immediate progenitor of Newton's absolute time.

Newton contrasts absolute with relative time (sc. Descartes' time) as follows:

Absolute, true, and mathematical time, of itself, and from its own nature, flows equably without regard to anything external, and by another name is called duration: relative, apparent, and common time, is some sensible and external (whether accurate or unequable) measure of duration by means of motion, which is commonly used instead of true time; such as an hour, a month, a year.[3]

After giving his equally famous definition of two kinds of space, Newton distinguishes absolute from relative motion, the former being change of absolute place in absolute time. He then argues that from the position of bodies "in our regions" it is impossible to determine whether they are at absolute rest or not. But from the inertial forces which belong to bodies only by virtue of their absolute motion, he argues that it is possible to show that a twirling bucket of water is in absolute motion while the fixed stars (which, assuming the bucket to be the geometrical point of origin, are in relative motion) are not in absolute motion. This is because a force must have been impressed upon the water, since it recedes from the axis of rotation.[4] From the bucket experiment, so-called, Newton concludes that the "relative quantities [of motion] are not the quantities themselves, whose name they bear, but those sensible measures of them (either accurate or inaccurate) which are commonly used instead of the measured quantities [of absolute space and time] themselves."[5] If we knew the forces acting upon the heavenly bodies, which it is Newton's purpose to discover, we could then determine their real and not merely their relative motions. These forces are gravitational and inertial, and given the laws of motion and impressed forces, Newton believed absolute motions, and hence positions in absolute time and space, could be discovered. These locations and quantities may be very different from what they appear to be in our frameworks of relative space and time, and Newton warns against confusing the measures, which are relative, with what is measured, which is absolute. "They do strain the sacred writings, who there interpret those words for their measured quantities; nor do those less defile the purity of mathematical and philosophical truths, who confound real quantities themselves with their relations and vulgar measures."[6]

Newton is more explicit about absolute space than about absolute time: and this is characteristic of most philosophers. It is infinitely easier to think about and to talk about space than time; there is something at least imaginably thing-like about space, but this is not true of time; whether right or wrong, it seems to make sense to speak of space as *existing*, whereas the existence of time is a much more obscure notion since, it may be thought, only part of time, viz. the present, "really" exists. After generations of Newtonism, we have learned to think about absolute space, and without any Pascalian horror; but we have hardly learned to think about absolute time—the time that would have flowed equably in the absence of anything *in* time, in the absence of anything happening. Yet to understand Newton we must make a double effort: to understand his novel notion of absolute space—a task difficult enough when he wrote, but speciously easy now—and to understand his conception of absolute time. Perhaps in his own day the latter was easier because it was less mystifying to those who thought they had a cogent conception of eternity.[7]

The best we can do, perhaps, is to apply, by analogy, what he says about absolute space to absolute time; for his two definitions are parallel. Both space and time are absolute in the sense of requiring nothing external for their existence. It is an accident of both that there are things in space and things which last through invervals of time. Space and time are empty receptacles into which God put the matter he created; but they would have existed exactly as they are had no body been created to occupy them. They are infinite and infinitely divisible; but whereas space is isotropic, time has a sense, flowing from future to past. They meet the requirements which philosophers at that time put upon substance: they exist without being dependent upon the existence of anything else, and they can be conceived without requiring the conception of existence of anything else. They are ontologically primitive and epistemologically objective.

Leibniz, as we shall see, saw seeds of infidelity and atheism in such a substantial conception of space and time. Here were two substances God did not create, waiting for him to fill them. Spinoza, just shortly before this time, had called extension (roughly, space) an attribute of substance (God), and Samuel Clarke, Newton's disciple, called space (and presumably time) a property of God.[8] We do not know what Newton thought on these matters; he did say that absolute space is "the sensorium of God", and he adumbrates the notion that absolute time is God's eternal duration. When Leibniz, Berkeley, and finally Kant show ontologically objective and absolute space and time to be unintelligible and to be no longer needed in cosmology, divine support for them, which was sought by Newton and Clarke, is no longer required. The world is enough for time.

A subtle shift has occurred. Eternity had been, metaphysically, conceived as timelessness. Time was irrelevant to reality and to God; we speak only in human terms (all we have) when we refer to the everlastingness of God, and we can hardly avoid ascribing a history—albeit a beginningless and endless history—to God. But Newton temporalizes eternity itself; eternity is for him the infinite mathematical time that was before the world and will last after the world is destroyed, but coeval with God.[9] All this belongs more to Newton's theology than to his cosmology, but never before or since, I think, has the eternal and the cosmically temporal been brought into so close a union. If absolute time is needed in the understanding of the world, then eternity is needed; Newton warns against confusing absolute and relative time, as we have seen, because that will "strain the sacred writings", i.e., will mix up ordinary temporal measurements with eternity. With every cosmological or metaphysical or epistemological step away from time's absoluteness there is a step towards making the world itself enough for time.

II. Locke
John Locke called himself "an underlaborour in clearing the ground a little, and removing some of the rubbish that lies in the way of knowledge" in "an age that produces such masters as the great Huygenius and the imcomparable Mr. Newton."

Locke provided an epistemology to ground Newton's cosmology, but we shall see how much rubbish he removed in Newton's own theory of time.

Locke discusses time as a simple mode of duration. Duration
corresponds to "expansion", which is the name he prefers to
"space" or "extension" when speaking of Newton's absolute
space independent of the existence of bodies in it. "Duration,
antecedent to all bodies and motions which it is measured by"[10]
is the Lockean counterpart to Newton's duration which, we have
seen, becomes first absolute time and then, through its infinity
and equability, eventually either eternity or a substitute for it.
"Expansion and duration do mutually embrace and comprehend
each other, every part of space being in every part of duration,
and every part of duration in every part of expansion."[11] That
is, every part of space exists at all times, and conversely. The
place of a body is that part of expansion it occupies, and time
is that part of duration lying between two things or between the
beginning and end of a thing.—So much for Locke's ontology of
duration, which is like but perhaps less "mystical" than Newton's.

By a simple mode Locke means "a modification of the same
[simple] idea which the mind either finds in things existing, or
is able to make within itself without the help of any extrinsical
object, or any foreign suggestion."[12] Examples of simple modes
are number ("the simple idea of an unit repeated") and space
and time. The simple idea underlying time is that of duration,
and the modes are "any different lengths" of it whereof we have
distinct ideas, as hours, days, years, etc., time and eternity."[13]
(Note especially that he says eternity is a mode of time; this is
not the language of Plato, or the theologians.) To understand
time, we must first consider the simple idea of duration.

One is aware of "a train of ideas which constantly succeed
one another in his understanding," and reflection on this fur-
nishes him with the idea of succession, the idea of his own duration during this succession, the idea of the duration of other
things co-existing with his own thinking, and, finally, "the idea
of the duration of things which exist while he does not think."[14]

Like St. Augustine, therefore, Locke finds the origin of our temporal ideas not in motion per se, but in one motion only, viz., the motion (change) observed in a sequence of ideas. It is not even the observation of change, but the change of observation, that generates our sense of succession and time. There is, as it were, an internal clock by which motion itself is measured, and motion which is too rapid or too slow to cause a sequence of noticeably different ideas does not measure time. "The constant and regular succession of ideas in a waking man, is, as it were, the measure and standard of all other successions."[15] But this standard is observable only by the individual; hence some motions "constant, regular, and universally observable by all mankind and supposed equal to one another, have with reason been made use of for the measure of duration."[16]

But, Locke reminds us, in a passage reminiscent of Newton, "We must carefully distinguish betwixt the duration itself, and the measure we make use of to judge of its length;"[17] but he makes this remark for a quite different purpose. Duration is, for him, the lastingness of things; there is no talk in Locke about an empty, eternal duration whether there are things enduring or not; but it is time, not duration understood as lastingness of things, which is infinite. Time, which is like number, can be extrapolated beyond the duration of things that exist, and just as there is no greatest number, so there is no maximum of time. Time is infinite; duration need not be and, because of the creation of the world, is not. Hence Locke can attach a quite precise meaning to applying "the measure of a year to the duration before the creation." It is the infinite extendability of the *measure*, not of what is measured, which gives rise to the conception of infinite time independent of the answer to the question about the beginning or end of the world. For eternity, we are given a mathematical property of a continuous infinite series.[18]

Locke thus supplies an epistemology for Newton's cosmology, but not for his theology and metaphysics or for those parts of his cosmology which depend upon absolute time considered as eternity. While Newton gives no argument for the infinity of absolute time and thus none for the eternity of God's duration—piety is no argument—Locke's theory does contain an argument based on the analogy of numbers as the measures of duration or motion with numbers which are indifferent to the nature and existence of things numbered, the latter being infinitely extendable.[19] Eternity was always something thought of as *given*, though beyond human comprehension; now it, or its substitute infinite time, is something constructed by human thought from human experience. Not that Locke drew any unusual theological consequences from this fundamental shift in his conceptual arrangements; he just as confidently as Newton ascribed his temporal concepts to "that Being which must necessarily have always existed."[20]

Before leaving Locke, I wish to mention two criticisms to which he was subjected. Berkeley objects to both Newton and Locke on the point that the time they speak of (both relative and absolute) is an abstract idea. He agrees with Locke that the simple mode (he calls it "simple idea") of time has its root in the succession of ideas in the mind, but when "abstracted" from that and ascribed the properties of flowing uniformly, of being participated in by all things, and of being infinitely divisible he finds himself (really Locke and Newton) "lost and embrangled in inextricable difficulties." Time is nothing if "abstracted from the succession of ideas in our minds;"[21] that is what time is, and not "only the sensible measure thereof, as Mr. Locke and others think."[22]

The reader of Locke is often baffled by the ease with which Locke moves from a simple idea to the simple and complex modes of it. To be sure, without the experience of succession it is difficult to see how one would gain the idea of time; but the properties of time are so different from the properties of any experienced succession that it is unclear how the latter could *originate* in the former. This is Leibniz's repeated complaint about Locke's derivations—that he leaves out the work of, and the predispositions of the intellect involved in, the movement from a simple idea to the simple and complex modes and ideas of substance. Thus he criticizes Locke: "A succession of perceptions awakens in us the idea of duration, but it does not make it. . . . Changing perceptions furnish us with the occasion of

thinking of time, and we measure it by uniform changes."[23]
Fully to understand and to weigh this criticism, however, requires that we understand Leibniz's positive doctrine of time.

III. Leibniz

Leibniz was the most unashamed metaphysician of the philosophers studied in this paper. Not for him any silent or reticent
piety and acknowledgment of the mystery of God; Leibniz
sometimes writes as if he were as privy to the councils of God as
he was to those of Hannover. He speaks with as much rational
assurance about God as about mathematics, physics, logic, history, and diplomacy. In this metaphysical assurance, he is perhaps more characteristic of the seventeenth than of the eighteenth century; but it is necessary to speak of him after Newton
and Locke since he was an explicit critic of them.

Against Newton and his metaphysical disciple Samuel Clarke,
Leibniz argues that Newton cannot distinguish between absolute and relative space and time, because he cannot establish
absolute motion through the study of forces. (In this he would
have agreed with Berkeley, and modern physics since Mach and
Einstein has sided with them as over against Newton.) Hence
the concept of an absolute time, independent of the things and
happenings that occur in it, is a useless conception in physics.
But, worse still, he finds the concept of absolute time to be
metaphysically and theologically dangerous. If there is an absolute time, the following question is intelligible and demands an
answer: why did God create the world at the moment (in absolute time) that he did, and not earlier or later? But this question
cannot *in principle* be answered, because in absolute time one
moment is exactly like any other moment; by Leibniz's principle of the identity of indiscernibles, moments in absolute time
are identical, and God therefore could have had no reason to
create the world at one moment rather than another. But, granting that there is absolute time, He did so; therefore He did
something wthout a sufficient reason, which is against His ra-
tionality. Therefore there is no absolute time.[24]

Leibniz has another reason for rejecting absolute time, this one being a logical instead of a theological reason. Everything that really exists (i.e., every substance, or monad) is an individual with attributes (properties and changes of properties) which inhere in it. All propositions about substances are propositions in which the predicates inhere in the substance and in the concept of the substance if that concept be complete. Real predicates are one-place predicates, dependent only on the subject of which they are predicated; and all true affirmative judgments are, either implicitly or explicitly, analytical of the subject-concept. Another way of saying this is: What is true of a single substance would be true of it if it were the only thing in the universe. Temporal predicates, such as "before . . ." and "at the same time as . . .", are two-place predicates; they cannot be true of a thing taken in isolation. They express relations, and relations are not a part of the ultimate ontological furniture of the universe, which consists exclusively of active substances and their states existing independently of, but in a preestablished harmony with, all other things. Each monad is essentially and dynamically unrelated to all the others, but each is a "living mirror" of the universe, reflecting it from its own point of view.

Thus, for Leibniz, there is no absolute time and space as ontological primitives; even relative time and space are not metaphysical realities. He says they are not real, but ideal; that is, they are representations in single monads of the *order* of their states and the states of the other monads. As representations, not true realities, they are phenomena; but the spatial and temporal locations assigned to things in each monad's reflection of the world are determined by what is genuinely real, and hence they are not illusory (unless taken to be more than they are). The illusion arises from thinking that the monads are physically real, extended things and therefore material; while in truth they are unextended spiritual agents. But correctly taken as phenomena without further pretensions, they are *phenomena bene fundata.*

It is therefore incumbent upon Leibniz to show what there is in the system of monads which is not spatio-temporal but which serves as the foundation of the phenomenal appearance of the world, which is under the condition of relative time and space. He says that time is the "order of possible inconsistents" or of non-compossible possibilities.[25] That is, two propositions which are mutually exclusive may both be true under one condition only, viz., that they are true *at different times;* two things which could not coexist (e.g., my youth and my old age) may nevertheless exist if there is time, a time when I was young and a time when I am old. Now God could have created a world (perhaps like Spinoza's "block universe," as Williams James called it) in which everything was logically consistent but in which the number of possibilities to be realized was limited by its instantaneous or permanent, unchanging character. But God in creating the best of all possible worlds created that one in which there would be a maximum of realized possibilities, and the condition under which this maximum is achieved is that they are realized, or at least represented, as occurring one after another. (Space is the order of incompatible things existing simultaneously—they exist at different places; time is the order of incompatibles existing at the same place—but at different times).

It is quite clear from this that God himself must have envisaged the world *sub specie temporis* as well as *aeternitatis;* he created a world in which non-compossible possibilities would be realized. That shows that there is nothing *necessarily* illusory about temporality, though God (as Augustine says) must have surveyed instantaneously or eternally what we men experience only under the form of time. Leibniz at least once says that space and time do not depend upon the actuality of things, but only upon their possibility; and without an actual world, space and time would be only ideas in God's mind.[26] More usually, however, Leibniz writes as if space and time are only the ways by which finite monads interpret relations between things which are not intrinsically spatio-temporal at all. For example, a state of a monad which is *logically* prior to another state is seen as *temporally* prior. Time is a phenomenal mapping of the ontological and logical relations between the states of a monad which are, in turn, reflections of the state of the entire universe. Loemker describes Leibniz's physics as "a phenomenal commentary on his metaphysics." The realm of nature (spatio-temporal) is an ectype of the realm of grace. Time is a moving image of eternity, in which what is ontologically necessary appears to be phenomenally contingent.

The idea of "mapping" logical or ontological relations phenomenally is easier to represent by a spatial than a temporal model. Ruth Saw's lucid model[27] is that of a cross-word puzzle. The logical relations are: The second letter in a nine-letter word meaning "elephant" is the last letter in the name of a great desert, the third letter is the initial letter in the name of the Greek god of time, etc. Such a "program" is logically independent of the spatial representation on the grid of a cross-word puzzle, but the latter is the more perspicuous representation of it for us men. Perhaps a graph in which one of the coordinates is marked "time" will serve as a model for the spatio-temporal representation of a mathematical function in which the values of one of the variables is logically ("eternally") fixed by the values of another.

Like Descartes and Newton, Leibniz distinguishes between duration and time, which is its relative metric and well-founded phenomenon. Duration is essential to substances, which persist and, according to Leibniz, cannot be destroyed. This means that there is a set of durational predicates which belong to each substance and not just to its phenomenal presentation. While it is literally true that God, the *monas monadum*, exists at all times, because he is coeval with the temporal world which is a manifestation of his choice of the best of all possible worlds, there is a constant danger of subreption, of a "category mistake" in using temporal predicates or durational predicates in describing the world in Leibniz's metaphysics.[28] Though without the attribution of time-like predicates to substances, his theory is unintelligible; in the phenomenal world where his theory of time is most at home, he has no more use for metaphysical duration than for absolute time.

IV. Kant

Kant agreed with Newton that time and space are absolute, that is, independent of the things and events which occupy them. But he agreed with Leibniz that time and space are not metaphysically objective, that is, more then well-grounded phenomena. Absoluteness and objectivity had not been clearly distinguished from each other before Kant, and it is not unusual to find even today, in popular scientific articles about the theory of relativity, the confusion which Kant was the first to remove. When reading about the theory of relativity, the reader often does not know whether it is relativity in the sense of relationality or relativity in the sense of subjectivity, i.e., relation to the knowing mind, that is being expounded; perhaps sometimes the author himself does not know.

For Kant, the question as to whether time is objective (real) and the question as to whether it is absolute (not relative) must be answered by quite distinct inquiries. We shall discuss Kant's theory of time under five somewhat overlapping rubrics in order to keep these two question as distinct as possible.

1. The metaphysical unreality of time. Kant teaches the "transcendental ideality", not the "transcendental reality", of time.[29] Time is *only* a form of experience and does not pertain to reality as it is in itself, about which we know and can know nothing. In his *Inaugural Dissertation of 1770*, he sees the purpose of his critical philosophy to be the isolation of the forms and principles of the sensible world (which are space and time) from the forms and principles of the intelligible world (which in 1770 he thought to be the categories of classical ontology). It is essential to prevent the use of the former in discussing the intelligible world, since Kant believed that most of the failures of classical metaphysics were a consequence of the "subreptitious" use of time and space as if they were forms of things in general instead of merely forms of human experience.

Kant's reason for believing that they are forms of experience instead of independent objects of experience is found in the pattern of his thought called his "Copernican Revolution." According to this, the necessary and imprescriptable features of what we know must be features determined by the operations of the mind independently of what happens to be the content or object of the experience. If time were real, and if it were experienced as a content or object (as it would be if it were real), we could at most say: Everything I have experienced has had a date, therefore in all probability everything I will ever experience will have a date. Our knowledge of time would be inductive and empirical.[30] But we do not say any such thing: We know *a priori* (i.e., we know it to be necessarily and unexceptionably true) that all experiences and all objects of experience will be temporal. Now all the other philosophers we have discussed knew this, but only for Kant did it pose a problem: How do we know something about every experience (viz., that it will be temporal) before we have it?

The term *a priori* is equivocal. It may describe that we know necessarily and universally to be the case. But it may also refer to what makes such knowledge possible. In this sense it refers to our "knowing apparatus", as it were, indicating that the universal and necessary form of knowledge "must lie ready for our sensations *a priori* [in the second sense] and so must allow of being considered apart from all sensations."[31] In this second sense (and only in this sense) Kant's theory resembles Descartes' theory of innate ideas, more especially in the modified form of it which Leibniz defended against Locke's attack. All our knowledge begins with experience, Kant and Leibniz say in apparent agreement with Locke; but not all of it arises out of experience,[32] and what does not arise out of experience is precisely that which we know *a priori* (in the first sense) because it is *a priori* (in the second sense).

Kant argues that if we think away all the temporal content, time itself, instead of disappearing along with that from which Locke thought it was an abstraction, cannot itself be thought away. The form of our perception, in the absence of any empirical content, becomes itself an object of a pure (not an empirical) intuition. Thus Kant concludes that time is (a) the form of all our experience and (b) the object of a particular kind of experience he calls pure intuition.[33]

2. *The absoluteness of time.* In the previous sentence I have anticipated this Kantian thesis: time is an *object* (though not an
empirical object, like a dog, who makes his presence known by
causing sensations in us) and not merely a relation between objects (for it subsists and can be known even when it is considered
as if it were empty of objects and events). Time is a very peculiar
thing, differing from all other things except space in that it is
not empirically known; but it is like every other thing in the
world in that it is an *individual*. That is, there is *one* time, and
what we call "times" are mere parts or limitations in it.[34] It is not
a concept like that of man, for we can understand the concept of
man without knowing whether there are any individual men and
without knowing how many men there are. But we know that
there is *one* time, since *any* two events are related to each other
as either successive or not, and of any two events which are not
simultaneous, one is before the other. All events are therefore in
one time; and Kant says time is given as an infinite magnitude.

Kant gives another proof of the absoluteness of space which
we may adapt, by analogy, for a proof of the absoluteness of
time.[35] The space-argument is known as the argument from
non-congruent counterparts. If space is merely a relation between things, as Leibniz believed, then when the relations among
the parts of two things are identical, there should be no discernible spatial difference between them. But this is not the case.
The relations between the fingers of a glove and the fingers of
the hand that the glove fits are identical; but the relations between the fingers of a right hand and those between the fingers
of a left hand are identical; therefore a left-hand glove should
fit a right hand. But it does not. In order to explain this phenomenon, Kant says, we must relate the hand and the glove "to
the whole of space." Since we easily make the distinction between left and right, and since this distinction is not a matter of
abstract geometrical relations but something which must be
seen or directly experienced or ostensively defined, we must
have a notion of the whole of space which is independent of the
things in it.

The preceding argument says that left and right are not analyzable without remainder into the mutual relations of the things occupying space; we must know also how things are oriented in absolute space. A similar argument can be contrived for time. Time has a *sense* which is not captured by Leibniz's relational analysis into the condition under which non-compossibles become possible, for this relation is the same whether one of the non-compossibles is earlier or later than the other. World history might as well have run backwards, so far as Leibniz's analysis of time is concerned; in fact, to Leibniz there would be no discernible difference—granting his relational analysis—between a world running one way and a world running the other. By analogy to the space argument, we can attribute to Kant the view that the difference between one direction and the opposite direction of time can be discerned only by relating temporal series to the one absolute time as an infinite *given* magnitude.

3. *Time sensible, not conceptual.* All our knowledge of existing things is the application of general predicates (universals) to particulars. We must be able to say something general about a particular, and we must bring any particular under some general concepts. The particular, to which we may refer as a "this", is the thing which we are talking about, and the general concept gives us information about the "this" by predicating of it that it is like or unlike something else. Concepts are the work of thought, but the identification of what they are about is the work of our senses. I *see* a this; I think *about* it.

There are logical forms (categories) which are our rules of thinking about things and expressing our knowledge of them in judgments which attribute a predicate to a subject. These categories are *a priori* and are related to logic. But Kant discovered a philosophical problem in identifying a particular to which the conceptual predicates are attributed. He asks: What are the *a priori* forms of our sensing particulars, analogous in function to the categories which are *a priori* forms for our thought about them? And he answers: Space and time are the two necessary forms of individuation, of identification of a "this", and of reidentification in two experiences of the same thing. Leibniz had held that two objects having all their properties in common would be indiscernible and therefore identical; Kant adds that though there could be (though there probably are not) things having all one-place predicates in common, they would still not be identical because they would be in different locations in space and time. He concludes:

"Time is not something that exists of itself, or which inheres in things as an objective determination. . . . Time is nothing but the subjective condition under which alone [knowledge of particular existing things] can take place in us. For that being so, this form [of knowledge] can be represented prior to the objects, and therefore a priori."[36]

Kant has said much the same about space, which he interprets as absolute but not as ontologically real, as a form of phenomena and therefore not as conceptually analyzable without remainder. But now Kant introduces an important difference between the two. Space, he says, is the form of our outer sense, while time is the form of our inner sense. This much is in agreement with Locke; and, as Locke saw, outer things and motions come under the form of time only by being represented in our inner sense, in our awareness of changes in our stream of consciousness. Hence Kant adds to the statement that "time is nothing but the form of inner sense" the statement: "Time is the formal *a priori* condition of all [phenomena] whatsoever."[37] Locke, in his naiveté, had not seen the problem involved in how we move from the awareness of the time of the passage of our ideas to the dating of events in the physical world which we perceive. Kant must show how we *construct* a public, objective time-series out of data which are private and, presumably, different for every observer.

Before we narrate Kant's efforts in this direction, however, we must take note of Kant's repeated use of the word "our" in referring to inner and outer sense. Unlike the categories, which are logically necessary, Kant holds that there is nothing *logically* necessary in our having the forms of sensibility which we do have. We can easily imagine that the inhabitants of other planets (whom Kant believed to exist) and angels (whom he did not believe to exist) and perhaps intelligent animals have quite different ways of identifying and re-identifying particulars, though we cannot imagine *what* these other forms and ways of particularizing may be. For all we know, space and time may be nothing more than forms of *human* sensibility and knowledge. It is only a short step from this view to the more extreme view that space and time are culturally determined, and that their study belongs in the sociology of knowledge. This is a step Kant did not take, and probably would have resisted had he thought about it. But those who argue that time as Western man understands it is not a necessary human form of organizing experience, and that other ways of organizing experience actually exist and are manifested in different linguistic and artistic and explanatory structures are only going one step beyond Kant along a path he first opened.

4. *The rehabilitation of relative time.* The problem in the penultimate paragraph of the previous section is that of moving from time as the form of inner sense to time as one of the forms of the physical world. In a happy example, Kant illustrates the process he is attempting to understand. I first see the basement and then the roof of a house; and I first see a ship pass under one bridge and then see it pass under a different bridge. Both of these pairs of experiences are temporally related: Each is one experience after another. But of the first I say that the house had a roof at the *same* time that it had a basement, and of the second I say that the ship was under one bridge and under another at *different* times. How do we do this? It would be easy if we could perceive (and not merely have a pure intuition of) absolute time; for then each thing we experience could be dated, and we would find the dates of roof and basement the same, and the date of passage under one bridge earlier than that of passage under the other. Since we cannot do that, we must be content to fix their dates only in relation to each other, but in a public time in which their relations may or may not be the same as the relations among the private experiences themselves. (Another example: I see the flash of a gun, and one second later hear the explosion; you see the flash, and hear the explosion two seconds later. What *a priori* principles are involved in our decision, confirmed by experiment, that the two occurred at the same time?)

Kant's answer to these questions is given in the most important, and probably the most difficult, chapter of the *Critique of*

Pure Reason, entitled "The Second Analogy of Experience."
What follows here will be a gross over-simplification of that
chapter but will not, I hope, substantially misrepresent it. In
brief, we attach temporal predicates to objects not just by seeing
them in time as the form of our *inner* experience, but by con-
ceptualizing the kinds of objects we are seeing. It is only because
of a vast background of empirical concepts and laws of nature
that we say that the roof of a house (in all probability) does not
exist without the continuing existence of its foundation; the
fact that we happen to see the roof before we see the basement
is dismissed as irrelevant to what the situation in the world is.
For similar reasons we know that an unanchored ship (in all
probability) moves down-stream, and this knowledge leads us
not to ignore the order in which we see it in different positions.
If I saw the roof first and then the basement, I would draw the
same conclusion that I would from seeing the basement and
then the roof. But if I see the ship under bridge one and then
under bridge two, I do *not* draw the conclusion I would draw
were I to see it first under bridge two and then under bridge
one: In one case, I say the boat is moving downstream, in the
other, upstream.

Now in these examples, it is mostly empirical knowledge
about houses, ships, streams, and bridges that permits us to
draw the conclusions we do. But Kant argues that all this empirical knowledge is content for *a priori* categorial forms which
are "schematized," i.e., manifested as *a priori* patterns of time.
In the case of the house, there is the *a priori* category of substance as the permanent in time; in the case of the ship, the
a priori category of causality which is a necessary sequence in
the states of a thing. Each of these *a priori* categorial principles
appears in a slightly different form in Newton's physics, for
which Kant supplies an epistemological foundation far sounder
than that provided by Locke.

5. *Time and the language of faith.* Kant appears to have had to
pay a very high price for this solution to the problems he inherited from Newton, Leibniz, and Locke. He has had to give
up any application of temporal predicates to reality (e.g., to
God, to the soul, and to things as they are in themselves apart

from their appearances to human beings). The history of creation, the eternity of God, the immortality of the soul, and other
favorite topics of the theologian and metaphysician are unat-
tainably beyond the reach of human knowledge. It seems, even,
that it does not make sense even to talk about them, much less
to claim to know any truths about them. Claims to know about
them are not only unfounded; but in giving them up, we have
paid no high price. On the contrary, they are dangerous, because, Kant says, *if* such talk were well-grounded, the metaphysical world could only be an extension of the spatio-temporal-
causal world of our scientific experience, and the other world
of metaphysics would be just the same old Newtonian world,
only vaster. In the Newtonian world, or in its metaphysical
duplicate, there would be no place for the assumptions which
Kant thought we have to make in order to take moral concerns
as valid. In spite of what Newton said, in a Newtonian world
there is no place for God; in a world of matter in space and of
motion in time, there is no place for an immaterial substance
(the soul) and its temporal predicate of immortality; no way in
which an event can occur without being determined, according
to the laws of motion, by a temporally earlier event, and hence
no freedom of the will, hence no morality.

But all of these dire consequences are ruled out once we realize that the form of time applies only to the world of phenomena, and that our knowledge is restricted to this. "I . . . found
it necessary," Kant says, "to deny *knowledge* in order to make
room for *faith.*"[38]

Two points in this famous sentence are worth noting. (A)
Kant says he found it *necessary* to deny knowledge. But this
does not mean that he called upon faith, *ab extra*, to limit or to
supplement knowledge. Kant is not fideistic. Rather he has
shown that the conditions of *a priori* knowledge can be met
only if knowledge is confined to the appearances of things, and
does not reach their reality *an sich*. The conditions that make
knowledge *possible* also restrict its scope. (B) Kant says he found
it necessary to deny *knowledge*. Kant is not in the long line of
Christian apologists who denied reason in order to make way

for faith, who appealed, in James' expression, to a *will* to believe against or beyond the evidence. Rather Kant insists that reason has two functions, one in knowing (theoretical reason) and one in guiding conduct (practical reason); it is the *same* reason in two functions, and it is as possible, and as necessary, to be reasonable in the conduct of life as it is to be reasonable in the conduct of inquiry. We cannot *know* that the will is free, or that God exists, or that the soul is immortal; but Kant thinks that it is reasonable to believe that they are in order to use reason in the conduct of our lives; hence these beliefs are articles of rational faith.

But it is only enthusiasm (*Schwärmerei*) to claim knowledge of them, and *Schwärmerei* is morally corrupting:

> Assuming that [nature] had indulged our wish and had provided us with that power of insight or enlightenment which we would like to possess or which some erroneously believe they do possess, what would be the consequence so far as we can discern it? . . . God and eternity in their awful majesty would stand unceasingly before our eyes . . . Transgression of the law would be shunned. . . . [But] most actions conforming to the [moral] law would be done from fear, few would be done from hope, none from duty. The moral worth of actions . . . would not exist at all.[39]

But, of course, human beings cannot be silent about the things they believe really exist, though they cannot know them (and most religious-minded people probably do not know that they cannot know them). They must talk a religious or metaphysical language using temporal and spatial metaphors in which they ascribe to God everlastingness and omnipresence and to the soul a future life. This is inevitable, and it is not dangerous if we take such locutions as symbolical expressions of faith and not as knowledge-claims. Thus men can talk an appropriate language of eternity;[40] but all their knowledge is of things in time and space.

V. Conclusion

I have written brief accounts of the theories of time formulated by four eminent philosophers of the eighteenth century, and written it as if Locke, Leibniz, and Kant were doing nothing but working over a system left in an unsatisfactory state by Newton. This, of course, is a fiction. Each of the three later philosophers had access to all the traditional treatments of time that were available to Newton, and perhaps made better use of them; and each of them was sensitive, to a degree to which Newton was not, to what was going on in the world outside the laboratories and halls of philosophy. I do not think it very fruitful to see great philosophers as if they were mere spokesmen for their times (though this may be effective when trying to understand second-raters), for they are more likely to be disposed to criticize than to celebrate the climate of opinion in which they live. Still, each philosopher is a child of his times, and I do not think it too far-fetched to see the general trend from Newton's to Kant's philosophy of time as at least obscurely reflecting some of the major shifts in the thinking of the Enlightenment about man and his place in the world and in world-history.

There is a sentence in *Finnegan's Wake* which reads: "Shake eternity, and lick creation." I do not know what this sentence means in the context of that book, but in isolation it suggests to me that man can master the world ("lick creation") if he breaks up the solid, static, Eleatic world ("shake eternity") of which the world of his knowledge and action was thought to be only a moving image—perhaps not exactly an illusory image, but at least one lacking the ontological dignity and perfection of true reality. Every one of our philosophers admits the eternal; Newton, and especially Leibniz, seem to be intimately acquainted with it, while for Kant it is only an object for rational faith and plays no part in the understanding of the world or our experience. Locke alone seems sincerely uninterested in it, though he too pays lip-service to it. If the Enlightenment can be characterized as a period of growing secularization, of decreasing need for other-worldly revelation and succour, of finding this world sufficiently rich in human challenges and opportunities, then we can say that the Enlightenment in general was bent upon shaking eternity so that it could lick creation. Human conceptions replace divine conceptions; the *sensorium dei* of Newton becomes the Kantian form of *human* sense.

There are at least two trends of thought in the eighteenth century as a consequence of which human time replaces divine eternity as the proper object and concern of man.

The first is what Lovejoy called "the temporalization of the great chain of being."[41] At the beginning of the century, the great chain was vertical; at the end, horizontal or perhaps gently sloping upward. At the beginning, the chain was suspended from a static eternity, and every link in it was characterized by its vertical distance from God. Thus does the great chain appear in Pope's *Essay on Man*. But there was empirical, scientific evidence against this conception of the great chain, in that occupants could not be found for every stage. The gaps, however, had once been filled (as we know from the fossil record). The plenitude of being is not representable by a chain hanging at rest, but by a temporal process in which some of the stages of being were occupied only in the past and some are to be occupied only in the future. The historicisation of nature develops into an eschatology of progress, in which time is itself almost a creative force begetting new forms of natural beings and new social arrangements among mankind and trending to a goal which is not eternally present but an ever-receding end. The heavenly city becomes the future city. Eternity had been shaken, and creation was in course of being licked. Hegel writes: "Enlightenment, proclaiming itself as the pure and true, here turns what is held to be eternal life and a holy spirit into a concrete passing thing of sense, and contaminates it with what belongs to sense-certainy [i.e., perception under the form of space and time]."[42]

The second is a vast increase in the amount of time available for the explanation of the present situation and for the pursuit of human goals.[43] There is something a little pitiable, to me at least, in Sir Isaac Newton, perhaps the greatest mathematical genius who ever lived, spending his time trying to calculate, from Biblical texts, the time of the ending of the world. The age of the world is sufficiently short for him to think that the world did not come, in time, to its present state but was formed in its present state by the hand of the Creator. Locke (in an aside, and by way of illustrating something else) appears to think that

5,639 years is a plausible conjecture, but he mentions a Chinese estimate of 3,269,000 years which he does not believe is true.[44] Kant, on the other hand, speaks of the age of the world in "millions of years or centuries," and gives calculations of tidal friction to determine how long the day was at various periods in the very distant past. For him, the universe at large is in a "steady state" —the material which once formed one solar system will be dissipated again into primordial chaotic dust from which new nebulae and solar systems will be formed, and formed by the slow inexorable processes of attraction and repulsion governed by Newton's laws. For Kant, there is world enough and time to explain all the present and all the different past and future states of the universe without appealing to an act of creation or special providence of the kind Newton believed was necessary for the establishment and stabilization of the solar system. Closer to the earth, Hutton, the founder of modern geology, held that there was in the geological record "no vestige of a beginning," nor even any sign of catastrophic changes which had had to be assumed when it was believed that the age of the earth was small.[45]

The history of mankind likewise requires more time than is allowed by Biblical chronology, and Enlightenment historiography gets along well without divine guidance and intervention; just think of the contrast between Bossuet and Gibbon! When the slow-moving processes of civil history are not allowed enough time to effect the great changes which the new study of antiquities showed must have occurred, it was easy, nay necessary, to appeal to another world, which is timeless, to account for this one. But when it is discovered that there is time *enough*, this appeal to eternity becomes less and less importunate.

So eternity was shaken, shaken out of the philosophy of nature and the philosophy of man. Its place was taken by a human phenomenon or invention, time. We were left with the time without any pretensions to eternity; time was quite enough.

Notes

1. *Physics IV*, 14.

2. *Principles of Philosophy*, I, §57.

3. *Mathematical Principles of Natural Philosophy*, Definition VIII, Scholium (Motte translation, New York, 1846), p. 77).

4. Ibid., p. 81.

5. Ibid., p. 81.

6. Ibid., p. 82.

7. The *Encyclopédie* (art., Eternité, ed. 1778, vol. 6, p. 45) says rather acidly that it has reported on the scholastic debates about eternity rather fully "because they serve to show into what labyrinths one is hurled when one wants to reason about something one cannot conceive."

8. *The Leibniz-Clarke Correspondence*, Clarke's Fourth Paper, §10. *Philosophical Papers and Letters*, translated by L. E. Loemker (Chicago, 1956), vol. II, p. 1127.

9. See Werner Gent, *Die Philosophie des Raumes und der Zeit* (Hildesheim, second ed., 1962), Vol. I, p. 165.

10. *Essay Concerning Human Understanding*, Book II, ch. xv, § 4. (edited by John W. Yolton, Everyman ed., vol. I, p. 161).

11. Ibid., § 12 (p. 167).

12. Ibid., ch. 13, §1 (p. 133).

13. Ibid., ch. 14, §1 (p. 146).

14. Ibid., §5 (p. 147).

15. Ibid., §12 (p. 150).

16. Ibid., §19 (p. 152).

17. Ibid., §21 (p. 154).

18. Ibid., §31 (p. 159).

19. Ibid., §30 (p. 158).

20. Ibid., §31 (p. 159).

21. *Treatise Concerning the Principles of Human Knowledge* §98.

22. Letter to Samuel Johnson, March 24, 1730, in *Principles, Dialogues, and Correspondence*, edited by Colin M. Turbayne (Indianapolis, 1965), p. 240.

23. *New Essays Concerning Human Understanding*, translated by A. G. Langley (LaSalle, 1949), p. 156.

24. *Leibniz-Clarke Correspondence*, Leibniz's Third Paper, ¶3 (Loemker, II, 1109).

25. *Leibniz's Correspondence with De Volder*, and "The Metaphysical Foundations of Mathematics" (Loemker, II, 865, 1083).

26. *Leibniz-Clarke Correspondence*, Leibniz's fourth paper, §41. (Loemker, II, 1123).

27. Ruth Lydia Shaw, *Leibniz* (Penguin Books, 1954), p. 109.

28. The great complexity of the problem led Bertrand Russell to discern *three* inconsistent theories of time in Leibniz, only two of which I have alluded to. See *Critical Exposition of the Philosophy of Leibniz* (London, 1900), §74. In *Early German Philosophy* (Cambridge, 1969) p. 270 I have discussed Wolff's theory of time and the appropriateness of Kant's tendency to ascribe Wolff's views to his master, Leibniz.

29. *Critique of Pure Reason* A 35 = B 52.

30. Ibid., A 40 = B 57.

31. Ibid., A 20 = B 34.

32. Compare the first paragraph of the Introduction to the *Critique of Pure Reason* with Leibniz's *New Essays* Book II, Ch. 1 (Langley, p. 111).

33. *Critique of Pure Reason* A 31 = B 46; A 32-4 = B 49-51.

34. Ibid., A 32 = B 47.

35. *Prolegomena to any Future Metaphysics,* §13.

36. *Critique of Pure Reason* A 32-3 = B 49.

37. Ibid., A 34 = B 50.

38. Ibid., B xxx.

39. *Critique of Practical Reason*, translated by L. W. Beck (Chicago, 1949), p. 248.

40. *The End of All Things* in *Kant on History*, edited by L. W. Beck (Indianapolis, 1963), p. 76.

41. *The Great Chain of Being* (Cambridge, 1936), Chapter 9.

42. *Phenomenology of Mind* (Baillie translation), p. 571.

43. See Stephen Toulmin and June Goodfield, *The Discovery of Time* (London, 1965), Chapters 4, 5, and 6.

44. *Essay Concerning Human Understanding*, Bk. II, Ch. xiv, §29 (Yolton, I, 158).

45. James Hutton, "Theory of the Earth, or an Investigation of the Laws Observable in the Composition, Dissolution, and Restoration of

Land upon the Globe," *Transactions of the Royal Society of Edinburgh,* vol. i, part ii, pp. 209–304 (1788), at p. 304. Reprinted in *James Hutton's System of the Earth, 1785; Theory of the Earth, 1788; Observations on Granite, 1794;* together with *Playfair's Biography of Hutton,* with Introduction by V. A. Eyles (Contributions to the History of Geology, ed. G. W. White, vol. 5. New York: Hafner Press, 1973), p. 128.

The Extended Moment: Time, Dream, History, and Perspective in Eighteenth-Century Fiction

Maximillian E. Novak

I shall begin this paper with two quotations from a novel written at the end of the eighteenth century. In the first, the heroine and narrator is about to be strangled by her frenzied brother, who has warned her that she must prepare for death:

> These words were a sufficient explication of the scene. The nature of his frenzy, as described by my uncle, was remembered, I, who had sought death, was by now thrilled with horror because it was near. Death in this form, death from the hand of a brother, was thought upon with indescribable repugnance.

A certain comic quality enters this passage because the passives seem to make the threatening action absurd and remote. But putting aside the idea that he might have been paid by the word and did not want to have his heroine say, "I remembered my uncle's description of his madness, and I was terrified," what is apparent is that the writing resorts to introspection and analysis of feelings in such a way as to prolong the experience of the reader with events that are actually occurring rapidly, much as the television serials, like *The Six Million Dollar Man*, use slow motion in order to give the impression of tremendous speed.

141

The second quotation is from the heroine's interview with
the man she loves, who believes that he has overheard her tell of
her sexual liaison with the villain:

> My sight was of no use to me. Beneath so thick an umbrage the dark-
> ness was intense. Hearing was the only avenue of information which the
> circumstances allowed to be open. I was couched within three feet of
> you. Why should I approach nearer? I could not contend with your be-
> trayer. What could be the purpose of such a contest? You stood in no
> need of a protector. What could I do but retire from the spot over-
> whelmed with confusion and dismay? I sought my chamber, and endeav-
> ored to regain my composure. The door of the house, which I found
> open, your subsequent entrance, closing and fastening it, and going into
> your chamber, which had been thus long deserted, were only confirma-
> tions of the truth.

What the lover believes he has heard is an error, and the entire
work depends on the errors caused by relying more upon hear-
ing than seeing—errors, in the case of the characters in Charles
Brockden Brown's *Wieland,* which result in a series of horren-
dous murders committed in the name of religious inspiration.
What I am interested in here is not the explanation of a seeming
supernatural occurrence by ventriloquism but rather the reliance
upon things perceived and observed, the near obsession with
what almost seems like voyeurism in the fiction of the end of
the century. Such interest in what is perceived could only have
come after a century dedicated itself to speaking about the ways
in which we know what we know. Those works of fiction written during this period that were concerned with depicting some
image of reality were, almost inevitably, involved in creating
systems of perspective, and in exploring inner and outer realities,
they inevitably slowed the pace of fiction, making it into that
sluggish form known as the novel.

I

Among the definitions of perspective supplied by Nathan Bailey's
English Dictionary (7th ed., 1735) is a distinction between what
he calls "*Speculative*" perspective, "the Knowledge of the Rea-

sons of different Appearances of certain Objects, according to the several positions of the Eye that beholds them," and "*Practical*" perspective, or the "Method of declinating that which is apparent to our Eyes, or that which our Understanding conceives in the Forms that we see Objects." Both of these definitions suggest a post-Cartesian, post-Lockean world, the first through its emphasis on our angles of vision, the second on the mental nature of perception. And they may even imply the notion that we have to learn how to see what we see. Whether Locke and Berkeley would have agreed with Owen Barfield's arguments that what we perceive are, in fact, communal representations which differ from society to society, is questionable, but they would hardly have been shocked by the concept. Eighteenth-century fiction came of age during a period when there was considerable sophistication about the relationship between the world of our perceptions.[1] From the beginning, writers of fiction realized that their job was not to act as creators of a mirror reflection of reality but to create a construct that would pass for the real in some way. The methods of achieving this were neither self-evident nor easily attainable. Each writer had to find his or her own way of creating the kind of illusion that suited his or her talents. Seldom were the methods the same.

One of the more fascinating theoretical statements of the relationship between fiction, perception, and reality occurs in Richard Burthogge's *An Essay Upon Reason*, which was published in 1694 and dedicated to John Locke. Burthogge argued that "*Consciousness of Seeing,*" as opposed to perception, was owing to the "difference of Conceptions, for if we were to see only one thing, we would have no more idea of seeing than if we were blind." Burthogge, following Locke in making conception and consciousness synonymous with idea and thought, proceeds to accept whatever is perceived as having some form of reality:

> Since it is as truly said, that one does think, or conceives such things, as it is of him that Dreams, or sees a Vision, that he does Dream, or see a Vision. Wherefore such Cogitables as these in respect of their Objective

> Existence may be referred to Realities of *Appearance* as Dreams and Visions are: for as the Act of Dreaming Really *is*, and the thing Dreamt both Really seem; so the Act that produces a Fiction Really is, and the Fiction also really seems.

Burthogge admits that there is some distinction to be made between our apprehension of a fiction and our perception of reality, but his solution is hardly conclusive. "There is this between the foresaid Cogitables," he writes, that " . . . Dreams and Visions do not only Really seem, but seem to be Real; Whereas Fictions, do only really seem, but do not seem to be Real; at least not always, and as Fictions."[2]

In spite of this distinction, such as it is, Burthogge suggests that the line between fiction and reality may, on occasions, disappear entirely. In speaking of Old Testament prophecy, he maintains that our apprehension of it is so vivid that it makes little difference whether we read it or experience it:

> External Causes that are not objects do yet impress the Faculties which they Act upon, in the same manner that Objects do; and therefore all the images that do rise from such Impressions, must be of things as present, and in being; because they Represent them as if Really they were Objects in Act, that had excited and stirred the Faculties.

I have quoted Burthogge at length to suggest that from an epistemological standpoint, the writer of eighteenth-century fiction could feel some comfort in his ability to compete with reality. The real question was whether he could write a fiction that was memorable and vivid.

Hence the simple illusionism fostered on Defoe by a variety of nineteenth-century critics and their twentieth-century followers will hardly stand examination. In wanting language to have the power of "the thing itself," and in believing that fiction was the most powerful method of conveying reality, he did not confuse the ability to bring objects and characters to life with the creation of some dull catalogue of specific details. As I have suggested elsewhere, his main achievement was to slow up the reader's time by various forms of repetition. Details were part of the process, but that method is far less important than the use of diaries, fantasies, and parallel fictions that are brought in to surround the main action. It was José Ortega y Gasset who commented most fully on the sluggishness of the novel, but he succumbed to the idea that some fictions might have a technique that operated like a completely clear glass through which we could see without being aware that we were seeing through a pane. In fact, there is no such mechanism. Even *trompe l'oeil* depends on deceiving the eye through conventions we have learned.

II

In attempting to look more closely at some works of fiction, I will start at the end of the century to underscore some of the points I made in speaking of *Wieland*. A good example may be found in a passage from Mrs. Radcliffe's *The Italian*, in which the heroine, Ellena, is attempting to flee from a nunnery after refusing to take the veil:

> As they crossed the garden towards the gate, Ellena's anxiety lest Vivaldi should have been compelled to leave it, encreased so much, that she had scarcely power to proceed. "O if my strength should fail before I reach it!" she said softly to Olivia, "or if I should reach it too late!"
>
> Olivia tried to cheer her and pointed out the gate, on which the moonlight fell: "At the end of this walk only," said Olivia, "see!—where the shadows of the trees open, is our goal."
>
> Encouraged by the view of it, Ellena fled with lighter steps along the alley; but the gate seemed to mock her approach, and to retreat before her. Fatigue overtook her in this long alley, before she could overtake the spot so anxiously sought, and, breathless and exhausted, she was once more compelled to stop, and once more in the agony of terror exclaimed—"O, if my strength fail before I reach it!—O, if I should drop even while it is within my view."
>
> The pause of a moment enabled her to proceed, and she stopped not again till she arrived at the gate; when Olivia suggested the prudence of ascertaining who was without, and of receiving an answer to the signal, which Vivaldi had proposed, before they ventured to make themselves known. She then struck upon the wood, and, in the anxious pause that followed, whispering voices were distinctly heard from without, but no signal spoke in reply to the nun's.

"We are betrayed!" said Ellena softly, "but I will know the worst at once;" and she repeated the signal, when to her unspeakable joy, it was answered by three smart raps upon the gate. Olivia, more distrustful, would have checked the sudden hope of her friend, till some further proof had appeared, that it was Vivaldi who had waited without, but her precaution came too late; a key already grated in the lock; the door opened, and two persons muffled in their garments appeared at it. Ellena was hastily retreating, when a well-known voice recalled her, and she perceived by the rays of a half-hooded lamp, which Jeronimo held, Vivaldi.

This is a highly dramatic moment in the novel and leads to an equally exciting climax as the hero and heroine discover that the gate leading out of the nunnery is shut and their quest for freedom seemingly prevented. Although there is some focus on Ellena's thoughts, the sensation that we experience as readers of an object or goal retreating before us as we move forward—the sensation of a nightmare—is achieved by a careful description of movement toward a given point, with accounts of Ellena's movements and her physical exhaustion. We are not so much concerned with what she thinks as with what she sees and expects to see, what she hears and expects to hear. In her day, Mrs. Radcliffe was praised for much the same things for which Defoe was praised—minute and accurate detail. But the matter is more complicated than that. What might in some novels simply amount to rushing to a gate to hear a signal is held up by dialogue, sounds, and various details. What might have been a moment is extended to not more than half a page, and it is done, not so much for the suspense, as for the sense of reality we experience in living longer with a scene. If realism in the cinema may be tested by the number of doors that are opened and closed rather than have the camera fade from one room to another, Mrs. Radcliffe would score well as a realist.

In what is still the best commentary on Anne Radcliffe's fiction, the anonymous author of the "Life and Writings of Mrs. Radcliffe," prefaced to *Gaston de Blondeville* (1826) remarked how in one of her early novels she had failed to achieve "local truth or striking picture":

Incredible events follow each other in quick succession, without any attempt to realize them. Those, who complain of the minuteness of Mrs. Radcliffe's descriptions, should read this work, where every thing passes with headlong rapidity; and be convinced of their error. In some few instances, perhaps in "The Mysteries of Udolpho," the descriptions of external scenery may occur too often; but her best style is essentially pictorial; and a slow development of events was; therefore, necessary to her success. . . . Escapes, recaptions, encounters with fathers and banditti; surprising partings, and more surprising meetings, follow each other as quickly as the changes of a pantomine, and with almost as little connection. . . . There are in this short story, incidents enough for two such works as "The Mysteries of Udolpho," where, as in the great romance, they should not only be told, but painted; and where reality and grandeur should be given to their terrors.

Yet compared to some narratives of the seventeenth and eighteenth centuries, Mrs. Radcliffe's first two fictions are relatively leisurely. In spite of the complaints of her critic quoted above, she does give her readers a few glimpses of the scenery of Sicily and Scotland.

For example, compare her most rapid pace with this passage from a picaresque narrative, translated from Spanish in 1707:

Having receiv'd my Letters and Money, I set out again for the Army, and all the next ways thro' the Frontiers of *Germany*, being then beset by the Enemy, was oblig'd to take a great Compass about, thro' *Hungary*. Coming to the Imperial Court, the Marques de *Castel-Rodrigo*, his Catholick Majesties *Ambassador Extraordinary*, gave me another Packet of Letters for the Army, with which I set forward very diligently, and entring *Bohemia*, pass'd thro' *Prague*, and came to Dresden, and the Duke of Saxony's Court. There I had Intelligence of the Army, being told it March'd towards *Leipzig*, after the Swedes. I made such haste that in four and twenty Hours, about a League from Leipzig, I discovr'd the two Armies drawn up in Battle, handling one another very Rudely, by way of Pelting and Hacking.

If Estevanillo Gonzales was attempting to get the sense of movement in time, he seems to have chosen the wrong method. This is not so much movement as the summary account of a headlong race from one point to the other, not the sense of time that we get from the picaresque with its travelling from inn to inn and city to city, but rather something like the racing in

Through the Looking Glass where one runs to get nowhere. Radcliffe's method, in even her earliest works is clearly the reverse. By having characters focus on given landscapes or scenes, she forces the reader to observe the world through which the characters move, and by making observations on the responses of her characters, she sets up an interaction between landscape and character that makes her fiction concrete in a way that writers like Fielding and Sterne would have found tedious.

In the age of Locke and Hume, when Identity seemed to be mainly one's idea of a continuous self, it was inevitable that narrative would become determinedly internalized. The famous footprint Crusoe finds on his island is stared at, measured, compared with his own foot, viewed from all sides. But its reality depends on the somewhat unreasoned terror that it produces in Crusoe. We are made aware of his responses to this strange phenomenon—the product of a devil, cannibal, or ship-wrecked sailor—in the same way as we learn of Ellena's feelings of terror, through a persistent focus on something out there, and a delineation of its psychological effects.

As I have argued elsewhere, this device of focusing on the object and expanding the time experience of the work of fiction was one of Defoe's major contributions to what we call realism. Take Colonel Jack's search for a proper tree to hide his first booty gathered as an apprentice pickpocket. That money literally alienates him from his former world, for he can no longer trust his fellow Glass-House boys with whom he used to sleep so peacefully in the warm ashes. Fearing that he will speak in his sleep about his money, he decides to hide it in a tree:

> When my crying was over, the Case was the same; I had the Money still, and what to do with it I could not tell, at last it came into my Head, that I would look out for some Hole in a Tree, and see to hide it there, till I should have occasion for it: Big with this discovery, as I then though it, I began to look about me for a Tree; but there were no Trees in the Fields about *Stepney*, or *Mile-End* that look'd fit for my purpose, and if there were any that I began to look narrowly at, the Fields were so full of People, that they would see if I went to hide any thing there, and I thought the People Eyed me as it was, and that two Men in particular follow'd me, to see what I intended to do.

This drove me farther off, and I cross'd the Road at *Mile-End*, and in the middle of the Town went down a Lane that goes away to the *Blind Beggars* at *Bednal-Green*, when I came a little way in the Lane, I found a Foot-Path over the Fields, and in those Fields several Trees for my Turn, as I thought; at last one Tree had a little Hole in it, pritty high out of my Reach, and I climb'd up the Tree to get to it, and when I came there, I put my Hand in, and found (as I thought) a Place very fit, so I placed my Treasure there; and was mighty well satisfy'd with it; but behold, putting my Hand in again to lay it more commodiously, as I thought, of a Suddain it slipp'd away from me, and I found the Tree was hollow, and my little Parcel was fallen in quite out of my Reach, and how far it might go in, I knew not; so, that in a Word, my Money was quite gone, irrecoverably gone, irrecoverably lost, there could be no Room, so much as to Hope ever to see it again for it was a vast great Tree.

As young as I was, I was now sensible what a Fool I was before, that I could not think of Ways to keep my Money, but I must come thus far to throw it into a Hole where I could not reach it: well, I thrust my Hand quite up to my Elbow, but no Bottom was to be found, or any End of the Hole or Cavity; I got a Stick off of the Tree and thrust it in a great Way, but all was one; then I cry'd, nay, I roar'd out, I was in such a Passion, then I got down the Tree again, then up again, and thrust in my Hand again till I scratch'd my Arm and made it bleed, and cry'd all the while most violently: Then I began to think I had not so much as half Penny of it left for a half Penny Roll, and I was hungry, and then I cry'd again: Then I came away in dispair, crying, and roaring like a little Boy that had been whip'd, then I went back again to the Tree, and up the Tree again, and thus I did several Times.

This example of what might once have been thought of as Defoe's unselective realism is actually a fine attempt to picture one aspect of growth. The world in which he had formerly felt entirely comfortable is now something outside and potentially hostile. Although we are told what he sees, his perception is colored by his fear of observation. We are never allowed to lose track of the child's emotions. And Romanticism notwithstanding, there are few characters who get to understand and know a natural object the way Jack gets to know the tree. Defoe also moves the reader about in time with implicit comparisons between the emotions of a small child and those of an adult and with Jack's own speculation about the future and the hunger he may have to face.

In scenes like this, Defoe achieved what Conrad said the novelist should do. He made his readers see and feel as they had never done before. And he did it not merely by focusing on small objects but by large and sublime scenes of shipwreck and mountain scenery. Crusoe surveys his island from its highest point and, like Mrs. Radcliffe's heroes and heroines, looks out over a calm valley of deliverance after a harrowing experience amid the snows of the Pyrenees. And Defoe as a traveller in the *Tour* frequently takes the opportunity to climb the highest peaks to see what lies below. He marvels at a valley filled with the lights from the cottages of weavers as they work through the night. In describing Chatsworth in Derbyshire, his mind moves swiftly from the peacefulness of the scenery to the possibilities of disastrous earthquakes in a land of sublime volcanoes:

> Nothing can be more surprising of its Kind, than for a Stranger coming from the North, suppose from *Sheffield* in *Yorkshire*, for that is the fisrt Town of Note, and wandering or labouring to pass this difficult Desert Country, and seeing no End of it, (just as was our Case) on a sudden the Guide brings him to this Precipice, where he looks down from a frightful height, and a comfortless, barren, and, as he thought, endless Moor, into the most delightful Valley, with the most Pleasant Garden, and most beautiful Palace in the World: If contraries illustrate and Place can admit of any Illustration, it must needs add to the Splendor of the Situation, and to the Beauty of the Building.

This use of contrast, the Gothic technique of watching a shipwreck from a safe place and being drawn into it complusively, is already implicit in Defoe's fiction as well as non-fiction. And in the end, Defoe may have to be viewed as a forerunner of the tradition of Gothic imagination as much as the founder of realistic, social fiction.

III

But Defoe provided only a single point of view, a narrative technique appropriate for an age that tended to think in terms of isolated consciousness. It was up to Richardson, in *Clarissa*, to provide the techniques that gave fiction the ability to handle various modes of statement through multiple points of view. As might have been suspected, Richardson's view was narrower in focus and more enclosed than Defoe's. Richardson might have enjoyed revising Defoe's *Tour*, but he was no traveller. At one point Clarissa is threatened with a trip to her uncle's moated and romantic house, but letters are written in chambers. The crucial scenes of *Clarissa* are played out in the enclosed spaces of rooms and cells, with only a hint of the arbors that appeared in earlier epistolary fiction from which he drew many of his techniques.

My interest in this paper is not in the technical maneuvering of point of view between Clarissa, Lovelace, Belford and others, nor in the way the arrangement of letters play with time in relation to the action. Rather I want to examine the ways in which the characters perceive themselves and the events in which they are involved. In such a pattern, Clarissa must appear as a moralist, Lovelace as a dramatist, and Belford as the true novelist.

To begin with Lovelace, I refer to his perspective as dramatic not only because he stages his letters to Belford as short comedies or dramatic skits but also because he is conscious of himself as the actor in a drama and is continually aware that whatever contradictions may be permitted him, he cannot drop his essential character. More accurately, we can say that he would like to think of *Clarissa* as written, produced, directed by, and starring Lovelace. (There is even a flurry of rivalry after Clarissa's death concerning who will write her story.) Like the actor whose role is more real than his own personality and who only feels himself truly in character when he is on stage, he collapses completely when Clarissa will not follow the script. And behind all his role playing, there is little except what Clarissa calls "vice itself." This is her discovery about him and about life in general— that in spite of his accomplished performance, there is little there that is real, that external polish means nothing without some inner moral meaning.

He takes a number of roles, but the part he must stick to is that of the libertine. That he is partly aware that much of what he thinks are ideas and emotions are only postures gives him an ambiguity that may explain the attraction he had for so many of Richardson's admirers. Marriage, he announces, would be out of character. A libertine should have a new marriage every spring. He maintains that a bit of raping will do Clarissa a great deal of good; and in his daydreams he dwells on raping Mrs. Howe, Anna, Mrs. Bevis, Mrs. Moore, and Mrs. Rawlins, not to speak of his Rosebud, whom he so ostentatiously spares. He also daydreams of his power. Every libertine may be a king; so he dreams of playing king to Clarissa's role as slave; and of being her play husband who must teach his wife to be a proper spouse. And when he has to deal with the Smiths, with whom the dying Clarissa is living, he plays the role of an impish tradesman.

The important point of all this is the effect of such imaginative moments on the reader. If the novelist must give us a sense of what Frank Kermode calls *Kairoi*, a feeling of timelessness, by extending his action through various kinds of explorations into the mind, nothing will give that effect so well as daydreaming or the reports of actual dreams, since they seem to open out into a world of fantasy which has the timelessness that writers like Mircea Eliade have ascribed to myth. Although I have cast Lovelace as the dramatist, his real attraction for us lies in those fantasies that Richardson would have considered the product of ungoverned passions. Nothing that Richardson did to darken the character of Lovelace in order to make us dislike him changed his true attraction.

The realistic novelist built into *Clarissa* is Belford. Lovelace has a regard to details, but he seldom uses such circumstantial descriptions except for comic effect. It is Belford who is truly alive to what details mean. His account of Clarissa's room is used for much the same effect that Balzac uses his description at the beginning of *Père Goriot*—to let minute description serve as history:

> A bed at one corner, with coarse curtains tacked up at the feet to the ceiling; because the curtain-rings were broken off; but a coverlid upon it with a cleanish look, though plaguily in tatters, and the corners tied up in a tassell, that the rents in it might go no farther. . . .
> Four old Turkey-worked chairs, bursten-bottomed, the stuffing staring out. An old, tottering, worm-eaten table, that had more nails bestowed in the mending to make it stand than the table cost fifty years ago when new. . . .

> Near that, on the same shelf, was an old looking-glass, cracked through
> the middle, breaking out into a thousand points; the crack given it, per-
> haps, in a rage by some poor creature to whom it gave the representa-
> tion of his heart's woes in his face.

This is not by any means an objective account of the room. Belford is filled with sympathy for the victims who have come
through the room over the years. Eventually, he used it as a foil
for his picture of Clarissa "in her white flowing robes . . . illumi-
nating that horrid corner; her linen beyond imagination white,
considering that she had not been undressed ever since she had
been here." Radcliffe too will make a room and its objects reveal a terrifying history, and from this standpoint, Richardson
gave something to the Gothic that no amount of sublime representation in Defoe could give. Even an object like Roxana's
dress, symbolic of past luxury and sensuality, does not function
in quite the same manner as Belford's vivid descriptions.

One reason for this may have something to do with Belford's
position in the action. He is close to the third person novelist,
commenting on the action without actually doing very much
about it. He urges Lovelace to do justice to Clarissa, and an
eventual convert to Clarissa's point of view, he can, nevertheless,
move between the two. Having been a rake himself, he can understand Lovelace's feelings painfully. As the repository of the
consciences of both Lovelace and Clarissa, he is in full possession
of their secret thoughts. Enough of a moralist to read a sermon
over the death of Mrs. Sinclair, he tends to be more tolerant
than Clarissa. If Fielding was right about the novelist possessing
the four qualities of genius, humanity, learning, and experience,
Belford obviously has the best equipment for the job.

As for Clarissa, one might think that she has a tendency
toward Lovelace's theatricality; she is a great lover of tragedies.
But whatever may be said of her psychology—of her seeming
longing for death after all hope of sexual fulfillment seems to
have passed, of her absurd posturing, of her refusal to be entirely true to herself—she is ultimately a more powerful, if less
attractive figure than Lovelace. If she lies to herself, it is in the
cause of keeping her passions in tune with her rational and
ethical nature. Granting this, there is much in her views of her-

self and of events that raises questions. We may ask whether the kind of person that Clarissa would really want is someone with a "gentle heart." Does she *really* think that marriage is the "highest state of friendship"? Is not Lovelace's low opinion of marriage closer to reality?

To ask such questions is necessary, because they arise from the way Richardson gives us the novel. A multiple perspective which includes characters of the force of Lovelace and Clarissa has something of the character of a debate. And while Richardson allows us little choice in deciding who has won and who has lost, this is not to say that the loser has not scored some points. Clarissa argues from the perspective of the Christian moralist, and she arrives at the compatible conclusion that the individual integrity of her life embodies a higher value than duty to her family. She dies with the sense that she has been right and that her family, some of her friends, and Lovelace have been wrong. If she is betrayed, it is not by her beliefs but by her life. And in so far as *Clarissa* is a novel and not merely a debate, we are impelled to ask questions about the relationship between her character and the events that betray her and the opinion she holds to her death. If we were to look at her behavior from the angle of an Eric Berne, we might say that she is playing the game, "look what you made me do now." But in her beliefs she remains constant to the end.

Moreover, she has the intelligence to perceive what is going on around her, to understand Lovelace's games and to defeat them to her satisfaction. And she has the ability to create and charge language with meaning as no one else in the novel. Lovelace becomes the "ready kneeler" and more simply, the "man." And when she tells him that she has a heart too proud for him to contend with, she knows what she is talking about. On the other hand, Lovelace's adherence to his role as a libertine betrays him. The principles work well enough for Lovelace the actor, and they may work for his friend, Mowbray; but for the real Lovelace, of whom we have glimpses by his inability to stay in character all the time, they are no good at all. In those moments when she takes on the role of the realistic novelist, as in her account of the dinner given by Lovelace to introduce her to his rakish friends, her choice of language is perfect.

IV

I have been arguing that it is not merely having several "speculative" perspectives on what may be a single action that provides the proper sluggishness that we want in a work of fiction but the quality and texture of those perspectives. If one of the most arresting elements in this process is the daydream, the ordinary dream is even more forceful in this respect. Like almost everything else in an epistolary novel, the dreams are related historically, but they belong to a world without time and need "no writing to the present" to achieve an effect of immediacy. Lovelace's dream about Clarissa interceding between Morden and himself has a near magical power:

> At this, charmed with her sweet mediation, I thought I would have clasped her in my arms: when immediately the most angelic form I had ever beheld, all clad in transparent white, descended in a cloud, which, opening, discovered a firmament above it, crowded with golden cherubs and glitterying seraphs, all addressing her with: Welcome, welcome, welcome! and, encircling my charmer, ascended with her to the region of seraphims; and instantly, the opened clouds closing, I lost sight of *her*; and of the *bright form* together, and found wrapped in my arms her azure robe (all stuck thick with stars of embossed silver), which I had caught hold of in hopes of detaining her; but was all that was left me of my beloved Clarissa. And then (horrid to relate!) the floor sinking under me, as the firmament had opened for *her*, I dropped into a hole more frightful than that of Elden; and, tumbling over and over down it, without view of a bottom, I awaked in a panic; and was as effectually disordered for half an hour, as if my dream had been a reality.

Like the end of *Don Juan*, the total picture is powerful even if the individual imagery seems to come from some bad religious painting that frightened Lovelace in his youth. Speaking of another dream, Lovelace remarks that matters occur "by some quick transition, and strange metamorphosis, which dreams do not usually account for. . . for dreams . . . confine not themselves to the rules of the drama." If this dream of judgment seems to satisfy his desire for self-punishment, the dream in which he is able to move from overcoming Clarissa to seducing Anna Howe to their having one boy and one girl, who eventually marry and enjoy Lovelace's estate, operates as pure wish fulfillment and fantasy.[3] It is very much like the satisfying end of *Wuthering Heights* in which young Cathy and Hareton find the kind of union the demonic lovers, Heathcliff and Cathy, cannot achieve on earth.

Clarissa refuses to regard dreams as anything but the product of imagination.[4] Nevertheless, she confesses that she wakes in a "great terror" from a vision of Lovelace stabbing her from revenge, throwing her body on "two or three half-dissolved carcasses" in a grave, and trampling on the earth with which he covers her. Such a moment in her epistolary narrative projects us into a possible future even while reflecting the general terror she feels at the imminence of her marriage to Solmes and her seemingly inevitable defloration without love. Its impact is ultimately even more powerful than the record of her ravings after the rape, for whatever Clarissa may believe about dreams, this one suggests that her unconscious has apprehended her fate even while her conscious mind continues to deny it. While contemporary thought allowed that most dreams might be caused by the imagination putting together the events and fears of the day, by excess eating, or by lying in the wrong position, no one denied that God could and did communicate by means of dreams. As a result, dreams have the potentiality of prophecy even when treated lightly.[5]

The dreams in Defoe's fiction function in precisely the same way. They are highly dramatic moments out of time by which an important message may be conveyed. In addition to dreams, Defoe also uses moments of vision which have the same effect. Moll calls out to her Jemmy, and he hears her miles away; Roxana has a sudden vision of her lover's death, and it comes true; and Crusoe dreams of a majestic vision of an avenging angel and turns to repentance:

> I thought, that I was sitting on the Ground on the Outside of a Wall, where I sat when the Storm blew after the Earthquake, and that I saw a Man descend from a great black Cloud, in a bright Flame ⸲° Fire, and

light upon the Ground: He was all over as bright as a Flame, so that I
could but just bear to look towards him: his Countenance was most inexpressibly dreadful, impossible for Words to describe; when he stepp'd
upon the Ground with he Feet, I thought the Earth trembl'd, just as it
had done before in the Earthquake, and all the Air look'd to my Apprehension, as if it had been fill'd with Flashes of Fire.

That the dream functions as a means of providing Crusoe with a
supernatural and at the same time personal explanation for the
earthquake which almost destroys him and may be read as a
type of problem-solving for his anxieties does not detract from
the terror that he feels and attempts to convey. "No one," Crusoe states, "that shall ever read this Account, will expect that I
should be able to describe the Horrors of my Soul at this ter-
rible Vision, I mean, that even while it was a Dream, I even
dreamed of those Horrors; nor is it any more possible to describe
the Impression that remain'd upon my Mind when I awak'd and
found it was but a Dream." What Crusoe stresses is the inability
of language to describe his experience. So far from the exactness of Belford's description of Clarissa's cell, we are in the
area of Burthogge's concept of the reality of dream. This, at
least, is what Crusoe seems to mean when he says "even while it
was a Dream, I even dreamed of those Horrors." Interestingly
enough, the dream impells Crusoe toward religious conversion
and toward a new vision of reality that makes his self and the island a meaningful sphere of action.

In realistic fiction from Defoe to Dostoevski, the dream functions as a radical element, giving an insight into a world at once
less substantial and more vivid than the world of "practical perspective." It represents a world that exists and does not exist
and events which, whether they come about or not, have the
power of prophecy. The angelic form that raises his spear against
Crusoe does not complete his threat that Crusoe must die, and
Lovelace's dream fantasy of fruition with both Clarissa and
Anna Howe ends in the reconciliation that life will not provide
for him. Clarissa may wonder why she trembles at her dreams
when reality appears almost equally terrifying, but she acts in
such a way as to make her dream self-fulfilling. Crusoe's dream,

on the other hand, comes with the force of what R. D. Laing calls "derealization," an event that shakes a person free from a false and numbing reality.[6]

Roger Caillois remarks that in primitive societies, when dreams come into competition with reality, it is the dreams that win out. He also points out that the act of reading a work of fiction has some affinities to participating in someone else's dream:

> The dream remains the common property of the sleeper who had dreamed it and of the waking person who remembers it; in an analogous sense the novel fulfills itself with a mediatation between the writer who has created it and the reader who is introduced for a brief instant, for an interlude, as a supernumerary character into a fictional world.[7]

Dreams in realistic fiction have the force of being the most powerful fantasy within a larger fantasy. If civilized man generally tends to put aside his dreams through repression or the conscious recognition that such fantasies have little to do with the ways in which we attempt to deal with ordinary life, a fiction about someone else enables us to take literary dreams very seriously.

In Gothic fiction, dreams became a central device for drawing the reader into the work, the best example being Lockwood's wonderful dream of Jabes Branderham and the lost child in *Wuthering Heights*. But unlike the realistic fiction with which it has so much in common, Gothic fiction tended to blur the distinction between the dream state and the waking state and to extend those techniques of fiction that tended to hold up the flow of time in narrative. Even in an early work like *A Sicilian Romance*, Mrs. Radcliffe continually attempts to build toward moments of anxiety. The wandering thoughts of the heroines extend the terrors of Clarissa's dream into fantasies of imagined dangers and horrors. We are told of the governess of the heroines, Emilia and Julia, that "Her utmost endeavors were unable to repress the anxiety with which the uncertain fate of Julia overwhelmed her. Wild and terrific images arose to her imagination. Fancy ordered the scene—she deepened the shades; and the terrific aspect of the objects she presented was heightened by the obscurity which involved them."

Radcliffe used dreams even more effectively in *The Romance of the Forest*, in which Adeline tells of a vision not very different from that in *Pilgrim's Progress*. She is shown a mirror in which she views herself "wounded and bleeding profusely," and suddenly hears the words, "Depart this house, destruction hovers here." And in a series of dreams at the end of the first volume, she has a vision of a dying Chevalier. He quickly disappears, but after imagining herself wandering through the dark passages of a castle in the series of dreams that follow, she discovers him once more, surrounded by mourners.

> Suddenly, she thought these persons were all gone, and that she was left alone: that she went up to the coffin, and while she gazed upon it, she heard a voice speak, as if from within, but saw nobody. The man she had before seen, soon after stood by the coffin, and lifting the pall, she saw beneath it a dead person, whom she thought to be the dying Chevalier she had seen in her fromer dream: his features were sunk in death, but they were yet serene. While she looked at him, a stream of blood gushed from his side and descending to the floor, the whole chamber was overflowed; at the same time some words were uttered in the voice she heard before; but the horror of the scene so entirely over came her, that she started and awoke.

This dream acts as a center of supernatural terror and as a means of propelling the plot forward. The scene is almost repeated in Adeline's waking state, a method that Jane Austen parodied in *Northanger Abbey*. But while Catherine Morland may have a troubled sleep after General Tilney mistreats her, Jane Austen is not going to allow her or any other heroine of hers to have vivid and compelling dreams. Her novels are defiantly free of evil visions arising out of anything but the experience of social life. Villains may be permitted to ride in romantically in the midst of a storm, but the kind of curiosity that hovers over all kinds of novels at the end of the eighteenth century and holds up the flow of the narrative is mostly absent from her fiction. She preferred dialogue and scene as methods of concentration.

Of course Mrs. Radcliffe had a variety of techniques as well. In *The Mysteries of Udolpho*, she relied almost exclusively on scenic descriptions to extend the reader's experience of the novel. Emily has a dream about her father after his death, but no central position is given to it. And even the kind of introspection that clots the flow of the narrative in *Wieland* is only intermittently present. Although there is a passage in which the heroine's moods are described in terms of the gloomy clouds that surge about the mountains and her thoughts of chaos in contrast to her optimistic feelings as she contemplates the green valleys of Italy, a remarkable number of descriptions have little involvement with either character or event.

Yet there is an additional layer in *The Mysteries of Udolpho*—that of the past and the barbarism of the human race before the Enlightenment. In Mrs. Radcliffe's novels, whatever the historical setting (*The Mysteries* takes place in 1584), the values of the hero and heroine always reflect the ways that her audience expected such people to behave. When Emily stares at the terrifying Momento Mori covered with worms, an experience never fully explained until the end of the novel, she faints away. "Horror," says Radcliffe, "occupied her mind, and excluded, for a time, all sense of past, and dread of future misfortune: she seated herself near the casement, because from thence she heard voices, though distant, on the terrace, and might see people pass, and these, trifling as they were, were reviving circumstances." Just as the view of the mountains suspends time through wonderfully sublime, almost Wordsworthian epiphanies, so this moment of terror, produced by a sudden vision of the grotesque past also stops the narrative flow. This incident is hardly an isolated one: everything that occurs at Udolpho seems like an historical throwback. There are rooms which have been used for torturing victims; and in the recesses of such a room, Emily discovers a corpse covered with blood. The villain, Montoni, is himself a throwback to grotesque figures of pure will and power such as Dryden's Maximin.

By way of giving further impact to such terrifying moments in history, Radcliffe even inserts a "Provencal Tale,"which the reader is told is "tinctured with the superstition of the times." In that world of the distant past, the ghosts, whose existence brings a mixture of skepticism and derision from the main characters, are permitted to function freely as examples of Gothic superstition. And as in all of her novels, the Catholic Church is depicted as an institution carrying into the present the terrors and superstitions that the modern world should have put behind it. This is an effect which may have dropped out of her novels for us; but its presence in the text is undeniable, and its intended effect upon the contemporary reader obvious.

The use of landscape, dreams, the terrors of the past and circumstantial realism are blended together skillfully in *The Italian*, which is, among other things, a study of the nightmarish and anachronistic institutions of Italy. Since it embodies her most modern setting, it also states her case most clearly. In the latter part of the novel, her hero, Vivaldi, suddenly enmeshed in the mysterious trial system of the still extent Inquisition, sounds like an indignant and naive member of the ACLU, demanding his rights and liberties in a world that continues to measure out its time in human pain.

But before these final scenes, there is a return to the dreams and fantasies of *The Romance of the Forest*. Vivaldi in particular has a tendency toward a hyperactive imagination. When a mysterious voice calls out, "Go not to the villa Altieri . . . for death is in the house," his mind immediately conjures up a vision of Ellena as already murdered. "He saw her wounded," writes Radcliffe, "and bleeding to death; saw her ashy countenance, and her wasting eyes from which the spirit of life was fast departing, turned piteously on himself, as if imploring him to save her from the fate that was dragging her to the grave." Even more vivid is the vision of a figure with a bloody finger that Spalatro sees just before going to murder Ellena. Spalatro is hardly anyone that we would take too seriously, but he is no Sancho Panza; he is a man who has killed before and would kill again. Nothing in the work explains such visions except some comments on the effects of an overheated imagination.

And once more Radcliffe treats us to a nightmare—this time the kind that appears to be duplicated by what is experienced on awakening. Imprisioned in the dungeons of the Inquisition, Vivaldi dreams that the monk who warned him not to go to the villa Altieri enters his call:

The Monk, whose face was still shrowded, he thought, advanced, till having come within a few paces of Vivaldi, he paused, and, lifting the awful cowl that had hitherto concealed him, disclosed—not the countanance of Schedoni, but one which Vivaldi did not recollect ever having seen before! It was not less interesting to curiosity, than striking to the feelings. Vivaldi at the first glance shrunk back:—something of that strange and indescribable air, which we attach to the idea of a supernatural being, prevailed over the features; and the intense and fiery eyes resembled those of an evil spirit, rather than of a human character. He drew a poniard from beneath a fold of his garment, and, as he displayed it, pointed with a stern frown to the spots which discoloured the blade; Vivaldi perceived they were of blood! He turned away his eyes in horror, and, when he again looked around in his dream, the figure was gone.

When, upon waking and discovering that very monk in his cell, Vivaldi attempts to draw the line between empirical reality and dream; but he finds that the task is almost beyond his capacities. And when the examiners of the Inquisition question him about Schedoni, the villainous murderer of the novel, Radcliffe tells us that he found his mind resembling "the glass of a magician, on which the apparitions of long buried events arise, and as they fleet away, point portentously to shapes half-hid in the duskiness of futurity. An unusual dread seized upon him; and a superstition . . . usurped his judgment. He looked up to the shadowy countenance of the stranger; and almost believed he beheld an inhabitant of the world of spirits." Thus he is highly susceptible when the monk of his dream and now apparently part of his waking experience warns him that he will behold an extraordinary event the next time he is taken to the "place of torture." To the monk's demand that Vivaldi accuse Schedoni, Vivaldi raises some civil libertarian scruples, but the monk, holding up a dagger, pronounces, "To-morrow night you will meet me in the chambers of death," and, seemingly, vanishes.

These scenes at the end of *The Italian* have the quality of dream and fantasy whatever the state of Vivaldi's mind. Locked in his dark cell, he feels part of a living nightmare. And when the guard insists that he saw no one in the cell with him, his worst fears seem confirmed. Time is measured out in words, pages, chapters, but the reader's sense of time is held up by the stasis that is the prison experience. And the Inquisition itself is a kind of throwback to a period of history which Radcliffe's heroine, Ellena, says should be ignored—ignored because contemplation of such institutions would cast too dark a pall over our idea of mankind. To believe that there might have been a time when a Roman emperor might have sacrificed thousands of slaves for the pleasure of seeing a mock sea battle, she tells Vivaldi is too grim for either contemplation or even real belief. Yet the existence of a Schedoni makes the knowledge of the past essential.

Probably the most fascinating blend of perspective, both speculative and practical, and the way the novel allowed modes of seeing to slow the pace of fiction occurs in the scene when Ellena is attempting to escape from Spalatro and encounters an even more dangerous enemy in Schedoni as she flees along the beach. The scene is reminiscent of Crusoe's discovery of the footprint on the shore of his beach; but no, with Radcliffe's third person point of view, both the subject and object are observable. And in this case, where the situation involves two persons observing each other, the exact angle of vision is not always clear. Ellena first sees Schedoni from a distance with his "black garments . . . folded round him; his face was inclined toward the ground, and he had the air of a man in deep meditation." Responding to his profession, she first assumes he must be a person of holy thoughts and actions: like so much in this work, closer observation of persons and things reveals a hidden evil. As she comes closer to him, he appears like a serpent winding his way toward her:

> He approached, his face still bent towards the ground, and Ellena advanced slowly, and with trembling steps to meet him. As he drew near, he viewed her askance, without lifting his head; but she perceived his large eyes looking from under the shade of his cowl, and the upper part of his peculiar countenance. Her confidence in his protection began to fall, and she faultered, unable to speak, and scarcely daring to meet his eyes. The Monk stalked past her in silence, the lower part of his visage still muffled in his drapery, and as he passed her looked neither with curiosity nor with surprise.

She thinks she may be able to find help elsewhere, but Schedoni weaves about her and cuts off her escape. Radcliffe, approximating Ellena's thoughts, remarks, "There was something also terrific in the silent stalk of so gigantic a form; it announced both power and treachery." Finally her efforts prove futile. Spalatro appears, and she is brought back to the house where she knows her life to be threatened.

From such a scene, a critic might draw some conclusions about a progressive darkening of the attitude toward the way humans perceive and the medium of time in which everything is observed. I would be reluctant to do so. From the beginning of the century, writers like Swift remarked on the paradoxes inherent in choosing to perceive in one way or another—too deeply or too superficially. Each of the writers I have discussed, Defoe, Richardson, and Radcliffe, would have had some idea, however superficial, that what they perceived was not exactly the mirror image of the phenomenal world, and each would have recognized the necessity of creating an autonomous reality within their fictions. This appears to me more important than that one might have been more interested in the concerteness of objects, or in character relationships, or in landscape than the others.

Angus Fletcher has argued that behind the realism of Defoe and the landscapes of Gothic fiction may be found the same kind of daemonic agency that haunts allegory.[7] Without wishing to enter into the complexities of this position, I would simply say that the intricacies of realism—particularly the relationship between fantasy and realism in the same work—still need exploration. Writers like Sterne and Fielding are of the same stamp as a Borges or a Nabokov. For them problems of time and perspective are solved within the artistic fabric which forces form and meaning upon the flux that exists outside the world of art. And in *Tristram Shandy* Sterne makes the novel into a vast ring in which problems of fictional and experienced time and the entire problem of human identity underlying perspective is wrestled to its knees. But we should recognize that those writers I have dealt with as realists were handling the same problems in other ways.

Notes

1. Edmund Law, writing in 1734 as a self-proclaimed follower of Locke maintained that both time and space were merely mental constructs.

Locke, of course, reduces time to a spatial concept but is unwilling to dismiss space as an "Idea" even if he questions whether our notion of it is either clear or distinct. See Law, *An Enquiry into the Ideas of Space, Time, Immensity and Eternity* (Cambridge: W. Thurlebourn, 1734), p. 131.

2. Burthogge, of course, is speaking of fictions like the chimera and the centaur, which Locke (*Essay Concerning Human Understanding*, Book II, Chapter xxx) dismisses as mere combinations of simple ideas. Burthogge treats them with more interest than Locke because he is fascinated by the notion that all ideas, as they exist in the mind, possess degrees of reality. What he says of these fictions may, without much distortion, be applied to literary fictions as well. Both are different from dreams and fantasies in being consciously willed into existence.

3. Modern readers may find Lovelace's imagination an appealing part of his character, but the author who claimed to be the first writer on "Consciousness" deplored dreams and daydreams as the products of appetites and passions and argued that those who indulged in too many imaginative flights were little better than beasts. See *Two Dissertations Concerning Sense, and the Imagination* (London: J. Tonson, 1728), pp. 81, 183-186. This work is sometimes ascribed to Zachary Mayne.

4. In *Sir Charles Grandison*, Harriet Byron has a dream which suggests her anxieties about her future husband's relations with other women. At first she finds herself rejected by him; then she sees him as a ghost and herself a widow. She speculates about her nervousness about such dreams, but she is unwilling to reject them entirely. Lady G. to whom she writes of her experience tells her to put aside any superstitious belief in dreams, arguing that Harriet's fears are merely something instilled in her by her nurses when she was a child. And she adds, "Do you think I don't dream, as well as you?" *Grandison* (London: Richardson, 1754), VII, 216-219, 287.

5. Most writers on dreams during the late seventeenth and early eighteenth centuries stressed natural causes: the particular position of the sleeper, upsetting foods, the nature of the humours and the passions. But few denied that it was possible for God or angels to communicate through dreams. For example, Moses Amyraldus, who argued that divine, allegorical dreams were "wholly expir'd," and that most dreams were from natural causes, conceded that dreams which were clearly prophetic of future events had to come from good or evil spirits. Andrew Baxter, writing in the middle of the eighteenth century, insisted that all dreams had be be caused by spirits. See Amyraldus, *A Discourse concerning the Divine Dreams Mention'd in Scripture*, trans. James Lowde (London: Walter Kettilby, 1676), pp. 15-16, 24-27, 113; and Baxter, *An Enquiry into the Nature of the Human Soul*, 3rd ed. (London: A. Millar, 1745), II, 172.

6. Some dreams in fiction function as purely literary cues for indi-

cating the direction of the plot and have few symbolic overtones. Of this type is the dream of the mother of the Cavalier in Defoe's *Memoirs of a Cavalier* that during her labor a man played a drum under her window. Roderick Random's mother dreams that she gives birth to a tennis ball, which the devil, who acts the part of a midwife, strikes with a racket. The highland seer she consults predicts that her son will be a great traveller, but she might have had that information out of contemporary dreambooks in which such dreams of tennis refer to travel to get wealth. See *Nocturnal Revels: Or, a Universal Dream-Book* (London: Andrew Bell, 1707), Part 2, p. 162.

7. "Logical and Philosophical Problems of the Dream" *The Dream and Human Societies*, ed. G. E. Grunebaum and Roger Caillois (Berkeley: University of California Press, 1966), p. 51.

"Dwarfs of Wit and Learning": Problems of Historical Time

Robert D. Moynihan

One of the pervasive themes in the seventeenth and eighteenth centuries is the contradictory definition and place accorded to historical time: specifically, whether history had the capability of not merely recording the past but of allowing its readers to predicate the inevitability of positive change. Any student of Herbert Butterfield,[1] or reader of the informative notes by H. R. Trevor-Roper,[2] knows of the coming of age of Whig historiography, a nineteenth-century phenomenon whose distracting exaggerations have been extracted, read, and reinterred. Nonetheless, essential questions about the theory of progress and history remain in spite of the cross-examination of George III and his historians. Butterfield, however, not discussing that specific problem, complains that the manipulation of the past, its semi-mythical forms and models, has created it own distortions:

> The very strength of our conviction that ours was a Graeco-Roman civilisation—the very way in which we allowed the art-historians and the philologists to make us think that this thing which we call 'the modern world' was the product of the Renaissance—the inelasticity of our his-

167

torical concepts, in fact—helped to conceal the radical nature of the changes that had taken place and the colossal possibilities that lay in the seed sown by the seventeenth century.[3]

The essential event of the seventeenth century that is distorted by the "classical" past is revolution, the turning aside of past forms of time and order, and the ensuing, irreconcilable debate about the right or wrong of the English regicide.

One method of analysis would be to establish the cause of that event as an early form of social disorder itself. Hiram Haydn sees "emergent democratic principles apparent in the writings of the sixteenth century [which] scoffed at the established hierachy of 'professions,' 'vocations,' and traditional castes."[4] But what is described here as an initiation comes to more complete expression in the next century. Lawrence Stone describes the time preceding the appearance of the vital mob, analyzed by George Rudé,[5] with its disrespect for social class and established order. Stone sees the period of the seventeenth century before the English civil war as a time of disorder, marked by a disrespect for ruling classes. Mobs jostled and threatened earls, overturned coaches. Gentry stopped welcoming returning aristrocracy to their lands; yeomanry no longer voted as directed.[6] The disagreements seem absolute, with the granting of titles for royal profit, public ostentation by the ruling classes, the contrast between city and country living, "the Puritan exaltation of the private conscience, . . ." and disagreements about "constitutional theory, methods and scale of taxation, forms of worship, aesthetic tastes, financial probity, and sexual morality."[7]

Originating in the period Haydn discusses, these differences became more irreconcilable in the next century. On no topic was there more increased and marked disagreement than the interpretation of historical time, which itself came to be one of the many indications of the state of mind of the outsider, the religious and social reformer, and eventually, the overt revolutionary who saw self, party, and cause as the inevitable projection of the future. The most commonly read work in the seventeenth century which redefined the historical past to the advantage of the present and the future originated in the period Haydn describes, Foxe's *Acts and Monuments,* the "Book of Martyrs." The achievement of this work is astonishingly innovative. Foxe, as a justification for the lowly, humble, and victimized, describes all past history as an epochal prelude to a Protestant ascendency which reveals the soul voyaging through the process of antagonism and rebellion to establish the new society of ordinary individuals, conscious of their superiority over the past. In one of the introductions to this work, Foxe as a Protestant chronicler interprets the pagan and the Papal-Roman periods as commonly decadent. However, he adds the notion of time as a perfecting resolution of divine will which is made present in expected changes necessary to establish the new order. Foxe makes Augustine's "city of God" a physical and political immediacy: England, the antithetical Babylon, initiates a national and religious destiny to build an empire of the spirit. At times the adherents of "truth" have been but a fragment, "yet . . . some remnant always remained from time to time which . . . stood in open defense of truth against the disordered church. . . ." These true religionists faced a series of persecutions, including the "Saxon yoke," which assured the slaying of the "Britain-preachers."[8] Yet even those Saxons embraced Christianity, but one episode of the past swept by Foxe's peroration to a distant but perfect future. The conclusion of this preface, "To the True and Faithful Congregation of Christ's Universal Truth," is emphatic:

> The God of peace, who hath power both of land and sea, reach forth his merciful hand to help them up that sink, to keep up them that stand, to still these winds and surging seas of discord and contention among us; that we, professing one Christ, may in one unity of doctrine, gather ourselves into one ark of the true church together; where we, continuing stedfast in faith, may at the last luckily be conducted to the joyful port of our desired landing-place by his heavenly grace.[9]

This view of time is as important to succeeding, dissident generations as Foxe's democracy of carnage, "the heaps of slain bodies, . . . men of all sorts, of all ages, of all degrees; lords [to] . . . artificers."[10] The martyrs themselves, "rescued from oblivion and enlisted in a religious crusade by the rage of an his-

torical scholar,"[11] are important because their opposition is
made requisite to the future. Their beliefs develop no matter
what the contradiction of past authority. Not unlike later rev-
lutionaries of the next century, Foxe defines existence by opposition. Time is volatile, changing, ordered to an inevitable future.
The power and the uniqueness of this view of time itself as historical agent is seen when one looks at Machiavelli's definition
of a supposedly "new" order, the possibility of change still tem-
pered by "fortune," the "ruler of half our actions."[12] Foxe's
definition is, indeed, more volatile, a projection of present into
a future that must be temporally realized. Such a theory makes
the past of conventional history, the emphasis on simple chronology, Machiavelli's stories of growth and decline, the mixing
of fable and actual historical persons, a negative example.[13]
Richard Baxter says as much in his seventeenth-century autobiography: "I am much more cautelous [cautious] in my belief
of history then heretofore. Not that I run into their extreme
that will believe nothing because they cannot believe all things."[14]
Baxter, a moderate Puritan, is cautious, for the process of recording contemporary biographical records, the past history of
the physical and psychological survivors of dissent, emphasizes
survival, the reordering of events whereby the antithetical process is celebrated as the progressive flux of time. The individual
records of survival, such as Baxter's, Bunyan's, and thousands of
others,[15] justifies a rewriting of personal experience and history
and their implications about the future order, when the waters
of the sea "cast up mire and dirt,"[16] a process of cleansing necessary for the new order. What such records lacked in biographical or historical accuracy, they compensated for by creating
a kind of hope that was intentionally destructive to the traditional past. They decidedly looked to the future as a means of
new historical pattern and self-justification, a process that was
never complete. Milton's statement in *Areopagitica* reveals the
energy and forward motion of the religious, personal, and historical process: "God is decreeing to begin some new and great
period in his Church, ev'n to the reforming of the Reformation
itself. . . ."[17] The redefinition of the writer as a witness of inevitable change, as initiator of change through rejection, is essen-

tially revolutionary. If the present is of greater importance than the past, the past is rejected because it is antithetical in religious and hierarchical value.

Manifestations of the new order, its amplification in science, politics, and literature insistently occur, and the controversy between the more radical English protestants and their established opponents are replicated in every generation of the seventeenth and eighteenth centuries. Foxe and his successors believed dissent to be justified as a means of growth, in the sense that the term "means the generation of a higher order. . . ."[18] The radical Gerard Winstanley combines these themes, the rejection of the past, the presumed foretelling of the future, the anticipation of communal plenty, the outsider redefining his own chronology. He describes *"the Despised Sons and Daughters of ZION, . . .* the objects of the world's hatred," but transforms that antagonism into the prediction that "redemption is near. . . ."[19] That promised future includes the change of the ownership of property as the righteous assert "that every one that is born in the Land may be fed by the Earth his Mother that brought him forth, according to the Reason that rules in the Creation."[20] The new order is rich, plentiful, made so by either the restructuring of society or the discovery of promised lands. As Thomas Goodwin describes the "new Indies," they are thought to contain "heavenly treasure," the sign of beneficient nature uncontrolled by past laws and circumscriptions. There is plenty, but "more . . . may be."[21]

Poetic reliance on these topics is overt. In Andrew Marvell's "The Horation Ode upon Cromwell's Return from England," the old order is presumed to be destroyed, for the new hero

> Could by industrious Valour climbe
> To ruine the great Work of Time,
>   And cast the Kingdome old
>   Into another Mold.
> Though Justice against Fate complain,
> And plead the antient Rights in vain:
>   But those do hold or break
>   As Men are strong or weak.[22]

And "Bermudas," compared with Foxe's conclusion of "To the

True and Faithful Congregation . . ." with its picture of the divine power "to still winds and surging seas of discord" to protect the "ark" of belief, and Goodwin's description of the "new Indies" with their rich store are combined. The rejection of the decline of nature, as expressed in Edmund Waller's earlier "Battle of the Summer Islands," is overt. So is the assertion of political success for the new doctrines which exalt haven and plenty, the new time of order and successful exile:

> 'He lands us on a grassy Stage;
> Safe from the Storms, and Prelat's rage.
> . . . .
> 'He makes the Figs our mouths to meet;
> And throws the Melons at our feet.
> But Apples plants of such a price,
> No Tree could ever bear them twice.'
> . . . .
>   Thus sung they, in the *English* boat
> An holy and a chearful Note;
> And all the way, to guide their Chime,
> With falling Oars they kept the time.[23]

The refutation of these ideas is insistent. Their different forms have been reviewed often, the struggle between "ancients and moderns," theories of temporal and physical regression, and revisions of Eleatic time.[24] The tactics are usually confusing in spite of their basic simplicity. To the radical Protestant's assertions that change was inevitable and that "improvement" was unerring, the conservatives asserted the opposite. They usually did not separate the questions very clearly. Change could have been admitted, but divided from "improvement."[25] The typical solution, however, was and is more primitive. Change is itself denied or is paraphrased from Hesiod's *Theogony*, and time is itself made an agent of regression. Following this tradition, the aristocratic Edmund Waller's "The Battle of the Summer Islands" inverted the idea of time as promise. He combined a regressive historical vision with flat and listless commonplaces:

> Bermudas, walled with rocks, who does not know?
> That happy island where huge lemons grow,
> And orange trees, which golden fruit do bear,
> The Hesperian garden boasts of none so fair;

> Where shining pearl, coral, and many a pound
> On the rich shore of ambergris is found.

The banal conclusion can be anticipated:

> Heaven sure has kept this spot of earth uncursed,
> To show how all things were created first. . . .[26]

Contrasted with "Bermudas," this poem shows one of the essential peculiarities of argument during this period. Waller's statements about the primacy of a creation that was once pure but fallen to a lower estate, except for the model of the "Summer Islands" which stands as an example by which to judge later inferiority, use the same "evidence" found in Marvell. The interest is not so much that the two poems oppose each other, or even that one is supposedly modelled on the other, but that they use the identical evidence to come to opposite conclusions.

It is this very act of an antithetical and primitive dialectic that gives the exchanges in the seventeenth and eighteenth centuries their modern and nominalistic nature. For the evidence is clear that each camp looked to a past that was familiarly represented but antithetically interpreted according to the idea of nature as either progressive or static. Foxe, followed by a radical Winstanley, or commonwealthmen such as Harrington, Molesworth, and Algernon Sidney, believed in the dynamic of change. Less reliant on the "spirit" for guidance in human affairs, the commonwealthmen used the identical records of the past, semimythical constitutions of the ancients, to support their arguments. Their opponents also argued from authority, used the same sources, but came to opposite conclusions. The past, representing a mythical perfection in the arts if not in ordered government far removed from factional strife, was such that its succeeding ages could only reveal imperfections, a failure of human ability, an unfortunate, not a fortunate, fall.

The question is not merely that every major historical argument of every age has its opposite, as George Boas mentions in his definition of the enlightenment,[27] but that historical and social arguments of the seventeenth and eighteenth centuries assumed such a perversely antithetical form. For one group which used a theory of time to realize a different order of literature, politics, and individuality, another asserted that the past, with its distant perfection, its "classicism," made any change impossible, makes any change, in fact, a sign of decline and cultural inanition. There is a mental limit for every suggested boundary, a Waller, or a Dryden, for every Marvell or Milton: for the frontier of the spirit, and later the mind of the enlightenment, there is the limitation of inadequacy. Man must admit his indebtedness. As Richard Harvey critically observed, "Persons of limited information, when they are at a loss to assign a cause for anything, very commonly reply that it is done by the spirits; and so they introduce the spirits upon all occasions. . . ."[28] Both sides in the controversy at this stage introduce "spirits" in the form of religion, but the conservatives do so to emphasize weakness and relatedness, to prove inadequacy before history and constrained religious belief.

The controversy about the historical past is a tedious one. George Hakewill in 1627 published a defense of the moderns, considering Sidney and Spenser equal to the ancients, believing that the science of the seventeenth century superior, Christianity preferable to paganism.[29] Joseph Priestley's *Lectures on History*, published in 1788, seems a paraphrase:

> That the state of the world at present, and particularly the state of Europe, is vastly preferable to what it was in any former period, is evident from the very first view of things. A thousand circumstances show how inferior the ancients were to the moderns in religious knowledge, in science in general, in government, in laws, both the laws of nations and those of particular states, in arts, in commerce, in the conveniences of life, in manners, and in consequence of all these, in *happiness*.[30]

The French form of the controversy originated with a courtly tribute to Louis XIV, but the arguments, while cut off from religious sources, are vital. Fontenell denies that "moderns" are less skilled in art or science and ironically asserts that "If the ancients were more intelligent than we, the reason must be that brains in those days were better arranged, made of firmer or more delicate fibers, and filled with more animal spirits. . . . Trees, too, then would have been taller and more beautiful; for if Nature was then younger and more vigorous, trees as well as hu-

man brains must have felt the effect of that vigor and youth."[31]
According to Fontenell, the myth of the past was tedious in its
enforcement of literary genre. The pastoral satisfies imaginations
with but "a kind of half truth," and is a literary form of "con-
cealing . . . meanness":

> If those who are resolved to find no faults in the ancients tell us that
> Theocritus had a mind to draw nature just such as it is, I hope that ac-
> cording to these principles we shall have some idyllia of porters or wa-
> termen discoursing together of their particular concerns, which will be
> every whit as good as some idyllia of shepherds speaking of nothing but
> their goats or their cows.[32]

Admittedly, some versions of the primacy of the past are so
overstated that they are merely quaint. Sir William Temple's assertions about the fraudulent *Epistles of Phalaris* are semi-comic:
"I think the Epistles of Phalaris to have more race, more spirit,
more force of wit and genius, than any others I have ever seen,
either ancient of modern."[33] Literary judgments of this kind
are usually gratuitous and relatively harmless, but Temple unfortunately moves to other ground. His question, "Has Harvey
outdone Hippocrates?" is but a part of a question that has reactionary overtones: "Have the studies, the writings, the productions of Gresham College . . . outshined or eclipsed the Lycaeum
of Plato, the Academy of Aristotle, the Stoa of Zeno, the Garden
of Epicurus?"[34] In spite of Bentley's astonishingly physical re-
tort ("Every living language, like the perspiring bodies of living
creatures, is in perpetual motion and alteration . . ."),[35] every
generation since has brought forth its second Temple of declin-
ing argument.

But the essential point about time and historical evidence remains: the debate of one generation is merely a rehearsal for the
same arguments in the next; the same evidence is used by both
sides, but is juggled for rhetorical effect. Beside the "burden of
the past," "dwarfs on giants' shoulders" and other mummeries,
rhetorical partisans use the same sources for opposite conclusions, and both sides in the struggles in seventeenth-century England used the past for their own intent. As a critic of Harrington's liberal political theories observed in 1659: "Antiquity is
considered with Veneration by almost all Men, and even They

who Professe to slight it, make great Advantage of it when they imagine it is on their side. He intitles to Antient Prudence that way of Popular Government which his Good applauds."[36]

The use of the past in such a dialectic is even more debilitating than the traps of perspective and tradition encountered in the history of science, Priestley, for instance, defining oxygen as "dephlogisticated air,"[37] or the opponents of William Harvey finding his work an opportunity for theological censure, preferring and using the works of Galen long past their correction.[38] But it is not merely the past. The dynamic of time itself is what proves most intimidating to the conservatives, Dryden among them, who defines nature as a frozen, static certainty, made dynamic only by erring man and his changing interpretations:

> Dim, as the borrow'd beams of Moon and Stars
> To *lonely, weary, wandring travellers,*
> Is *Reason* to the *Soul.* . . .

Dryden himself sets the political tone in the preface of this 1682 poem, an attack on "the Doctrines of King-kill and Deposing . . . still maintain'd by the whole Body of Nonconformists and Republicans" who will be worthy of civil respect as "true Englishmen" only "when they obey the King, and true Protestants when they conform to the Church of Discipline."[39] What is most regrettable to Dryden, however, is the use of the evidence of the scriptures, reinterpreted to justify change: "the Sectaries furnished themselves with the . . . Weapons; and out of the same Magazine, the Bible. So that the Scriptures, which are in themselves the greatest security of Governours, as commanding express obedience to them, are now turn'd to their destruction." Similarly, the danger of the past as a prediction, or justification, for political change, particularly by animated individuals (or "heroes") is just as suspect. Neither the scriptures nor the past justifies the kind of changes threatening England, namely, an unsuccessful republican past still touted as the ideal form of government for the future. Only a strong central government, a monarchy, discourages the formation of multiple sects, the reformers reforming, whom the past proves victims of incapacity, "dwarfs of wit and learning," in Dryden's phrase. The age "is only fit for Satyr," significant for its "ingratitude to the Government." His catalogue of the past is a combination of academic prepossession and the propagandistically useful theory of weakening succession:

> not only the Bodies, but the Souls of Men, have decreas'd from the vigour of the first Ages; that we are not more short of the stature and strength of those gygantick Heroes, than we are of their understanding, and their wit. . . . How vast a difference is there betwixt the productions of those Souls, and these of ours! How much better *Plato, Aristotle,* and the rest of the Philosophers understood nature; *Thucydides,* and *Herodotus* adorn'd History; *Sophocles, Euripedes* and *Menander* advanc'd Poetry, than those Dwarfs of Wit and Learning who succeeded them in after times![40]

One of the more inventive devices used by the Puritans and radicals to counter such views of authority and to anticipate restatements was to view the past from another vantage; they did not merely repeat the formulas about the Greek and Roman civilizations. The citation in their writing of the divinely inspired seekers of promise and independence, the Jews, is insistent and clever strategy. Writing to Cromwell in 1651, signing himself "A true Lover of Commonwealths, Government, Peace, and Freedom," Winstanley addresses the "General of the Commonwealths Army": "God hath honored you with the highest Honor of any man since *Moses* time, to be the Head of a People, who have cast out an Oppressing *Pharoah:* For when the *Norman* power had conquered our Forefathers, he took a free use of our English Ground from them, and made them his servants. And God hath made you a successful Instrument to cast out that Conqueror. . . ."[41] But the example had practical, civil applications. Harrington in *Oceana* uses the institution of the "Church of God" for a governmental model with divisions of responsibility between *Synagoga magna* and *Sanhedrin,* "first elected by the people."[42] Sir Henry Vane, a supporter of the Commonwealth who was to lose his life after the Restoration, uses Israel as the example of government of the elect, "As Moses did, . . . Take and choose you able and wise men, . . . that they may be made

Heads over the People. . . ." Vane believes that this ancient tradition endows its own kind of validity, "which was shewn unto
Moses in the Mount; in the wisdom of which Word he was then
taught to see the most excellent platforme of Civil Government,
as having its root and inward principles, as well as its outward
administration flowing from Divine Institution & revelation. . . ."
According to Vane a "Ruling Senate" elected "by . . . free suf-
frage" is the "most exact platforme of the purest kind of Government, and that which hath its foundation and first pattern
in the Word of God, in the practices of Israel's Commonwealth,
and so plainly of Divine Creation and Institution." It will be
but the prelude "to the setting up Christ as King throughout the
whole earth . . . when the Heads of the People and the Tribes of
Israel are gathered together before the Lord in the day of their
Assembly."[43]

But it is the day to day reform of government that is of greatest concern, the more extensive use of the ballot, a more representative voice in the interest of civil order. Harrington combines
the practical and the prophetic: "The use or Practice of the *Ballot* hath been very Ancient in the Eastern Countries; and *Postel-
lus* conceiveth, that the *Venetian* use of the *Ball,* is the same
with that, which was of the *Lot* in the Commonwealth of *Israel,*
and of the *Bean* in *Athens.*"[44] These points are elaborated in
Aphorisms Political, where "Popular Election" would occur
"according to the Precept of Moses, and the Rule of Scripture. . . ." But it is the comparision Harrington makes between
Israel and his hopes for a successful commonwealth, at once
visionary and practical, that is defined in the last of his statements in this acutely argued pamphlet: "The highest earthly
Felicity that a People can ask or GOD can give, is an equal and
well-ordered Commonwealth. Such as one among the Israelites,
was the Reign of GOD. . . ."[45] The use of these arguments was
undeniably successful. The model of ancient Israel as a pretext
for republicanism, confirmed by divine plan, was made the
more notorious by Cromwell's tacit readmission of the Jews to
England at the request of Menessah ben Israel. Those final mes-
sianic appeals, heard in December, 1655, look to the future, the
prophetic coming of the new age.[46]

The strategy of stopping the threat of such theories was simple. If change is difficult, but inevitable, it arouses the first conditions for revolution, improbable when there has been no hope, no period in which expectations have risen.[47] In other words, the traditionally conservative reaction to change is either to deny it in itself, or to deny the definition of time which includes expectation: Divine ordinance does not favor change, but stability derived from nature as a static and fixed state. Once again, this can be established by using the evidence of the historical "record." The Israelites did not favor a commonwealth, but absolute monarchy. Matthew Wren in *Monarchy Asserted* uses this simple inversion. The "commonwealth" Moses founded is not a republic. It is an example of absolutism. Moses was the agent of the godly, omnipotent "He," of a literally divine monarch: "to the People of *Israel* He was pleased to own a more particular Concernment, And did by an express Declaration of his Will to and by Moses, both at first enact their Lawes and Modell their Government, and reserve to himself the Result of the most important Affaires."[48]

As before in his conservative statements in the preface to Plutarch and in the *Religio Laici*, Dryden's tactic in *Absalom and Achitophel* is as simple as it is *un*original.[49] Yet, in its own way, the achievement is a brilliant reversal of time and historical analogy as used by radicals. In the poem, the time is the present. England, to grant the essential thesis of Harrington and the other disputants, is Israel, but it is not the semi-mythic commonwealth where the vote inevitably results in the selection "of the best representatives." Rather, the ethnocentric claim that "God is English"[50] comes to bear with appropriate devastation of radical intentions, which are left awkwardly dangling by their roots. The ideal past is transformed into the vexing present, where God's own chosen people are fractious and childlike. This simple and effective inversion is, in a narrow sense, the major dialectical achievement of the poem, which Dryden makes more ironic by turning the sexual license of Charles II (David) into a tribute to primordial, undiminished nature. Most important to Dryden's argument, however, is his use of time as a foil for evidence. The rebellious search for historical sources ends in primi-

tivism "when no rule, no president was found/Of men, by Laws
less circumscrib'd and bound,/They led their wild desires to
Woods and Caves,/And thought that all but Savages were
Slaves."[51] In spite of its irrelevance, the argument is devastatingly
preemptive, moving the reference of time to an unalterable and
irrefutable state, that of unrecorded proto-history without pre-
cedent or president.

What is most striking about these exchanges is not what they
indicate about the seventeenth- and eighteenth-century states of
mind, the aristrocratic ruse of the decline of art, morals and society, but that the views of the past and their expression in art
are overtly political. The conclusion, however regrettable, is
that the literature celebrating the golden age and the decline of
the present has, and had, social consequences, either by sup-
porting a particular but temporary *status quo*, by propagandizing
class bias, profit, by advocating a hoped for public admiration
of monarchical authority and order, or simply by being overtly
reactionary for the sake of property. The problem of the past,
of Milton and the poetry of the serious Marvell, is not that they
set an artistic model that is intimidating to their successors, but
that they viewed time and history as dynamic, if not revolutionary. It is this view which is embarrassing to their conservative
successors: to them, time itself becomes one of the topics of
refuge, its essential hypotheses unvarying from the acceptable
"ancients," no matter what the nature of evidence is that may
be introduced for refutation.

Paul Fussell notes that the imagery of the Augustans "operates generally as polemic rather than as revelation or epiphany.
What it bodies forth are public moral arguments, not private
apperceptions."[52] In the literature of the periods succeeding the
seventeenth century, however, private apperceptions are indeed
the basis for public moral arguments and political theory such
as that found in these lines at the end of the eighteenth century:

> It is now towards the middle of February. Were I to take a turn into the
> country, the trees would present a leafless wintery appearance. As
> people are apt to pluck twigs as they go along, I perhaps might do the
> same, and by chance might observe that a *single bud* on that twig had

begun to swell. I should reason very unnaturally, or rather not reason at all, to suppose *this* was the *only* bud in England which had this appearance. Instead of deciding thus, I should instantly conclude that the same appearance was beginning or about to begin everywhere; and though the vegetable sleep will continue longer on some trees and plants than on others, and though some of them may not blossom for two or three years, all will be in leaf in the summer, except those which are *rotten*. What pace the political summer may keep with the natural, no human foresight can determine. It is, however, not difficult to perceive that the spring is begun.[53]

That this passage is as much an illumination for Shelley's "Ode to the West Wind" as Foxe is for Marvell's "Bermudas" may illustrate the dynamic intensity of this time, its reversal, and its consistent restatement. Like most things English and protestant, this single most revolutionary idea, the transcending spirit's redefinition of the future as an extension of the changing present, is basically simple, sturdy, and recurrent.

Acknowledgments

My sincerest appreciation is due the National Endowment for the Humanities for granting periods of study and research at Yale University.

This paper traverses several morasses of argument discussed by Isaac Kramnick, J. G. A. Pocock, R. F. Jones, Judith Shklar, and many others. I aim, however, to correct the thesis of W. J. Bates's The Burden of the Past and the English Poet *and theories of anxiety and art that have followed. The essential anxiety in English literature following the mid-seventeenth century arose from the fear of political instability and a loss of order. Milton may be a "father poet"; he was also a primary radical who intimidated his English successors, extending his forceful image by the historical mirror of the French Revolution.*

I am in debt to several colleagues for their suggestions and encouragement, particularly Max Novak and Paula Backscheider. However, The genesis of this work occurred some time ago: I especially thank Henry Pettit for his example as teacher and scholar.

Notes

1. *George III and the Historians* (New York, 1959), Butterfield's preface to *Man on His Past* (Cambridge, 1969), xii, is more expansive: "The historian who survives seems to be the one who in some way or other has managed to break through into the realm of enduring ideas or gives hints of a deeper tide in the affairs of men."

2. The preface to *Critical and Historical Essays on Thomas Babington, Lord Macaulay* (New York, 1965).

3. *The Origins of Modern Science* (New York, 1958), 189-190.

4. *The Counter-Renaissance* (New York, 1950), xiv.

5. *The Crowd in History* (New York, 1964).

6. *The Crisis of the Aristocracy* (Oxford, 1965), 746-747.

7. Stone, 748-749.

8. *Acts and Monuments*, ed. George Townsend (reprint, New York, 1965), I, xx.

9. *Acts*, I, xxiv.

10. *Acts*, "To the Persecutors of God's Truth, Commonly Called Papists," I, xii.

11. Peter Gay, *The Loss of Mastery* (Berkeley, 1966), 15.

12. *The Prince*, ed. Max Lerner (New York, 1940), 21. Machiavelli as a "modern" is recently celebrated in J. G. A. Pocock's *The Machiavellian Moment* (Princeton, 1975).

13. Machiavelli's example of Moses as an antithetical figure is weakened by mixing several fables in the medieval style: "It was thus necessary that Moses should find the people of Israel slaves in Egypt. . . . It was necessary that Romulus should be unable to remain in Alba. . . . It was necessary that Cyrus should find the Persians discontented. . . . Theseus could not have shown his abilities if he had not found the Athenians dispersed." *The Prince*, 21. See Edward Halle's 1548 *The Union of the Two Noble and Illustre Families of Lancastre & York:* "father Moses had, by divine inspiration in the third age, invented letters. . . . Likewise Mercury in Egypt invented letters and writing, which Cadmus after brought into Greece." *Tudor Poetry and Prose*, ed. J. W. Hebel, et al. (New York, 1953), 587.

14. *The Autobiography of Richard Baxter*, ed. J. M. Lloyd Thomas (London, n.d.), 126.

15. Owen C. Watkins, *The Puritan Experience* (New York, 1972).

16. John Bunyan, *Grace Abounding to the Chief of Sinners*, ed. Roger Sharrock (Oxford, 1962), 33. The phrase is from Isaiah, 57: 2l-22.

17. *The Works of John Milton*, ed. F. A. Patterson (New York, 1934), IV, 340.

18. Helmut Kuhn, "The Case for Order in a Disordered Age," in *The Concept of Order*, ed. Paul G. Kuntz (Seattle, 1968), 448.

19. "The Breaking of the Day of God," in *The Works of Gerard Winstanley,* ed. George H. Sabine (reprint, New York, 1965), 87.

20. "The True Levellers Standard Advanced," Sabine, 257.

21. Christopher Hill, *The World Turned Upside Down* (New York, 1972), 297.

22. *The Poems of Andrew Marvell,* ed. Hugh Macdonald (Cambridge, Mass., 1956), 119.

23. Ibid., 12-13.

24. It is probably unnecessary to mention that these issues continue through several generations, reaching their climax in the late eighteenth century in the Burke controversies. My own biases are derived from Alfred Cobban, Peter Gay, and Conor Cruise O'Brien. J. H. Plumb's short essay, "Edmund Burke and His Cult," *In The Light of History* (New York, 1972), 95-101, is refreshingly blunt. Eleatic time is recently discussed by G. E. L. Owen in *The Pre-Socratics,* ed. Alexander P. D. Mourelatos (New York, 1974), 275 ff. "Parmenides expressly concludes, from his polemic against the possibility of change, that his subject *remains* the same."

25. Richard Schlegel, *Time and the Physical World* (East Lansing, 1961), 17: "It might be argued that a statement about time's direction is without significant content. The changing world goes through a succession of states, and the direction of time, we might say, is merely as given by the passage from one state to the next; the succession of states, whatever it may be, determines the direction of time. It is tautological then to speak of time's direction as being 'forward'. . . . The statement that time moves from past to future is, however, more than a definition of those terms, and is in fact a statement about the nature of our world." It should be emphasized, however, that a similar error would be to assure that time is regressive.

26. *The Poems of Edmund Waller,* ed. G. Thorn Drury (New York, 1893), 66.

27. "In Search of the Age of Reason," in *Aspects of the Eighteenth Century,* ed. E. R. Wasserman (Baltimore, 1965), 1 ff.

28. In A. R. Hall, *The Scientific Revolution* (Boston, 1956), 148. The statement is from the *Second Disquisition to Riolan* (1649).

29. J. B. Bury, *The Idea of Progress* (London, 1928), 88-89. Bury does not mention that Hakewill was responding to Bishop Godfrey Goodwin's 1616 *The Fall of Man, or the Corruption of Nature.*

30. In John T. Marcus, *Heaven, Hell, and History* (New York, 1967), 74.

31. "A Digression on the Ancients and Moderns," in *The Continental Model*, ed. Scott Elledge and Donald Schier (Ithaca, 1970), 358.

32. "Of Pastorals," Elledge, 347.

33. "Ancient and Modern Learning," (1690), in *Five Miscellaneous Essays* by Sir William Temple, ed. and intro. by Samuel Holt Monk (Ann Arbor, 1963), 64.

34. Ibid., 62.

35. "Dissertation upon the Epistles of Phalaris," in *The Works of Richard Bentley*, ed. Alexander Dyce (New York, 1966), II, 1.

36. Matthew Wren, *Monarchy Asserted* (Oxford, 1659), 2.

37. S. E. Toulmin, "Crucial Experiments: Priestley and Lavoisier," in *Roots of Scientific Thought*, ed. Philip P. Wiener and Aaron Noland (New York, 1957), 481 ff.

38. Although he was not a historian of science, Thurman Arnold's description of the process of ignorance has too much verve to be rejected: "We see the master, seated on a sort of throne at some distance from the cadaver, with Galen's book open before him. Below, a robed assistant with a pointer indicated those portions of the human body which are relevant to illustrate the text. The actual dissection is being done by a menial who is not permitted to wear the robes of learning. Students stand around, but do not dissect. It is not surprising that such methods always proved the text of Galen. . . . Differences could be explained by pointing out that the human constitution had degenerated since the days of the constitutional fathers. . . ." *The Symbols of Government* (New Haven, 1935), 23.

39. Preface to *Religio Laici*, in *The Works of John Dryden* (Berkeley, 1972), II, 108.

40. Dedication to *Plutarch's Lives*, in *The Works of John Dryden*, ed. S. H. Monk (Berkeley, 1974), XVII, 227. The comment about satire is on page 229 of the same essay. See note by Monk on pages 436 and 437 of the same volume: "The evidence suggested that in the 1660's and 1670's [Dryden] had acknowledged progress but that in the late 1670's he questioned its likelihood." As well, see Achsah Guiborry, "Dryden's View of History," *Philological Quarterly*, 52(1973), 187-204.

41. *Works*, ed. Sabine, p. 501.

42. *The Political Writings, . . .* ed. Charles Blitzer (New York, 1955), 64.

43. *A Needful Corrective of Ballance in Popular Government* (London, n.d.), 1, 8, 10–11. The work is an amicable response to Harrington's *The Prerogative of Popular Government*.

44. *The Benefit of the Ballot* (n.p., n.d.), 1.

45. Second edition (London, 1659), 18. The same point is emphasized in Harrington's *The Art of Law Giving*, Book 2, "Shewing the Frames of the Commonwealths of Israel," in *The Oceana and Other Works*, ed. John Toland (London, 1747).

46. The primary documents are edited by Lucien Wolf, *Menessah ben Israel's Mission to Oliver Cromwell* (London, 1901). See, as well, Heinrich Graetz, *History of the Jews* (reprint, Philadelphia, 1956), V, 27 ff., Albert M. Hyamson, *The Sephardim of England* (London, 1951), Cecil Roth, *A History of the Jews in England* (London, 1964), Harold Fisch, *Jerusalem and Albion* (New York, 1964), and S. B. Liljegren, *Harrington and the Jews* (Lund, 1932).

47. James C. Davies, "Toward a Theory of Revolution," *American Sociological Review* XXVII(1962), 17.

48. Wren, 64.

49. The preceding references amplify and change the contexts of R. F. Jones's "The Originality of *Absalom and Achitophel*," *MLN*, 46 (1931), 211-218. The essay is useful for its observation about the conservative use of the parallel between David and Charles II, but it fails to provide the reasons or the political meanings for the analogy. Dryden's use of time and the analogy are unoriginal in their conservatism.

50. A gloss in John Aylmer's *An Harborowe for Faithfull and Trewe Subjects*, quoted by William Haller, "John Foxe and the Puritan Revolution," in *The Seventeenth Century*, ed. R. F. Jones, et al. (Stanford, 1951), 209.

51. Dryden, II, 7, 11. 53-56.

52. *The Rhetorical World of Augustan Humanism* (Oxford, 1965), 140.

53. Thomas Paine, *The Rights of Man*, ed. H. H. Clark (New York, 1961), 233.

Reason Dazzled: Perspective and Language in Dryden's
Aureng-Zebe

David W. Tarbet

> Our corporeal eyes we find
> Dazzle the opticks of our mind.
> *Denham*

The invention of pictorial perspective in the Italian Renaissance depended upon the incorporation of the idea of distance within painting. That distance found two expressions. The first, more obvious and well known, involved the technical questions of how to mathematisize represented relations among objects. Renaissance theorists thought they had solved the problem of the "rationalization of space" and ended the debate on the portrayal of visual fact.[1] There have since been sceptical objections to this confidence, and I shall address such objections shortly. But I wish to mention the second expression of distance within painting before I undertake that topic. Although Alberti, for example, seemed most innovative in his technical expositions, he was not concerned solely with the accurate translation of images. Once pictures became realistic, their purpose was not fulfilled. The vividness and authenticity of the represented objects served another end—that of the picture's significance or *istoria*. This second distance between image and thought presented a conceptual distance that opened the painting to a discursive "reading" and proper understanding. I will return to the importance of this second and conceptual space later in this paper.

Realistic representations of figures and buildings appear in the works of Giotto, but they are illusionistic fragments in an unincorporated space. Alberti's *Della pittura* altered this condition by expounding the theory of a unified "point of view" in a painting which established precise relations between the position of the artist or viewer and the represented image, and between the objects within the picture.[2] Both distances, that between the viewing eye and its objects, and that between the objects in the painting itself, were made subject to mathematical relationships which created the illusion of spatial coherence and uniformity. The painting appeared true to life because it allowed the usual power of vision to determine not only the objects represented, but also the distance between viewer and objects and their distance from each other. The technical sophistication of competing theories all serve one end: the unification of pictorial space and the inclusion of the perception of distance within the visual experience of painting.

The revolutionary importance of the idea of distance in perspective theory has, however, tempted critics to move too quickly beyond its stated concern with accuracy. Recognition of distance implies a split between viewer and scene, subject and object. Exaggerated stress on this division can lead to the current "Nietzschean" view of perspective in which objective accuracy falls under the dominance of a subject for whom all facts are illusion. Arthur Danto describes Nietzsche's doctrine of "perspectivism" as the belief that "there are no facts but only interpretations." The germ of Nietzschean perspectivism may be in Alberti and later theorists, and a tradition of scepticism almost as radical as Nietzsche's existed in the seventeenth and eighteenth centuries, but it was a remote adversary.[3] Renaissance perspectivism stressed fact, and the distance it recognized did not entail division or alienation. It was a mimetic enterprise in the service of reality. If a painting incorporated the viewer's distance from a scene or object, it also showed his way to it. The measure marking the separation also established a link.

Early perspective theorists committed themselves to accurate reproduction. They believed that paintings signified their objects with an ontological confidence in the translation of scene to pictorial image.[4] Much of the same confidence continues into the eighteenth-century thought, and I will assume that this, rather than the Nietzschean view of perspective, is most appropriate for the discussion of Dryden and Restoration drama.

Although perspective theory did not undermine epistemological confidence, it did shift the grounds of certainty. The introduction of the idea of distance into painting required the corollary development of an individual viewpoint. Such a viewpoint could adequately claim accuracy, but never absoluteness. Claudio Guillén explains that "it is not the thought of God . . . or the cohesion of things as they really are on which the *system of painting* rests, but the perception and understanding of the observing human being."[5] Divine and metaphysical sanctions yield to the particular terms of perception; fact resolves itself into the truth of human vision. This alteration in the basis of authority is important not only in itself, but also as the clue to understanding the translation of perspective theory into other artistic mediums. We are considering literature, not painting. How does "distance," which in painting concerns spatial relations, appear again in the non-spatial medium of language? It is possible to retreat into metaphor, but that, fortunately, is not necessary.

Timothy J. Reiss has edited an issue of *Yale French Studies* which addresses itself to precisely this problem. In his introduction, Reiss identifies the Classical age as the period in which the discoveries of Renaissance perspective theory re-express themselves in thought about language. He argues that Galileo's telescope (a "perspective glass") made subsequent thinkers aware of the distanced and mediated relationships between observers and the objects of their view and study, and further, that the Galilean experimental model found a natural linguistic and grammatical parallel: "Eventually the word, so to speak, passed down the telescope with the image until it was conceived of as a simple mental creation, having a quite arbitrary connection with the thing." This in turn made science assume a perspectival stance:

"Experimental language is not at first an attempt to describe the thing itself, so much as a description of the human *sighting* of that thing, of a *particular* relationship between an object clearly defined in space and time and the mind perceiving it under the same restrictions. Language stands for the distance."[6] Scientific language uses the terms of perspective theory to separate itself from metaphysics and theology. Whether the separation means that language is "arbitrary" is, however, another question.

Once language assumes an intermediate position marking the distance between subject and object, it does not necessarily lose status. It may, in fact, gain importance. On the one hand, it becomes merely an indicative element mediating between thought and its object. It loses absolute status and becomes no longer a mark on the world, but a sign system pointing toward things essentially separate. This process of division underlies Michel Foucault's account of classical thought in *The Order of Things* and is fully developed in that important work.[7] But, on the other hand, it becomes the sole agency for rejoining thought and object, and, thus, parallels the mathematical unification of space in Renaissance art which heals any possible breach and asserts its own authority. Jay Rosenberg and Charles Travis see a contest in seventeenth-century philosophy from which language emerges triumphant:

> Traditionally, necessity has been held to carry with it a set of metaphysical properties. . . . For example, in seventeenth- and eighteenth-century writers such as Descartes and Leibniz it is common to find accounts of at least some kinds of necessary truths in terms of the nature of God. Given that God exists necessarily, any fact about the world which follows from God's nature should also be necessary. . . .
> It is more usual nowadays to attempt to account for necessity in terms of language. This attempt is part of a tradition that goes back at least to Hobbes, though it reached ascendancy only in the late eighteenth and nineteenth centuries.[8]

Language in the classical period, therefore, first opens a distance between object and thought and then becomes the only means of rejoining these elements. The referential and signifying role of language implies a separation of words from objects, but also generates the need for justification which links them again. Just as the incorporation of distance in painting created the double measure of the viewer's separation from and connection to a scene, classical theories of the indicative quality of language divide the sign from the thing as the first step in a process which solidifies the truth of the reference.

Drama possesses a special ability to expose the mediate quality of language because action and speech appear simultaneously. In soliloquy, aside, reflection and debate, characters can deliver their interpretation of events at the same time that they act their parts. Although dramatic conventions change and playwrights may at times reject or repress the opportunity to accompany action with an explicit verbal commentary, Restoration dramatists embraced this possibility with enthusiam. Under the influence of a new sense of language and with the architectural encouragement of the new perspective stage settings, they developed a double presentation of passionate action and dispassionate analysis.[9] Life in Restoration drama, especially in the serious heroic or tragic plays, is at once represented and hypothesized. Actions unfold for the sake of explanation, until, perhaps, it may be said that Restoration theater became a theater of ideas in which the true stakes were not in the feelings of the characters but in the ideologies and problems revealed through them. Its problems and resolutions were intellectual, and this is particularly true in the plays of John Dryden.

Anyone familiar with Dryden's plays will not require an example of the strongly distanced and reflective quality of his dramatic works. But if proof of the obvious is needed, I suggest examining the first act of *All for Love*. The scene between Ventidius and Antony was one of Dryden's favorites. Any reader of it should be struck by its unwillingness to let action unfold without commentary. Even when there appears no need, speeches register responses evident to the audience, as if actions cannot be assessed or confirmed without them. When Antony throws himself to the ground in despair, Ventidius observes:

> How sorrow shakes him!
> So, now the tempest tears him up by th' roots,
> And on the ground extends the noble ruin. (I. i. 213-215)

And when Ventidius cries in response to his observation of Antony's ignoble condition, Antony in his turn remarks:

> By heav'n he weeps, poor good old man, he weeps!
> The big round drops course one another down
> The furrows of his cheeks. (I. i. 266–268)

This sounds like a ready excuse for bad acting, but clearly it is not. It is part of Dryden's deliberate effort to distance speech from action and to emphasize the need for language to bridge the distance it creates. The counterpointing of action and commentary generates the problem of reference which is fundamental to this play and represents a theme more basic than any other in Dryden's drama. That theme is the adequacy of language to life and character. It appears throughout his work, translating the questions of Renaissance pictorial perspective into literary terms. Speech separates actions and characters only to rejoin them by description, just as Renaissance perspective separates viewpoint from pictorial images only to reunite them in a mimetic representation. There is, perhaps, a difference in emphasis. Literature can be more explicit about the problem because it can include reflections on the process.[10] And among Dryden's plays, the one that reveals these processes most fully is his last rhymed heroic play, *Aureng-Zebe.*[11]

Aureng-Zebe is a strangely passive hero. He fights on behalf of his father, but will not assert his own status and rights. He pursues his personal claims non-violently and justifies his inaction by explaining that anything he may do threatens his "name"—his assigned, or inherited, linguistic description. If he attacks his father to claim his love, he forfeits the title of "loyal son," (I. i. 107) and, in addition, is obliged to accept Indamora's insistence that only his loyalty will make him her "lover." (I. i. 453–460) Aureng-Zebe accepts both titles: "I to a son's and lover's praise aspire,/ And must fulfill the parts which both require." (I. i. 465–466) This automatically prevents his doing anything on his own behalf. He can only repeat the names proper to him until others recognize them. Any effort to enforce his claim will alter and destroy the semantic authority on which he bases his appeal. If words justify him, his only weapon is the reiteration of the titles he owns. When Dianet forces action on Aureng-Zebe with his offer of assistance in a rebellion, Aureng-Zebe repeats that

> Ill-treated and forsaken as I am,
> I'll not betray *the glory of my name.*
> 'Tis not for me, who have preserved a state
> To buy an empire at so base a rate. (II. i. 528–531; emphasis mine.)

Dianet can only see this as an illusory logic of romance and insists that the world is immune to such poetic nonsense:

> The points of honor poets may produce:
> Trappings of life, for ornament, not use.
> Honor which only does the name advance
> Is the mere raving madness of romance.
> *Pleased with a word,* you may sit tamely down
> And see your younger brother force the crown. (II. i. 532–537; emphasis mine).

But the logic of Dryden's play is that of poetry and language, not of power. Political authority must have a semantic ground. Arimant's early description of Aureng-Zebe as a "loyal son" and "lover" encompasses all of the hero's responsibilities and legitimate hopes. As a son, he answers public demands in a dutiful and disinterested way. He fulfills, in short, the requirements of "honor." Under his second title, he claims the personal and visionary goals of his desires in the terms of "love." Some conventional readings of heroic drama put these two elements at odds, but in this play, they are entirely consistent, or, at least, they remain consistent as long as everyone recognizes the authority of language. Love and honor are by definition compatible, and Aureng-Zebe must seem justified to anyone who understands the language. Any denial of Aureng-Zebe must, in turn, be a denial of language. The "name of father" has grown "hateful" to the Emperor (I. i. 88), and he wishes to escape its consequences. If he were to acknowledge his proper titles of "king" and "father" as Aureng-Zebe asks, (I. i. 294–311) there would be neither political nor personal disorder in the state. But the Emperor is not satisfied with what language allows: he wishes to say that he is not only "a father, but a lover too." (I. i. 289)

In order to do what he wishes, the Emperor must attempt to escape language—to be unnamed. What state or primitive condition of man exists outside language? Filmer could see none since his theory of government depends upon the family relationships the Emperor denies. Hobbes, however, does imagine such a state: it is the "state of nature," where words, along with everything else are subject only to individual will. The institution of government fixes language, and authorizing speech is one of the agencies of political control.[12] The Emperor's urge to escape names in *Aureng-Zebe* returns the state to a primitive chaos of warring wills, and only his resumption of "fatherhood" reestablishes political order. When language assumes this status, the work of a poet must appear constitutional.[13]

Dryden, however, uses another metaphor for the world beyond language. It is not only a reversion to clashing wills, but more, it suggests that humanity as well as politics depends upon language. Hobbes' state of nature is bestial ("nasty, brutish, and short"), and Descartes divided men from beasts by the possession of speech. A movement beyond language is a retreat to animality. When Morat refuses to accept the just claims of Aureng-Zebe to kingship and Indamora, Aureng-Zebe charges:

> But the brute soul, by chance, was shuffled in.
> In woods and wilds thy monarchy maintain,
> Where valiant beasts by force and rapine reign.
> In life's next scene, if transmigration be.
> Some bear or lion is reserved for thee. (III. i. 305–309)

As it happens, Morat is civilized before the end of the play, but only because he is returned to the world of words and discourse through the conversation of Indamora.

Dryden may sympathize with primitivism in plays like *The Conquest of Granada*, but there is no "noble savage" in *Aureng-Zebe*. This play condemns all forms of withdrawal and all supposed sanctions that antedate or surpass the bounds of custom and society. The speech of characters who imagine such conditions or claim such rights loses power and significance. The Lear-like retirement of the Emperor: "The fort I'll keep for my security,/ Bus'ness and public state resign to thee," (III. i. 174–175) heralds what he thinks of as the life of an epicurean god, (III. i. 180–189) but proves to be his untitling and impotence (III. i. 190–196).[14] Nourmahal's daring invitation to incest is an even more shocking withdrawal from social convention. Her wishes revert to a primitivism that threatens all distinctions of language, culture, and morals. But I must postpone the investigation of this extreme case; I only wish to stress that *Aureng-Zebe* allows no privileged secondary language of pastoral bliss or transcendent idealism. Excellence, order—all that is necessary for political stability and personal contentment—occur in ordinary language. Trouble comes only from those who try to oppose, circumvent or retreat from ordinary speech.

The anti-social cannot reveal an imagined literary world, since such positions or wishes are extra-linguistic. But this does not prevent the Emperor's withdrawal or the excesses of Morat and Nourmahal. What keeps language from altering to serve those who wish to avoid or abuse social life? It is important to note first that, for Dryden, acceptable language depends less on custom than on right. Only three characters in the play, Aureng-Zebe, Indamora, and Melesinda, maintain it, and their persistence is often misunderstood by others. (I have already quoted Dianet's incomprehension of Aureng-Zebe's allegiance to his "name.") The world, paradoxically, cannot be the measure of social good, since it cannot see how the best characters maintain their interests. The isolated and outcast characters, therefore, represent true social concern.

How is it that without the encouragement and sanction of ordinary language so many characters are perverse, or at least fail to interpret things clearly? This question returns me to the ideas of distance and perspective which I may appear to have forgotten. I have not forgotten them, and I hope now to use them to argue that the proper understanding of language in the play depends upon an adjustment in vision guided by the rules of Renaissance perspective theory and its consequences. No one in this play can name characters or attitudes properly unless they see them correctly. By a deliberate misreading yet deeper understanding of Aureng-Zebe's words, we can argue that "the snare in sight is laid." (I. i. 416)

Misperception is often a synonym for error, but in *Aureng-Zebe*, error—that is, mistaking of fact—is unimportant. The hero of the play is most often mistaken. He believes at times that a schemer at court has alienated his father, that Indamora does not love him, that Nourmahal will help him. Yet all these mistakes are unrelated to any real source of trouble. The "false optics" that Aureng-Zebe believes have distorted the facts about him (I. i. 317) are themselves falsely accused. It is not a mistaken image, but an incorrect relation to true ones that generates the difficulties of the play. Dryden underscores the problem with a masterful allusion to the Orpheus myth. Aureng-Zebe confirms the truth of Indamora's love at the expense of discovering his father's rivalry: "So the fond youth from hell redeemed his prize,/ Till, looking back, she vanished from his eyes." (I. i. 469–470) Visual confirmation of fact is the beginning of difficulty. At the moment Orpheus turns to make sure that the true Euridyce follows him, he loses her. He could have preserved her only by resisting the attraction of the image and disciplining his sight, since it is not its truth but his attitude that is in question. This becomes the pattern of the deeper problems in the play and isolates the difficulty of the wrong or villainous characters: The Emperor, Arimant, and Morat succumb to the sight of Indamora; and Nourmahal surrenders to the attractions of Aureng-Zebe. They do not see a false image; they establish the wrong relation to what they see.

The problem of relation shades into the question of distance. Both the Emperor and Arimant are drawn to Indamora at the same time that they recognize the requirements and limits which force them away from her. They want to destory or ignore the distancing forces and accept only the attraction. Both Arimant and the Emperor, with some implausibility, argue against themselves as they continue to pursue Indamora:

> All arguments in vain I urged and weighed;
> For mighty love, who prudence does despise,

> For reason showed me Indamora's eyes.
> What would you more? My crime I sadly view,
> Acknowledge, am ashamed and yet pursue. (II. i. 457–461)

This combination of analytic vigor and intransigence often appears in Dryden's plays (and in Restoration drama generally).[15] It is a contest between the attraction of an emotionally charged image and a linguistic inhibition. They approach Indamora as "lovers," but the verbal categories she offers refuse their claims and distance them from her. She gives Arimant the title of "friend" (II. i. 50) and recalls the Emperor to his obligations as husband and father (II. i. 143–147 and 187–192). Her restraint is linguistic, and they partly confirm it, since they acknowledge no proper sense in which they can be lovers.

In so far as Arimant and the Emperor admit the linguistic problem as a curb on their wills, they remain within the reach of reform. They finally prove their merit, but that is less important than the weakness they reveal. Both Arimant and the Emperor, as they repudiate their proper titles, move out of the world of discourse. This is especially true of the Emperor whose speech discloses his retreat from reason and the increased dominance of vision. This is not clear-sighted vision, but the charmed vision of "Indamora's eyes." The Emperor shows that his weakness encourages the collapse of thought into image. In this process, words lose their potency, arguments fade and reason yields. At its extreme, the process is one that Foucault has called "dazzlement."[16] In this play, dazzlement threatens many characters, but it claims only one victim, Nourmahal.

Incest is un-relational. Even the pun holds—incest succeeds only if family relationships dissolve. The basic terms of culture for the organization and perpetuation of the family fail, and all discriminations, including those of language, disappear.[17] Incest is also dazzling. In this state, nothing has true significance; the objects of sight lose sure reference, and vision turns on itself as if in a dream. The oneiric quality of Nourmahal's invitation to incest is obvious:

> I dreamed your love was by love's goddess sought,
> Officious cupids, hov'ring o'er your head.
> Held myrtle wreaths; beneath your feet were spread

What sweets soe'er Sabean springs disclose,
Our Indian jasmine, or the Syrian rose.
The wanton ministers around you strove
For service, and inspired their mother's love.
Close, by your side, and languishing, she lies,
With blushing cheeks, short breath, and wishing eyes;
Upon your breast supinely lay her head,
While on your face her famished sight she fed.
Then, with a sigh, into these words she broke
(And gathered humid kisses as she spoke):
"Dull and ingrateful! Must I offer love?
Desired of gods, and envied ev'n by Jove,
And doth thou ignorance or fear pretend?
Mean soul! And dar'st not gloriously offend?"
Then pressing thus his hand—(IV. i. 98-115)

Nourmahal tempts Aureng-Zebe not with argument, but with an opulent and absorbing vision. Her speech withdraws from narration and turns to pictorial evocation. She captures herself in the picture she paints and begins to act in the terms she describes. But Aureng-Zebe preserves moral discriminations by returning from sight to speech and from vision to discourse with his insistence that he will "hear no more." He reestablishes distance by creating the right relation to Nourmahal's painting, interpreting its promise of bliss as a conscious access to crime.

If we recall the remarks of Rosenberg and Travis, we see how modern philosophers had an important stake in preserving the mediating and signifying function of language. They were Aureng-Zebes, and like him, needed to resist the appeal of the image. It is interesting, therefore, that Descartes should already have discovered an escape from the non-signifying dream, if we can believe Baillet's *Vie de Monsieur Descartes.*[18] Baillet's account is the only source of information we have on the three dreams Descartes had on the night of 10 December, 1619. The dreams were very important to Descartes; he called them the miraculous start of a universal and fundamental science. The first two dreams were concerned with personal purity and the possibility of certainty. The second of them records an experience of dazzlement in which Descartes imagines that the room is filled with sparkling lights ("étincelles de feu") He cannot determine whether the flashes of light come from within the room, or from a failure in his own eyes or power of vision. This inspires the third dream, which is concerned with discriminating appearance from reality and shows the recovery of true distinction after the confusing and dazzling dominance of the sparkling lights over the second dream. The third dream is the longest and most elaborate, but its resolution is simple. Descartes discovers the stance or attitude he must take to distance the images in his dreams and make them reveal their truth;

Ce qu'il y a de singulier à remarquer, c'est que, doutant si ce qu'il venoit de voir étoit songe ou vision, non seulement il décida, en dormant, que c'étoit un songe, mais il en fit encore l'interprétation avant que le sommeil le quittât.

He begins his interpretation and then awakens to continue it. Little is said about the details of the interpretation (he explains that it is not completed until a few days later after he talks to "un Peintre Italien"). The dream's importance is in the distinguishing of its images from the process of interpretation and thought. Descartes feels secure when he identifies the dream as a dream, not a vision; he is confident of his explanations, once he separates himself from the absorbing power of the image, *i.e.* from the dazzlement of his second dream.

I noted at the beginning of the paper that Renaissance perspective theory incorporates two distances, one spatial and the other interpretive. The first functions in sight and adjusts vision, but it has consequences for language. It permits a reading of painting in terms of its significance or *istoria*. Spatial distancing begins to control the dazzling presence of the image by providing a dimensional context and set of relations to other objects. But the reading continues and completes this process of definition. The end of painting for Alberti is not a realistic reproduction of things. He welcomes realism and developed the mathematical techniques for perfecting a visually mimetic reproduction of things, but he also believes that those things are there to reveal their meaning or *istoria*. This, as the name implies, is a narrative and discursive feature; and it is the proper end of pictorial art. Alberti's requirement that a painting realize an *istoria* means that it implicitly divides itself from its images by projecting a reading or interpretation of them.[19]

Alberti did not seem to think that interpreting a painting was problematic. He does not devote himself to innovation nor see any need for refinement in technique here. He assumes that those skillful enough to paint well can convey their meaning. The same assumption, or a near parallel, appears in Descartes' account of his third dream. He worries about the possibility of instituting a separation between image and interpretation; but once formed, the interpretation is unproblematic. He wishes to know only that it functions as interpretation, that it is distinct from the images it explains. Once he guarantees the distance and detachment, he ceases to worry. This is exactly the case in *Aureng-Zebe*. Concern centers finally on those who cannot distance themselves from their wishes or interpret what they do. Nourmahal loses herself in the image ("Poor helpless I/ See all, and have my hell before I die! [V. i. 665-666]) and remains beyond help. Arimant and the Emperor keep some distance on their desires and, once they come to understand them, are redeemed.

It is interesting that reason is not their salvation. Reason, as we have already seen, cannot save them because it yields to the power of the image ("Indamora's eyes"). Characters in Dryden's plays only become reasonable under the antecedent impulse of "pity." Characters appeal to pity so frequently in *Aureng-Zebe* that I can only sketch in its importance and use. The word includes the common elements of its definition: compassion, charity, sympathy, but it also develops a more elaborate meaning in the play. Melesinda is the theoretician of "pity" and the way she uses the word indicates its expanded function. As Morat begins to give way to the enchantment of Indamora's eyes, Melesinda asks: "And can you then deny those eyes you praise?/ Can beauty wonder, and not pity raise?" (III. i. 493-494) She, in effect, points out the proper response to Indamora—not to make her a static and absorbing image "wonder," but to recognize what she says, to pity her and respond to her request. Pity, then, is the feeling that prompts interpretation and corrects mistaken visionary states. How? By being the one emotion whose function requires and encourages reciprocity. True pity must incorporate distance because of its reference to another. Recognition then reveals reciprocal obligations. Arimant finally sees Indamora and Aureng-Zebe as true lovers and realizes, therefore, that he can only act, and die, as their "friend." The Emperor sees his only possible relationship to them as protective "father." Morat presents a greater problem since he believes he can replace Aureng-Zebe and therefore sees no reason to acknowledge him. Melesinda must offer a further elaboration of "pity" as the only true form of self-interest:

> Heav'n does a tribute for your pow'r demand:
> He leaves th' oppressed and poor upon your hand.
> And those who stewards of his pity prove,
> He blesses in return with public love.
> In his distress some miracle is shown;
> If exiled, Heav'n restores him to his throne.
> He needs no guard while any subject's near,
> Nor like his tyrant neighbors lives in fear.
> No plots th'alarm to his retirements give:
> 'Tis all mankind's concern that he should live. (III. i. 425-434)

Pity rests on mutual recognition of right and assures concord and peace.

Morat seems to learn the lessons of pity. He even wants to adjust interpretations so that they soften unpleasant truths. When Asaph announces the supposed death of Aureng-Zebe, Morat requests that he:

> Pity the Queen, and show respect to me.
> 'Tis ev'ry painter's art to hide from sight
> And cast in shades what, seen, would not delight. (V. i. 146-148)

Pity, perspective and painting meet in one passage. Pity can correct wrongs, but never institute changes. Both Descartes and Dryden assume that if language and thought are allowed to operate properly, (*i.e.* free of the dominance of imagination and image), it will reveal its own incorporation of moral and political right. The one change allowed in the play, the end of the custom of killing all other brothers when the eldest succeeds to the throne, is obviously the righting of a wrong rather than a political innovation. And the other mistaken characters, the Emperor in particular, merely return to the acknowledgement of their own proper names and titles. Pity is a conservative rather than progressive force and posits an original unity; it cannot suggest new resolutions or reinterpretations. This makes Morat's reformation seem illusory, even to Aureng-Zebe, and creates some difficulties for the last act and resolution of the play.

The problem, however, goes deeper than consistency of character. Dryden suggests a theory of language in *Aureng-Zebe* that unites description and identity. He may, on the one hand, merely be anticipating Bertrand Russell who wished to claim that any true act of naming has to have some possible existing object as its referent.[20] Like Russell, Dryden formalizes his world, excluding the unacceptable as the unnamable. He wants language to be explicit and authoritative, and to act as a guarantee of reality. But he also knows its ambiguities and may even yearn to preserve them for the sake of extraordinary and unusual characters and feelings. Morat suggests the temptation in *Aureng-Zebe*, and *All for Love* opens with the striking statement that "Portents and prodigies are grown so frequent,/ That they have lost their name." Names and descriptions, hence the nature of existence, may change. Such an alteration requires more than an interpretation of given conditions in a settled language; it suggests a reinterpretation and novelty. *All for Love* makes characters labor to define Antony when words to describe him are unavailable, and the play testifies to a love between Antony and Cleopatra which ordinary terms cannot acknowledge.[21] Dryden develops his greatest play, therefore, around a central problem of his adopted theory of language. That he could incorporate this abstract concern into the substance of his play, testifies to his deep understanding of his linguistic theme and reminds us of the powerful intelligence that critics since Samuel Johnson find characteristic of Dryden's work.

Notes
1. William M. Ivins, Jr., *On the Rationalization of Sight with an Examination of Three Renaissance Texts on Perspective*, The Metropolitan

Museum of Art Paper No. 8 (New York, 1938). John White, *The Birth and Rebirth of Pictorial Space* (London: Faber & Faber, 1957).

2. Leon Battista Alberti, *On Painting,* trans. John R. Spencer (New Haven: Yale University Press, 1966). See also the very fine and comprehensive essay by Claudio Guillèn, "On the Concept and Metaphor of Perspective," *Literature as System* (Princeton, N.J.: Princeton University Press, 1971), pp. 288-293.

3. Arthur C. Danto, *Nietzsche as Philosopher* (New York: Macmillan, 1970), p. 77. On the sources of scepticism and the seventeenth-century "classical" reaction, see Richard H. Popkin, *The History of Scepticism from Erasmus to Descartes* (New York: Harper & Row, 1968). For Dryden's relation to the tradition of scepticism, see Phillip Harth, *Contexts of Dryden's Thought* (Chicago: University of Chicago Press, 1968). Harth corrects earlier mistaken identifications of Dryden with the tradition of radical scepticism.

4. Alberti does not, however, reduce painting to a *trompe l' oeil.* The images in a painting communicate an *istoria.* The *istoria* represents the discursive and intentional element which makes painting an artistic and humanistic activity. I will return to the importance of *istoria* later in the paper.

5. Guillèn, p. 290. On the question of the relation of viewpoint, distance, and certainty, I recommend the remarks of Eugenio Donato, "Levi-Strauss and the Protocols of Distance," *Diacritics,* 5 (1975), 2-12.

6. "Introduction: The Word/World Equation," *Science, Language, and the Perspective Mind, Yale French Studies,* 49 (New Haven, Conn., 1973), pp. 4, 6.

7. *The Order of Things* (London: Tavistock Publications, 1970). Foucault's opening discussion of Velasquez' *Las Meninas* (pp. 3-16) is particularly relevant, but see also pp. 58-63 and pp. 81-92. There have been some recent American challenges to Foucault. See George S. Rousseau, "Whose Enlightenment? Not Man's: The Case of Michel Foucault," *Eighteenth-Century Studies,* 6 (Winter, 1972-1973), 238-256; and George Huppert, "*Divinatio et Eruditio:* Thoughts on Foucault," *History and Theory,* 13 (1974), 191-207.

8. *Readings in the Philosophy of Language* (Englewood Cliffs, N.J.: Prentice-Hall, 1971), pp. 7-8.

9. It is interesting that the Restoration stage settings themselves had become perspective pictures. For this development see Richard Southern, *Changeable Scenery: Its Origin and Development in the British Theatre* (London: Faber & Faber, 1952).

10. Foucault argues, however, that Velasquez makes the question explicit for painting.

11. John Dryden, *Aureng-Zebe*, ed. Frederick M. Link, Regents Restoration Drama (Lincoln, Neb.: University of Nebraska Press, 1971). All citations to the play are included parenthetically in the text.

12. Hobbes develops his notions of the limits of free speech in the second part of *Leviathan*, Chapters 21 and 29. The authority of language itself can, however, claim different grounds. See the remarks of Edward Said on "natural" origins and conventional "beginnings" in the article, "Beginnings," *Salmagundi*, 2 (1968), 36–55.

13. See Earl Miner's arguments for the important public role implicit in Dryden's assumptions about poetry: *The Restoration Mode from Milton to Dryden* (Princeton, N.J.: Princeton University Press, 1974), pp. 15–16 and passim.

14. William Frost reviews the Lear theme in *Aureng-Zebe:* "Aureng-Zebe in Context," *Journal of English and Germanic Philology*, 74 (1975), 26–49.

15. See also III. i. 321–324. For Arimant's parallel reflections, see his dialogue with Indamora, II. i. 39–113.

This state of mind fascinates writers through the eighteenth century, expecially those in the "sentimental" tradition. See Roy Roussel's interesting discussion of distance and desire in Richardson's novels: "Reflections on the Letter: The Reconciliation of Distance and Presence in *Pamela,*" *ELH*, 41 (1974), 375–399.

When reason loses its teleological privileges and becomes only an instrumental device in the service of emotional ends, sentimental arguments are the only ones available to moralists. If "Desire's the vast extent of human mind," (II. i. 55) reason becomes impotent. The only hope is that some attitude will distance emotion and allow an approved emotion (usually pity) to measure other desires. I will return to this later.

16. *Madness and Civilization* (New York: Random House, 1967), pp. 92–96.

17. It is significant that Nourmahal is not Aureng-Zebe's natural mother. Incest prohibitions depend on culture and law, not on biology. The danger of incest is linguistic, since it destroys clear reference and confuses signification. Levi-Strauss and Lacan confirm Dryden's view that incest breaks down the operation of language. Jacques Lacan, *The Language of the Self*, trans. Anthony Wilden (Baltimore, Md.: Johns Hopkins University Press, 1968), p. 40: "The primordial Law is therefore that which in regulating marriage ties superimposes the kingdom of culture on that of nature abandoned to the law of copulation. . . . This law [against incest],

therefore, is revealed clearly enough as identical to an order of Language. For without kinship nominations, no power is capable of instituting the order of references and taboos which bind and weave the yard of lineage down through succeeding generations." For Wilden's discussion of incest prohibitions, see pp. 251–254.

18. *Oeuvres de Descartes*, ed. Charles Adam and Paul Tannery (Paris: Leopold Cerf, 1908), X, pp. 179–188.

19. Painting may itself resist interpretation and try to exclude narrative elements that allow for a reading. Svetlana Alpers gave an interesting paper on this topic at the 1975 English Institute meeting.

20. "Descriptions," in *Readings in the Philosophy of Language*, ed. Rosenberg and Travis, pp. 166–175.

21. In analytic terms, the characters surrounding Antony may confuse "mentioning" and "meaning" when they attempt to describe Antony. See P. F. Strawson, "On Referring," in *Readings in the Philosophy of Language*, ed. Rosenberg and Travis, p. 181.

III. SPACE

Concepts of Space

Ivor Leclerc

By the nineteenth century, the phrase "a spatial extent" came to make sense; it would not have done so prior to about the mid-eighteenth century. In fact, the adjective "spatial", according to the O.E.D., was of mid-nineteenth-century origin.[1] Previously the phrase "spatial extent" would have been a pleonasm; it would have meant "extensive extent." The introduction of this adjective, meaning "of or pertaining to space," signifies a new meaning of the word "space," one which has now very much come to be taken for granted, indeed by most as the basic meaning of the word.

Until the seventeenth century, the word "space" had the general meaning of "extent," and in English, back to the fourteenth century, was used in two main specific senses, one in regard to time, an extent or lapse or interval of time, and the other in respect of linear distance, an extent or interval between two or more points, and consequently also a superficial extent or area. This general meaning with these specific uses was also that of the Latin *spatium*, the word deriving from the Indo-European stem giving *spaein* in Greek, "to draw, stretch out," from which specifically "a certain stretch, extent, area of ground, an expanse," especially such an extent used for running races—whence *spadion* in Doric Greek and *stadion* in Attic Greek. From this general meaning of *spatium* as an "extent, stretch, interval" various derivative meanings arose, in Latin and later other languages, such as *de loco, in quo ambulatur*, "a place or extent in which to walk," whence the verb "to space," meaning "to walk"—Latin *spatiari*, Italian *spaziari*, Spanish *espaciar*, French *espacer*, German *spazieren*. The older general meaning of "space" as "extent, stretch, expanse, interval" still continues; this has not been superseded or rendered obsolete by the new meaning developed in the eighteenth century. It is a meaning distinct from and not derivative from the new meaning, as is too often supposed.

The new meaning emerged as the outcome of a long development, from the sixteenth to eighteenth centuries; and some appreciation of this development is important for a proper comprehension of the new meaning.

A new conception of nature emerged in the early seventeenth century, the conception of nature as "matter." Contrary to the antecedent view of nature, the conception of nature as "matter" entailed that nature was entirely without qualitative features such as colors, sounds, etc.; its features were purely quantitative: shape, size, etc. And further, matter *qua* matter was in itself changeless, always remaining just what it was, "matter," without any internal process of change or becoming. The only change possible for matter was change in respect of place, *i.e.* locomotion. The new physical science, *i.e.* knowledge of nature, of the seventeenth century was a mechanics, culminating in Newton's *Philosophiae Naturalis Principia Mathematica* in 1686. In this science it was not matter *per se* which was the object of study, but the *motion*, more strictly *locomotion*, of matter. Nature was investigated and understood in terms of a mathematical analysis of the locomotion of matter. The fundamental laws of nature were laws of motion, and these were expressed in mathematical formulae.

The scientific measurement of motion meant the measurement of the change or transference of a body from one *place* to another. This necessitated clarification of what was meant by "place." "Place," Aristotle had argued, is evidently dimensional, and it could be neither larger nor smaller than the dimension of the body in it. That is, the dimension of the place of the body had to be coincident with the dimension of the body. However, the dimension of the place could not be identified with the dimension of the body; for if it were, this would entail that the body takes its place along with it when it moves, in which case measurement from one place to another would be impossible. Aristotle resolved this issue by defining place as "the innermost limit of the enclosing body,"[2] the definition of place which was accepted until the sixteenth century. Then it came under attack for its identifying place with superficies, boundaries, whereas it was the entire *inner volume*, it was argued, which was to be identified with place. It was to express this conception that the word *spatium* was brought into use: place was to be conceived as *spatium vel locus internus*, "space or internal place." That is to say, what we are concerned with in "place" is the "extent" (*spatium*) constituting the "internal place" (*locus internus*).

The problem then arose as to the ontological status of this *spatium vel locus internus, i.e.* what kind of being or existent it is. It was generally argued that this *spatium* (extent) of place had to be distinguished from the extent of the body occupying it, and that it had to be left behind when the body moved. But when the body moved, did this imply that the *spatium* (extent) of the place remained vacant? Gassendi, who had resuscitated the ancient atomist doctrine in the 1620's, maintained that it did, in other words, that we had to accept the validity of the conception of "void extents." The overwhelming majority of thinkers, however, rejected this on the ground that a "void extent" (or "empty space") strictly meant an "extent of nothing," which was a contradiction, for "nothing" could not be extended. That is to say, the space or extent constituting the internal place had to be filled with something, for extent had to be the extent of something. This led to Descartes' solution that the physical universe had necessarily to be a plenum, and that extension was the very essence of the physical *res* or existent. This entailed that there could be no "void place." What we think of as *spatium vel locus internus* was a distinction of reason: "space or internal place and the corporeal substance contained in it, are not different otherwise than in the mode in which they are conceived by us."[3]

This doctrine entailed that when motion occurred, place had to be conceived relatively. For in Descartes' theory, motion "is the transference of one part of matter or body from the vicinity of those bodies that are in immediate contact with it, and which we regard as in repose, into the vicinity of others."[4] The difficulty is that the respective "vicinities" had to be regarded "as in repose," for if they were themselves moving, there would be no way to measure the motion from one place to another; but there could be no assurance whatever that the "vicinities" would not themselves be in motion.

Newton came to see very clearly that accurate measurement could not be possible if the places moved. It was therefore indispensably necessary to physical science, which was fundamentally the measurement of the motion of bodies, that place be not "relative," but on the contrary that it be "absolute," for "that the primary places of things should be movable, is absurd."[5] It was indispensable therefore to admit ultimate, absolute places; and these absolute, immovable places, Newton said in the first *Scholium* of his *Principia*, "constitute, what I call, immovable space *(spatiumque constituant quod immobile appello)*."[6]

This again made acute the problem of the ontological status of these "places" or "space"—Newton now using the term "space" for the "totality of places," a usage which thereafter became common, for example being accepted too by Leibniz and by Kant.[7] Newton was far more acute a philosophical thinker than most of his contemporaries, including Leibniz, acknowledged him to be. He saw very clearly that the supposition that space or the totality of immovable places be ascribed the status of a self-subsistent being or existent was quite untenable. Accordingly the supposition of space as a physical something had to be entirely rejected, and an entirely different analysis and conception of space produced. Newton had a highly ingenious solution to the problem. In common with all thinkers of the period, Newton accepted the doctrine of God as agent creator of the universe. This entailed, Newton held, that God, as creating agent, was active, acting, *i.e.* creating beings, *everywhere*, and *everywhen.* "Where" God acts, creating a body, is the "place" of that body. That is, "where" or "place" neither pertains to nor is derivative from the body; on the contrary, the "where," the "place," pertains to God's acting as being "there" and "then."

It is interesting to see that Newton's philosophical doctrine was mostly not taken account of or simply discounted by his contemporaries, with the consequence that he was understood to be holding a conception of space as some kind of actual existent as a "container" in which everything is, including God's acting. Even Leibniz was guilty of this misconception of Newton. Samuel Clarke, Newton's follower and protagonist, in his famous correspondence with Leibniz, tried hard to disabuse Leibniz of this error:

> God does not exist In Space, and In Time; but His Existence causes Space and Time. And when, according to the Analogy of vulgar Speech we say that he exists in All Space and in All Time; the words mean only that he is Omnipresent and Eternal, that is, that Boundless Space and Time are necessary Consequences of his Existence; and not, that Space and Time are Beings distinct from Him, and IN which he exists.[8]

Almost universally from the early eighteenth century onward the doctrine of space and time as some kind of absolute, self-subsistent beings or existents was ascribed to Newton, and has continued till today to be regarded as the "Newtonian doctrine." Not only that, but the doctrine came increasingly to be accepted, more particularly by scientists, as true. Some philosophers in the eighteenth century, notably Berkeley and Hume in Britain, rejected it as fallacious—though still erroneously ascribing it to Newton.

In Germany, and elsewhere on the Continent, Leibniz's conception of space as essentially a relation was the accepted doctrine, included by Kant in his pre-critical period. By 1768, however, Kant came to see fundamental difficulties in the relationist conception. On this view, place and the totality of places, i.e. space, was the result, the outcome, of acts of relating. Kant came to see that, contrary to this, place was *presupposed by* the act of relating; for example, to perceive a thing meant relating to the thing, but this presupposed that the thing was "there;" its "being there" was not dependent upon the act of perceiving, and thus a result of the perceiving. This meant that the "thereness," *i.e.* "places," of things had to be absolute and not relative. But what was entailed in holding that space, or the place of things, was absolute? Kant faced this issue in his dissertation *De Mundi Sensibilis* (1780) inaugurating not only his occupancy of the Chair of Logic and Metaphysics in the University of Königsberg, but also of his new "critical" philosophy. The currently accepted views of space he found quite unsatisfactory:

> Those who defend the reality of space, either conceive it as an absolute and boundless receptacle of possible things (the view commends itself to most geometers, following the English), or hold that it is itself a relation of existent things, vanishing therefore if things be annihilated, and not thinkable except in actual things (as, following Leibniz, most of our countrymen maintain). The former is an empty figment of reason [*illud inane rationis*], since it imagines an infinity of possible relations without any things which are so related, pertains to the world of fable.[9]

In his *Critique of Pure Reason* (1781) he dismissed this doctrine as the conception of a "non-entity" (*unding*).[10] Contrary to these two views he maintained a momentously new position:

> *Space is not something objective and real,* neither substance nor accident, nor relation, *but subjective and ideal;* and, as it were, a schema, issuing by a constant law from the nature of the mind, for the co-ordinating of all outer sensa whatsoever.[11]

In his *Metaphysical Foundations of Natural Science* (1786) Kant formulated his doctrine alternatively as follows:

> Space in general does not belong to the properties or relations of things in themselves, which would necessarily have to admit of reduction to objective concepts, but belongs merely to the subjective form of our sensible intuition of things or relations, which must remain wholly unknown to us as regards what they may be in themselves.[12]

This new Kantian conception of space came into some appreciable acceptance only in the next century—except by avowed Kantians of course. It was the conception of space mistakenly attributed to Newton which persisted, despite the criticism of Leibniz and of Kant, throughout the eighteenth and nineteenth centuries. This doctrine gained widespread adherence, not least by scientists, among whom a philosophical interest had sharply dwindled in the post-Newtonian epoch. It was found easy to accept the statement, "there is space," without troubling to face the difficult question as to the meaning of "is" in that statement, *i.e.* to ask what kind of "being" space was supposed to have. In other words, it was easy to reify "extension" without facing the fact that, as Kant said, we thereby have an *unding*, a "non-entity."

On the plus side, this doctrine had the definite advantage that it freed the concept of "place," required by mathematical physics, of the relativity which was inevitable if extension were fundamentally the extension of matter, as Descartes had maintained.

Further, this so-called Newtonian conception of space as an actual existent had another important advantage. If extension pertained fundamentally to the physical or matter, and this material extension were essentially mathematical, it meant, as Descartes had correctly maintained, that the *object* of mathematics, and of geometry in particular, was matter, and thus that pure mathematics was the study of the essence of the physical. This raised a serious difficulty, however, as to the difference between mathematics and physics. In the course of the seventeenth century, it came to be increasingly clearly recognized that the two sciences of physics and mathematics were not identical. The so-called Newtonian conception of space as an actual existent enabled the "objects," and thus the subject-matters, of physics and mathematics to be separated. The object of physics was the physical, *i.e.* matter; while the object of mathematics, and of geometry in particular, was space. This was why this conception of space, as Kant said, "commends itself to most geometers." I might add that the discovery of non-Euclidean geometry in the early nineteenth century constituted the first chapter in the destruction of this conception of space.

To pursue this topic, however, is beyond the scope of this paper.

Notes

1. By Whewell in *Philosophy of the Inductive Sciences.*

2. Aristotle, *Physics*, 212a 20-21.

3. Descartes, *Principles of Philosophy*, Pt. II, Princ. X.

4. Descartes, *Principles of Philosophy*, Pt. II, Princ. XXV.

5. Newton, *Philosophiae Naturalis Principia Mathematica*, Andrew Motte, ed. F. Cajori (Berkeley: University of California Press, 1961), p. 8.

6. Ibid., p. 9.

7. See my paper "The Meaning of 'Space' in Kant" in *Proceedings of the Third International Kant Congress*, 1972, pp. 393-400.

8. In G. W. Leibniz, *Die Philosophischen Schriften*, ed. C. J. Gerhardt, Vol. VII, p. 427.

9. Kant's *Inaugural Dissertation*, tr. J. Handyside (Chicago: University of Chicago Press, 1928), pp. 61-62.

10. Kant, *Critique of Pure Reason*, A39 B56.

11. Kant, *Inaugural Dissertation*, p. 61.

12. Kant, *Metaphysical Foundations of Modern Science*, tr. J. Ellington, pp. 23-24.

"Never Finding Full Repast:" Satire and Self-Extension in the Early Eighteenth Century

Hopewell Selby

IN this Design of Martin to investigate the Diseases of the Mind, he thought nothing so necessary as an Enquiry after the *Seat* of the *Soul;* in which at first he labour'd under great uncertainties. Sometimes he was of opinion that it lodg'd in the Brain, sometimes in the Stomach, and sometimes in the Heart. . . . At length he grew fond of the *Glandula Pinealis*, dissecting many Subjects to find out the different Figure of this Gland, from whence he might discover the Cause of the different Tempers in mankind. . . . He was confirm'd in this by observing, that Calves and Philosophers, Tygers and Statesmen, Foxes and Sharpers, Peacocks and Fops, Cock-Sparrows and Coquets, Monkeys and Players, Courtiers and Spaniels, Moles and Misers, exactly resemble one another in the conformation of the *Pineal Gland*. He did not doubt likewise to find the same resemblance in Highway-men and Conquerors: In order to satisfy himself in which, it was, that he purchased the body of one of the first Species (as hath been before related) at Tyburn; hoping in time to have the happiness of one of the latter too, under his anatomical knife.[1]

Like his serious and satirical forbears, Martinus Scriblerus is a hero with a quest. That he is a mock-hero, one whom we would call "Augustan" for lack of a better term, is suggested by his object, his method, and his attitude. Scriblerus investigates madness, "the Diseases of the Mind." His weapon is his scalpel, his method the dissection of the dead. He likens people to animals, conquerors to criminals; he seeks the "happiness" of a conqueror under the knife. The preposterous project blends comedy with cruelty in a way that surprises no one familiar with the work of Arbuthnot, Swift, Pope, and the others in the "club." Like Scriblerus, they often question the relationship between the mind's diseases and the body's deformities; like Scriblerus, they often construe this relationship as a problem of both "space" and "place." This essay will explore some meanings and values attached to the terms "space" and "place" in post-Cartesian philosophy and Augustan satire. Throughout the seventeenth and early eighteenth centuries, spatial concepts play an important part in philosophical and satirical portrayals of the human dichotomy between mind and body, spirit and flesh. I propose that we trace this dichotomy through some of its more bizarre formulations, first in the writings of the philosophers and then in the satires of Swift and Pope. This survey of the so-called "mind-body problem" will take us to the garret and the kitchen, as we examine some ways in which both satirists connect debased modes of writing with depraved habits of eating. Scriblerus will be our guide into this nether world: his *Memoirs* can help us identify the philosophical questions from which the satirists draw "hints" for many of their works. One of these questions is concerned with the nature of space; it appears in the crazy experiment. This question can be traced back to the pre-Socratics; it subsequently provoked debates as vehement as they were prolonged. Its first word is: where.

Where is the soul? That is what Scriblerus feels he must know to understand "the different tempers of Mankind." The question itself is old: Alcmaeon of Croton (sixth century B.C.) is generally credited with having been the first to designate the brain as the center of both consciousness and perception; his views were rejected by Aristotle, who, like Homer and Hesiod before him, continued to place thought and consciousness within the chest.[2] What makes Scriblerus' experiment "modern" is its unexamined assumption that problems of personal identity can be formulated in spatial terms. Ultimately, the mock-polymath gives geometrical answers to psychological questions: he decides that individual temperament depends on the shape of the pineal gland. The obvious butt of the joke is Descartes, whose *Passions of the Soul*, published less than a century before the *Memoirs*, first asserted the importance of the "small gland in the brain in which the soul exercises its functions more particularly than in the other parts."[3]

Considered as a piece of anti-Cartesian wit, the Scriblerian episode is far from original: Descartes' theory of the pineal gland appears, to the modern reader at least, to be one of the most overworked topics of early eighteenth-century satire. Even Swift, despite his protests against "endless Repetitions upon every Subject," has a go at it—in *The Mechanical Operation of the Spirit*, of course.[4] Pope is credited with having designed most of Scriblerus' experiment, probably from "hints" furnished by Arbuthnot. The experiment, in both method and conclusions, resembles the *Account of the Death and Burial of Dr. John Woodward, as also of What Appeared upon Opening his Body:* this satire, formerly attributed to Arbuthnot, describes in unquotable detail the physician's liver, intestines, and spleen before concluding that his *"Pineal Gland* was perfectly flacid *[sic]* , so that it seemed to have been incapable for some time of giving any proper Directions to the Will."[5] Prior sports with Descartes' theory in the doggerel of his *Alma, or, the Progress of the Mind;* Elijah Fenton mocks the "Sage Cartesians who "Assert that Souls a tip-toe stand/ On what we call the Pineal Gland."[6] Addison devotes a satirical *Spectator* (#275) to the imaginary dissection of a beau, whose pineal gland is encrusted with mirrors, "insomuch that the soul, if there had been any here, must have been continually taken up in contemplating her own beauties."[7] Even Berkeley, posing as "Ulysses Cosmopolyta," writes two *Guardian* Papers on the subject, describing a visit to the pineal gland—a "place narrower than ordinary"—of a free-thinker who (predictably) turns out to be Anthony Collins.[8]

The joke grows stale, but persists. Its persistence suggests that, like many jokes, it derives from anxieties which cannot be dispelled by more "rational" means. The Scriblerian episode clarifies these anxieties by referring directly to what Descartes said—or rather, to what his readers thought he said—about where the self really "is." Scriblerus describes personality in geometrical terms because he believes that the gland really "encloses" the soul: he thus imagines "that in factious and restless-spririted people he should find it sharp and pointed, allowing no room for the Soul to repose herself; that in quiet Tempers it was flat, smooth, and soft, affording to the Soul as it were an easy Cushion."[9] Descartes' theory, as presented here, is ludicrous: we can't help but laugh at the image of the soul tumbling inside of a gland in the brain. And this is true of all spatial formulations of the self—when made explicit, they are all literal nonsense of the sort expressed by the statement "I just had a thought four inches behind my eyebrows." Still, they persist, in some of the most rigidly codified locutions of the language. Almost all, we may note, attach positive value to the idea of "inside," negative value to that of "outside." We may not make it our everyday practice to affirm that we are "inside of" our bodies, but we know now as in the eighteenth century, that those who say anything else are presumed to be "out of" their minds. Even this idiom, which describes so many victims of Augustan satire, admits of no variation: we say "out of," not "outside of." Scriblerus' experiment is funny because it literalizes our habitual metaphor and thereby tries to trivialize it and make it go away. But go away it will not: we, like Scriblerus, believe that our "selves" are inside of, and distinct from, our bodies. No wonder that we speak of "self-aggrandizement," "belittlement," "megalomania" and the like; no wonder that we seek what Ernest Becker has termed "the prerogatives of limitless self-extension, what we might call 'cosmic significance.'"[10] We "live" in two radically different realms: the physical space of the body and the symbolic space of the mind. The mind's inner realm affords us all the room there is: the infinite reach of thought. The body, however, is finite in space as well as time: "a little earth upon the head," as one eighteenth-century essayist quoted Pascal, "*& en voila pour jamais.*"[11] The mind's inner freedom, paradoxically, requires simultaneous affirmation and denial that the body's prison exists; *"Ubi sum?"* is therefore an ironic question asked in every life. It assumes a special poignancy in the seventeenth and eighteenth centuries, when, as G. S. Rousseau has written, "man's conception of himself suffered an unprecedented trauma, one that left him fragmented and materially divisible."[12] Scriblerus' dissections are both serious and "mock."

"The manner whereby the Soul and Body are united, and how they are distinguished, is wholly unaccountable to us. We see but one Part, and yet we know we consist of two; and this is a Mystery we cannot comprehend, any more than that of the Trinity."[13] From the pulpit, Swift advocates repression, deliberate incuriosity about the spirit's union with the flesh. Pope, as moralist, portrays man as "In doubt, his Mind or Body to prefer,/ Born but to die, and reas'ning but to err."[14] And Arbuthnot reflects upon his aging body in his poem "Know Yourself:" "Am I but what I seem, mere flesh and blood/ A branching channel, with a mazy flood?/ . . . New matter still the mouldr'ing mass sustains/ The mansion chang'd, the tenant still remains."[15] For all three writers, the dualism is epistemological as well as moral and physiological, as revealed by their distinctions between seeing and knowing, desiring and thinking, seeming and being. Arbuthnot thinks of himself as "tenant" in the "mansion" of his body: his architectural metaphor, like his question about the validity of inferential knowledge, reflects the strains of the so-called empirical age, when the question "who am I?" comes to mean both "where am I?" and "what do I truly know?"

Locke, of course, is credited with having achieved this synthesis by enclosing the mind in the brain's "dark room" and by leaving it with only inferential knowledge of the world "outside." Solipsistic fear is therefore often termed the legacy of his *Essay;* critics ever since Berkeley have argued that its model of the mind affords us only (private) knowledge of our own ideas, and leaves us unable to verify the existence—let alone the nature—of anything external to ourselves. This fear has rightly been termed a concern of eighteenth-century writers;[16] but solipsism, I believe, is but one aspect of a more ominous problem which could be termed that of the relation between "brain-space" and "mind-space." Briefly stated, the problem is this: if the mind is "in" the brain, and if reality is "in" the mind, then where is the brain? Logic requires saying that the brain is "in" the mind, but this conclusion leads to a tautology which leaves the mind literally nowhere. Two possible solutions to the problem are the appeal to God, and the appeal to language. The first way is Berkeley's; the second will be ours, as we examine how both Henry More and Locke, in the very process of trying to refute Descartes, only fortify the cell in which they think he has enclosed the thinking self.

We return to the pineal gland, to compare what Descartes says with what his readers think he means. In fact, Descartes begins by saying that the soul "is of a nature which has no relation to extension, nor dimensions, nor of the other properties of which matter is composed;" he continues, however, with this apparent contradiction:

> The part of the body in which the soul exercises its functions is in nowise the heart, nor the whole of the brain, but merely the most inward of all its parts, to wit, a certain very small gland which is situated in the middle of its substance and so suspended above the duct whereby the spirits in its anterior cavity have communication with those in its posterior, that the slightest movements which take place in it may very greatly alter the course of these spirits, and reciprocally that the smallest changes which occur in the course of these spirits may do much to change the movements of this gland.[17]

At issue in the passage is Descartes' celebrated dualism—his division of reality into the mutually exclusive categories of material and immaterial "substance," *res extensa* and *res cogitans*. The defining property of the first category is its extended or spatial nature, what we might call "space-ness." The defining property of the second is its unextended or non-spatial nature. By "unextended," Descartes means "having no relation to space;" his readers, however, interpret the word as meaning "taking up no space." The source of the misinterpretation appears, quite simply, to be that Descartes thinks of space in one way; his successors, in another. The difference is that of the two concepts of space which come to coexist in the seventeenth century—without, it now appears, anyone fully recognizing their radically different implications for epistemology and psychology alike.

The two concepts may be summarized in the phrases "space as place" and "space as container."[18] According to the first concept, there can be no space without objects: this is the *topos* of the Aristotelian plenists. According to the second, there can be no objects without space: this is the *kenon* of Democritus and the atomic vacuists. The first concept is geometric and makes objects more important than space; the second is kinematic and makes space more important than objects. "Space as place" is the concept of Descartes; "space as container" the concept of Newton and More. The difference is nicely illustrated by the first of the *Guardian* essays in which Berkeley attacks Descartes. Descartes terms the pineal gland "the part of the body in which the soul exercises its functions immediately;" Berkeley writes that "Descartes was the first who discovered a certain part of the brain, called by anatomists the pineal gland, to be the immediate receptacle of the soul."[19] For Descartes, the gland is a place; for Berkeley, a "receptacle." For Descartes, the gland is a material—that is, "extended" and thus geometrically definable—substance whose importance is teleological: its movement makes possible the soul's interaction with the body and with matter in general. Berkeley, however, conceives of the gland as the receptacle *within* which the soul moves; Scriblerus, we recall, does likewise. The misprision appears slight, but, as E. A. Burtt explains, it has important consequences: "The universe of mind, including all experienced qualities that are not mathematically reducible, comes to be pictured as locked up behind the confused and deceitful media of the senses, in a petty and insignificant series of locations inside of human bodies."[20] For Descartes' successors, the problem becomes one of "breaking out," one of extending the limited realm accorded to the perceiving mind.

Henry More's solution is to "assign to *Spirits* their proper extension, and leave to *Matter* hers."[21] According to Descartes, immaterial "substance" is unextended; this, as construed by More, means that the soul—and hence all spiritual entities, including God—are nowhere, *nullibi*. Hence his attack upon the *"Hobbians [sic] and Nullibists"* who "have taken all Amplitude from Spirits, because their imagination is not sufficiently defecated and depurated from the filth and unclean tinctures of *Corpority.*"[22] But this task requires a conception of space that is independent of—and therefore superior to—the material world. By conceiving of space in this way—that is, as a container—More brings God back into the world, "through the same door," as he puts it in his well-known metaphor, "by which the Cartesian philosophy seeks to let Him out."[23] With Him, however, comes the whole host of incorporeal spirits—Genii, apparitions, witches and the like—which cause More's readers such embarrassment. Having separated space from matter, and having granted spirits an extension of their own, More is obliged to admit that spirits may exist without matter as well: "there is no more difference between a *Soul* and an aerial *Genius*, than betwixt a Sword in a Scabbard, and one out of it."[24] Both ideas—that of "space as container" and that of the extension of spiritual "substance"— permit More to accept Descartes' localization of the mind while denying its consequences. For Descartes' pineal gland, More substitutes the fourth ventricle of the brain as the "seat of the soul;" he denies, however, that the soul is confined in it.

Spiritual extension, for More, means not only the power of expansion—what he calls "spissitude"—but also the power of departure. For the Cartesian dualism which places all perceived reality within the mind, More seeks to substitute the kind of spiritual extension that would permit us to say, when perceiving an "external" object, that we are really "extended" in space. Furthermore, he seeks to show that the perceiving self or soul "is really and locally separable from the whole body."[25] In the attempt, however, he makes two mistakes. First, he continues, while trying to refute Descartes, to retain Descartes' definition of reality as that which is subject to mathematical treatment— that is, extended. Secondly, he retains many of Descartes' ideas about the topical nature of space: this appears in his assertion that "there is a substance in us which is ordinarily called the soul, really distinct from the body." More's use of the preposition "in," together with his elaborate discussions of the way in which the brain's fourth ventricle functions as "conarion" or "common sensorium," show his failure to establish a viable geometry of mind. Nonetheless, his idea of space re-emerges as the "absolute space" of Newtonian physics, whose internal counterpart appears in Locke's epistemology.

In his *Essay*, Locke synthesizes (muddles?) both seventeenth-century concepts of space. He retains space as a "primary" property of matter, calling it "extension," while also making space independent of matter and calling it "expansion."[27] Both co-exist in his model of the mind: as *Tabula rasa*, it retains some features of the Cartesian *topos;* as "dark room," it is both place and container. He portrays the mind as place when he compares it to "white paper" and asks, "Whence comes it by that vast store which the busy and boundless fancy of man has painted on it with an almost endless variety?" (II. i. 2). But he conceives of the mind as container when describing the memory as the "storehouse of our ideas" which "very often are roused and tumbled out of their dark cells into open daylight, by turbulent and tempestuous passions, our affections bringing ideas to our memory, which had otherwise lain quiet and unregarded" (II. x. 1, 8). Locke thus retains Descartes' localization of the mind, but adds to it the features of Newtonian space which enable him to describe learning and thinking in terms of motion. Locke's inner space resembles Newton's outer space in two principal ways. First, it is empty—this enables Locke to describe learning in acquisitive terms. Secondly, despite its emptiness, Locke's space possesses as inertial character—it is the necessary precondition for motion. This enables Locke to describe thinking in kinematic terms which lend to common idioms (*e.g.* "Quickness of parts," "dullness") the authority of Newton's mechanics. These features enable Locke to relate "brain-space" and "mind-space" not by placing the self "out there," but rather by bringing the world "in here." By construing the mind's inner space as independent of its ideas, Locke is able to grant the thinking self an extension which—though limited—at least saves him from the charge of nullibism. And by construing the mind as the place without which the self could not exist, he is able to refute More's notion that the soul "is really and locally separable from the whole body." In "furnishing" the mind with ideas, Locke makes it both palace and prison, both storehouse and strongbox.

Or does he? Does the *Essay*, as Locke himself seems to believe, vanquish both the nullibists and the ubiquitists, the followers of Descartes and More? Richard Bentley, in the second of the Boyle lectures of 1692, comes perilously close to demonstrating that it does not. Entitled *Matter and Motion Cannot Think; or, a Confutation of Atheism from the Faculties of the Soul*, the sermon seeks to demonstrate "that if these powers of cogitation, and volition, and sensation, are neither inherent in matter as such, nor predictable in it by any motion and modification of it, it necessarily follows, that they proceed from some cognitive substance, some incorporeal inhabitant within us."[28] The ease with which Bentley equates "cognitive substance" and "incorporeal inhabitant within us" should be noted here: it exhibits exactly the same fallacy that appears in Locke's familiar attack on the Cartesians and their belief "that the soul always thinks." According to Locke, "We know, certainly, that we *sometimes* think; and thence draw this infallible consequence, that there is something in us that has a power to think" (*Essay*, II. i. 10). The "consequence" is anything but infallible: Locke's inference from activity to substantial agent ("something") might be termed a fallacy of literally misplaced concreteness. Bentley, with the phrase "incorporeal inhabitant within us," tries to have it both ways. But the preposition "within" (on which Locke's entire epistemology depends, as Berkeley makes only too clear) is precisely what Bentley is forced to abandon after several pages of valiant, but futile, argument.

Bentley starts out auspiciously enough, reiterating the Lockean distinction between primary and secondary qualities to assert that "whiteness, and redness, and coldness, and the

like are only ideas in us that see and feel; but can no more be
conceived to be real and distinct qualities in the bodies themselves, than roses or honey can be thought to smell or taste their
own sweetness."[29] So far, so good: we would agree that the
rose can only "smell" intransitively, that the honey does not
taste itself. But then, in attempting to refute the mechanism of
the Cartesians, Bentley proposes that we

> carry in our minds this true notion of body in general, and apply it to
> our own substance. . . . We observe, then, that in this understanding
> piece of clock-work, that this body as well as other senseless matter, has
> colour and warmth, and softness, and the like. But we have proved it
> before, and 'tis acknowledged that these qualities are not subsistent in
> the bodies, but are ideas and sensations begotten in something else: so
> that 'tis not bones and blood that can be conscious of their own hard-
> ness and redness; and we are still to seek for something else in our
> frame and make, that must receive these impressions. Will they say
> these ideas are performed by the brain? But the difficulty returns again;
> for we perceive that the like qualities of softness, and whiteness, and
> warmth, do belong to the brain itself, and since brain is but body, these
> qualities (as we have shown) cannot be inherent in it, but are the sensa-
> tions of some other substance without it. It cannot be brain, then,
> which imagines those qualities to be in itself.[30]

Having set out to demonstrate the existence of an "incorporeal
inhabitant within us," Bentley is forced to conclude from his
Lockean premises that the brain's thought is performed by
"some other substance without it." That he (rightly) senses
danger here is suggested by his revisions in the sermon's second
edition. In the first edition, he concludes by saying that "the
brain is not that nature which imagines those qualities of itself;"
in the second, he substitutes the phrase "to be in itself" for "of
itself." The revision suggests his awareness, however limited, of
the spatial difficulties with the preposition "without"—a preposition which he is forced to use because he has just demonstrated that the brain, "within" which the mind supposedly
exists, is itself, like the rose and the honey, a mere collection of
secondary qualities—"softness, and whiteness, and warmth"—
which are "only ideas in us that see and feel." He has almost
demolished the walls of the mind's "dark room," has almost

shown that the extended cranium of Cartesian science in a mere collection of secondary qualities "within" the mind. Accordingly, he abandons the argument, and, after a somewhat desultory treatment of "mere motion," resorts to a lame—but nonetheless Lockean—joke: "It would behoove the Atheists to give over such trifling as this, and resume the old solid way of confuting religion. They should deny the being of the soul, because they cannot see it."[31] But that, of course, is precisely what the Atheists do—that is why they say that matter and motion *can* think. Bentley's "confutation" has left the Atheists' arguments almost intact—just how intact is indicated by the weak attempt at humor with which the sermon concludes: "But if they will be still squeezing understanding out of atoms, they should make use of their own understanding as an instance. Nothing, in my opinion, could run us down more effectually than that. For we readily allow, that if any understanding can possibly be produced by such a senseless clashing of atoms, 'tis that of an Atheist that has the fairest pretensions and best title to it."[32] Bentley has shown that solipsism is not the only problem in Locke's epistemology—has shown, that is, that even a belief in Locke's non-deceiving God (*Essay*, II. viii. 13) is not enough to answer the question of where our perceptions, and the realities they "resemble," exist.

Locke tries, in the third and fourth books of the *Essay*, to answer this question through language. He admits that "having the idea of anything in our mind, no more proves the existence of that thing, than the picture of a man evidences his being in the world, or the visions of a dream make thereby a true history" (IV. xi. 1). This is, indeed, a problem: we may possess intuitive knowledge of our own being, but "being in the world" needs further demonstration—demonstration, first, that the world itself is real. In proving that we do receive ideas from "without," Locke turns to his own writing for evidence:

> Whilst I write this, I have, by the paper affecting my eyes, an idea produced in my mind which, whatever object causes, I call *white;* but which I know that quality or accident (whose appearance before my eyes causes the idea) doth really exist, and hath a being without me. . . .

I can no more doubt, whilst I write this, that I see white and black and that something really exists that causes this sensation in me, than that I write or move my hand, which is a certainty as great as human knowledge is capable of, concerning the existence of anything, but a man's self alone, and of God (IV. xi. 2).

Locke seems unaware of the obvious difficulties of this argument, which Alexander Campbell Fraser calls "an old and inadequate illustration" because "'writing' and 'moving the hand,' although intraorganic, need to have *their* reality vindicated as much as the sight of black and white does."[33] Locke's unawareness suggests that he may be bringing to the argument certain paralogical velleities—of the sort, perhaps, that led More to hypostasize "spissitude" as a measure of the soul's extension throughout the body and beyond it as well. This possibility might account for the difference between Descartes' and Locke's meditations on their writing. Descartes makes the paper before him an object of doubt; Locke makes it an object of certitude.

Scribo ergo sum: writing, for Locke, is a way out as well as a way back in. From the motion of his hand, and from the words on the page, Locke convinces himself of the reality both of his body and of the world "outside." Still, he admits that even if our ideas do give us accurate information about this "outer" realm, they are nonetheless known only to ourselves:

MAN, though he have great variety of thoughts, and such from which others as well as himself might receive profit and delight; yet they are all hidden within his own breast, nor of themselves can be made to appear. The comfort and advantage of society not to be had without communication of thoughts, it was necessary that man should find out some external signs, whereof these invisible ideas, which his thoughts are made up of, might be made known to others (III. ii. 1).

Words, then not only verify our existence, but also provide the means of overcoming our existential isolation; they "stand as marks for the ideas within the mind, whereby they might be made known to others, and the thoughts of men's minds be conveyed to one another" (III. i. 2). One achievement of the third book of the *Essay* is that it helps us to understand the verbal nature of existence—and therefore of heroism, both "serious"

and "mock"—in the eighteenth century. Swift's virtuoso correspondents dashing off their epistolary accounts of fanaticism in
all its forms, the *Tale's* mad scribbler venting his private speculations for the universal good, Gulliver's writing his memoirs to
reform mankind, Pope's re-creations of himself as grotto-bound
moralist and as unjustly maligned satirist—their *esse* (to paraphrase Berkeley) is *scribere*. The same could be said, though
with different import, of many of Defoe's and Richardson's
novelistic characters. All use language to transcend the limits of
their individuality by gaining the "re-cognition" of others.
Locke's achievement is to redefine the immortality traditionally
granted by the written word—the temporal extension of Shakespeare's "black ink"—and give it spatial significance in the here
and now as well. Writing is Locke's manner of healing the Cartesian dualism. Through the words on the page, *res cogitans* becomes *res extensa*—the unextended self, that is, acquires a spatially extended character. And this, paradoxically, makes it possible to transcend the limitations of body, to overcome what
Henry More called "the filth and unclean tinctures of *Corpority*."

Thus, in a double sense, "self-aggrandizement" is the promise
of the printed page. As Becker puts it,

> man is not just a blind glob of idling protoplasm, but a creature with a
> name who lives in a world of symbols and dreams and not merely mat-
> ter. His sense of self-worth is constituted symbolically, his cherished
> narcissism feeds on symbols, on an abstract idea of his own worth, an
> idea composed of sounds, words, images, in the air, in the mind, on
> paper. And this means that man's natural yearning for organismic acti-
> vity, the pleasures of incorporation and expansion, can be fed limit-
> lessly into the domain of symbols and so into immortality.[34]

Becker relates symbols and self-love in a way that clarifies the
irony of Swift and Pope alike. Both writers, in their serious as
well as satirical works, view the human condition in terms of
the wish to overcome "corpority;" both, however, portray the
extension of the page as a fraud. Both consider the wish for
symbolic immortality as inevitable; both, however, portray the
belief in symbolic self-extension as a megalomaniac delusion,
madness. And so they seek to demonstrate that writing, far

from being a way to escape the body's bounds, is essentially a physical act. This is the significance of the crowd as a recurrent feature of their satiric landscapes: as image, it puns on the word "press" to establish the fundamental similarity of physical and verbal competition. In the *Tale*'s endlessly quoted anecdote about the crows gathered around the mountebank in Leicester-fields, Swift employs the device to dramatize the situation in the world of letters since the expiration of the Licensing Act: *"Among the rest, a fat unwieldy Fellow, half stifled in the Press, would be every fit crying out, Lord! what a filthy Crowd is here; . . . Z——s, what squeezing is this!"*. The adjacent weaver speaks for Swift: *"Bring your own Guts to a reasonable Compass (and be d——n'd) and then I'll engage we shall have room enough for us all"* (*Tale*, p. 46). The incident, inserted in a mock-panegyric on "the Multitude of Writers whereof the whole Multitude of Writers most reasonably complains" (*Tale*, p. 45), demonstrates Swift's awareness that writing itself is an act of physical aggression. Of course the "fat fellow" won't shrink; neither will Swift himself; "We all behold with envious Eyes,/ Our *Equal* rais'd above our *Size;*/ Who wou'd not, at a crowded show,/ Stand high himself, keep others low?".[35] As indicated by these lines from his verses on his own death, Swift views "rising" as the only alternative to "squeezing." But this escape requires either the *"Edifices in the Air"* which makes possible a *"superiour Position of Place"* (*Tale*, pp. 56, 60) or—as we shall see—the defiance of gravity by (ironically) denying the body's demands. Swift, then, construes writing as a physical process whose goal, paradoxically, is to overcome the limits of corporeal individuality and achieve "pre-eminence" by gaining the attention of others. In the *Dunciad*'s heroic games, Pope inverts the metaphor to portray the "motley mixture" of scribblers who race, waddle, stumble, and plunge to gain "pre-eminence" *below* each other; "'Here strip my children! here at once leap in!/ Here prove who best can dash thro' thick and thin,/ And who the most in love of dirt excel,/ Or dark dexterity of groping well./ Who flings most filth, and wide pollutes around/ The stream, be his the Weekly Journals, bound'" (II. ll. 263-268, *Poems*, p.

393). In the excremental image, Pope stresses the word "wide" to show that the dunces seek depth to achieve breadth. Swift's writers swell so that they might rise, Pope's dunces sink so that they might spread. Both satirists, in portraying the "extent" of art, insist on the physicality of its creation.

As indicated by the emphasis on "guts" and "filth," Swift and Pope reinforce this lesson by comparing mental and physical digestion. Many of their works develop isomorphic etiologies of writing and eating, which are related not analogically but causally. The relation of the two activities is, of course, a commonplace of the age, another version of the trite anti-Cartesian joke exploited by writers who, in Scriblerus' manner, consider locating the "seat of the soul" in the stomach. Thus one of the speakers in Prior's *Alma* concludes that "whatever you maintain,/ Of ALMA in the Heart, or Brain,/ The plainest Man alive may tell Ye,/ Her Seat of Empire is the Belly."[36] Similarly, the author of *The Right of Precedence between Physicians and Civilians Enquired into* declares "that, contrary to vulgar notions, the stomach is the seat not of honour only, but of most great qualities of the mind, as well as of the disorders of the body."[37] These jokes, like those about the pineal gland, betray anxieties about the question of where our "selves" really exist. Spatially considered, the stomach, like the brain and the page, is both place and container as well: the jokes express fear that the stomach's emptiness may determine the "contents" of brain and page alike. And this fear reveals two ways in which the alimentary preoccupations of the Augustans differ from those of earlier writers such as (to take a frequently-invoked example) Rabelais. The first difference—of which more later—is that revealed by the jokes' assertion that the "seat of the soul" must be the stomach instead of the head. The choice of stomach over head expresses anxiety at the possibility that we, like Descartes' endlessly debated animals, are mere machines, whose physical processes go on without "our" consent. Thus there is nostalgia in the *Dunciad*'s invocation of Swift "in Rab'lais' easy Chair" (I, l. 22, *Poems*, p. 721). Rabelais' celebration of life's physicality is unambiguously comic in part because he, like many

Renaissance writers, considers food as only one course in what is so often called the "banquet of sense."[38] Rabelais can enjoy this "banquet" because it never occurs to him to fear the mechanistic determinism of the Cartesians: when he locates the "seat of the soul" in the stomach, it for the purpose of admonishing his readers to "devour" his words and to laugh.

The Augustans also speak of devouring words, and they also laugh. But their laughter is ironic, for reasons which betray the other difference between their alimentary jokes and those of their predecessors. This difference derives from the spatial similarities between the brain and the stomach. Both are originally empty; in the late seventeenth century, the interest in the primacy of empty space places a new stress on the metaphors of "filling up" which express the acquisitive *ethos* of empiricism. To be human, in empirical terms, is thus to be an omnivore in every "sense." And because both the brain and the stomach are containers, their activities can be described in the vocabulary of the Newtonian mechanics, as Locke demonstrates when labelling words the means of "conveying" ideas from one mind to another. Swift, in another of the *Tale*'s crowd-images, satirizes the Epicurean analogue of Locke's metaphor by taking it literally—that is, orally:

> Air being a heavy body, and therefore . . . continually descending, must needs be more so, when loaden and press'd down by Words, which are also Bodies of much Weight and Gravity, as is manifest from those deep Impressions they make and leave upon us; and therefore must be delivered from a due Altitude, or else they will neither carry a good Aim, nor fall down with a sufficient Force. . . .
> AND I am the readier to favour this Conjecture, from a common Observation; that in the several Assemblies of these Orators, Nature it self hath instructed the Hearers, to stand with their Mouths open, and erected parallel to the Horizon, so as they may be intersected by a perpendicular line from the Zenith to the Center of the Earth. In which position, if the Audience be well compact, every one carries home a Share, and little or nothing is lost (*Tale*, pp. 60-61).

Pope, in a variant of the metaphor, describes himself as a victim of a seemingly endless "bombardment" of trivial gossip: "As one of *Woodward's* patients, sick and sore,/ I puke, I nauseate—

yet he thrusts in more" ("Satires of Dr. John Donne," IV, 11.
152–153, *Poems*, p. 684). Swift and Pope here relate the space
of mind, stomach, and page by insisting that words and food are
akin, both ways of "taking in" the world "outside."
  "The head of man," says Arbuthnot's *Dissertation on Dumpling* in a mock-encomiastic pun on this notion of "contents,"
"is like a Pudding: and whence have all Rhymes, Poems, Plots
and Inventions sprung, but from that same Pudding? What is
Poetry but a Pudding of Words?"[39] Swift, making a similar
comparison, reverses the cliché that "we are what we eat" to
proclaim that we eat what we are: he imagines, in his verses on
his death, that his poems were sent "with a Load of Books/ Last
Monday to the Pastry-Cooks" (*Poems*, II, 563, 11. 259–260).
Tempus edax rerum: Swift elaborates upon the proverbial formula to demonstrate that oral aggression holds the chain of being together in space as well as in time:

> So, Nat'ralists observe, a Flea
> Hath smaller Fleas that on him prey,
> And those have smaller Fleas to bite 'em,
> And so proceed *ad infinitum:*
> Thus ev'ry Poet in his Kind,
> Is bit by him that comes behind
> ("On Poetry: A Rhapsody," ll. 337–340, *Poems*, II, 651).[40]

Swift here answers the seventeenth-century distinction between
"words and things" by including the world of language in the
world of nature: the analogy between poets and fleas "works"
because—in the very act of reading—words are "swallowed up"
by those which "follow" on the page. Pope suggests this idea
when, in the *Essay on Criticism*, he describes the "editorial"
perversions of those who "on the leaves of ancient Authors prey/
Nor Time nor Moths e'er spoil'd so much as they" (11. 112–113,
Poems, p. 147). But this vision is tame in comparison with that
of Swift, who, in a horrific riddle on the subject, portrays the
space-time continuum as a giant's insatiable appetite: "Ever eating, never cloying,/ All devouring, all destroying,/ Never finding
full Repast/ Till I eat the World at last" (*Poems*, III, 930).
  Esse est aut edi aut edere: Swift and Pope are not alone in ap-

plying the Berkeleian formula to relate what we eat and what we write to what we know. The spatial connections among the three activities are evinced by the title of the anonymous *Philosophical Dissertation upon the Inlets to Human Knowledge*, whose author states that "Words are the necessary Vehicles of Thought, or as *Plutarch* very justly expresses it in his excellent Treatise of Education, Words are the Food of the Understanding, I cannot help observing by the by, that there is perhaps the strongest analogy between the Nourishment of the Mind and the Body, that is to be met with."[41]

Pope exploits the analogy in the *Dunciad* to portray textual exegesis as a process of eating others' words. Thus the medievalist "Wormius" is "on parchment scraps y-fed" (III, 1. 188, *Poems*, p. 758), and Aristarchus makes this vow: "In Ancient Sense if any needs must deal/ Be sure I give them Fragments, not a Meal,/ What Gellius or Stobaeus hash'd before/ Or chewd by old blind Scholiasts o'er and o'er" (IV, 11. 229-232, *Poems*, p. 779).[42] Like the *Essay on Criticism*, and like Swift's "Digression Concerning Criticks," the *Dunciad* portrays the "descent" of scholarship from admiration to regurgitation: the Pope-Warburton note on the scholiasts describes their transmission of knowledge as "taking the same things eternally from one mouth to another" (*n*. to 1. 232, *Poems*, p. 779). Swift develops the comparison in the *Tale* by equating learning with eating; wisdom is thus "a *Cheese*," "a *Sack-Posset*," "a *Nut*" (*Tale*, p. 66). Hence the zany "modern" project of "distilling" knowledge from "*fair correct Copies, well bound in Calf's Skin, and Lettered at the Back, of all Modern Bodies of Arts and Sciences whatsoever, and in what Language you please.*" The moderns— they are always seeking shortcuts—"convey" the books' words to the brain not by the mouth but by the more direct route of the nose, so that the "Elixir" distilled from the books "*will dilate it self about the Brain (where there is any) in fourteen Minutes, and you immediately perceive in your Head an infinite Number of* Abstracts, Summaries, Compendiums, Extracts, Collections, Medulla's, Excerpta quaedam's, Florilegia's *and the like, all disposed into great Order, and reducible upon Paper*"

(*Tale*, pp. 126-127). Swift here portrays the state of contemporary learning in quantitative as well as qualitative terms: to be modern, he says, is literally to "face" a near infinite number of words which must be either "pre-digested" or "distilled" into order. In the search for this order Swift, like his contemporaries, turns to a familiar "Ancient" for help.

"Tables should be like pictures to the Sight,/ Some dishes cast in shade, some spread in Light":[43] William King's Horatian *Art of Cookery* goes beyond mere parody to assert that literary and dietary styles are fundamentally related, both formal expressions of "taste." In one of his Horatian imitations, Pope conceives of his poetic *oeuvre* as a similar banquet of dishes; he, however, emphasises that the difference between Horace's audience and his own is that his readers insist on satisfying only their separate and specialized preferences:

> But after all, what wou'd you have me do?
> When out of twenty I can please not two;
> When this Heroicks only deigns to praise,
> Sharp satire that, and that Pindaric lays?
> One likes the Pheasant's wing, and one the leg;
> The vulgar boil, the Learned roast an Egg;
> Hard task! to hit the Palate of such Guests,
> What Oldfield loves, what Darteneuf detests
> (*Ep.* II, ii, ll. 80-87, *Poems*, p. 652)

The *Tale's* mad narrator, who invokes the image to declaim against "the pernicious Custom of making the Preface a Bill of Fare to the Book" (*Tale*, pp. 130-131), defends his disorganized book by equating the corruption of literary form with the decadence of dietary custom. Because his readers are specialists, he must, in order to please them all, fill his book with miscellaneous bits of wit and knowledge both: "the late Refinements in Knowledge running parallel with those of Dyet in our Nation, which among Men of a judicious Taste, are dresst up in various compounds, consisting in *Soups* and *Ollio's, Fricassees* and *Ragousts*" (*Tale*, p. 143). Thus, he literally crams his treatise with everything "inside" his head: "Therefore hospitably considering the number of my Guests, they shall have my whole Entertainment at a Meal; And I scorn to set up the *Leavings* in the Cupboard. What the *Guests* cannot eat may be given to the *Poor* and the **Dogs* under the Table may gnaw the *Bones;* this I understand for a more generous Proceeding, than to turn the Company's Stomachs by inviting them to morrow to a scurvy Meal of *Scraps*" (*Tale*, p. 184). The "Dogs," as might be expected, turn out to be us—the critics. No wonder that *The Right of Precedence between Physicians and Civilians Enquired Into* was for so long attributed to Swift: it declares that "A writer's stomach, appetite, and victuals, may be judged from his method, style, and subject, as certainly as if you were his mess-fellow, and sat at a table with him. Hence we call a subject dry, a writer insipid, a pamphlet empty and hungry, a style jejeune; and many such-like expressions, plainly alluding to the diet of the author."[44]

But the style of the author is, in turn, the diet of the reader: this is the point of Pope's conversation, in the second dialogue of the "Epilogue to the Satires," with the friend who says "This filthy simile, this beastly line/ Quite turns my stomach." Pope answers, "So does flattery mine" (11. 181-182, *Poems*, p. 702). In this way, Pope suggests that both stylistic and dietary corruptions are signs of moral—and therefore political—sickness. In this poem, Pope revitalizes the timeworn comparison of the human microcosm and the political macrocosm to show that the "court style" is debased in every sense: "Let courtly Wits to Wits afford supply,/ As Hog to Hog in Huts of *Westphaly;/* . . . From tail to mouth, they feed, and they carouse;/ This last full fairly gives it to the House" (11. 171-172, 179-180, *Poems*, pp. 700, 701). As in the *Epistle to Bathurst*, where Balaam's moral degradation begins when "lo! two puddings smoak'd upon the board" (1. 360, *Poems*, p. 585), Pope attributes this sickness to "luxury"—that is, to the use of money for gratuitous aesthetic elaboration that becomes increasingly valued for its own sake. Thus affluence, used at first to stimulate the sensory "inlets to human knowledge," ironically leads to the denial of the truths which the senses—particularly that of smell—tell us about ourselves. *Gulliver's Travels*, Swift's most fully developed attack upon "luxury," is thus an attempt to re-present to us the senses' "testimony" so that we may judge ourselves. In the third voyage, Swift uses food to demonstrate just how "inhuman" the Laputans are in their political and personal relationships. The Laputans, who enslave the populace below by manipulating their island's magnetic field, who refuse to make love to their wives, and who need "flappers" to stimulate their attention, pervert the natural forms of their food into geometical shapes. Thus Gulliver describes a Laputan dinner as consisting of "a shoulder of Mutton, cut into an AEquilateral Triangle; a Piece of Beef into a Rhomboides, and a Pudding into a Cycloid" (*Prose*, XI, 161). This is Cartesianism with a vengeance; as we might expect, the Laputans' inhumanity is reflected in their preference for the mathematical "harmony" of music over the cacaphony of words. They are among the least verbal of Swift's satiric creations; their style, of course, finds its ultimate expression in the calculations of the *Modest Proposal*.

Both Swift and Pope view these stylistic and dietary perversions as the result of egocentricity, "delusions of grandeur." The relevance of the idiom is evinced by the way in which bad writers, in their satires, may be divided into two general groups—those who starve themselves and scribble, and those who stuff themselves and sleep. Swift's satire exhibits a predominance of the first type; Pope's, of the second. Swift's "The Progress of Poetry" relates both types sequentially—or rather, consequentially. When "fresh in Pay," the Poet cannot write: "With good Roast Beef his Belly full,/ Grown lazy, foggy, fat, and dull:/ Deep sunk in Plenty, and Delight,/ What Poet e'er could take his Flight?" He produces only when he starves:

> With hungry Meals his Body pin'd,
> His guts and Belly full of Wind;
> And, like a Jockey for the Race,
> His flesh brought down to Flying-Case:
> Now his exalted Spirit loaths
> Encumbrances of Food and Cloaths;
> And up he rises like a Vapour,
> Supported high on Wings of Paper;
> He singing flies, and flying sings,

While from below all *Grub-street* rings
(11. 17, 21-24, 37-46, *Poems*, I, 230-231).

The poem could be termed a panegyric on starvation as the origin of art: the poet's "progress" is that of leaving the realm of matter for the realm of words. According to Swift, the antithetical relationship between physical ingestion and verbal production is a matter of exchanging one form of "self-aggrandizement" for another, of exchanging the physical predominance of size for the verbal preeminence of height.

Pope's dunces "sink" because they eat too much. "The Man who 'rose to the *Rotund*/ He sunk him down in *dull Profound*"— this, according to the authors of the 1729 *Martiniad*, is Pope's characteristic treatment of corpulence.[45] A note to the couplet glosses the word "Rotund" as "An Expression in *Scriblerus* for Plump, denoting, as he says, *Obesity*, and he is of Opinion, that a Fat Man cannot be a Man of Wit; For although he seemeth to admit *Guts* in a *Man's Brain*, He will not allow of *Brains* in his *Guts*."[46] The note is correct: the *Dunciad* begins at night, when "May'rs and Shrieves all hush'd and satiate lay/ Yet eat, in dreams, the custard of the day" (I, 11. 91-92, *Poems*, p. 724). The head is a pudding indeed: surfeit begets sluggishness, then silence. Pope's counterpart to Swift's portrait of the starving poet is the "progress-piece" about the "Young Aeneas" who makes the "grand tour" in the *Dunciad*'s fourth book. He

Try'd all *hors-d'oeuvres*, all *liqueurs* defin'd,
Judicious drank, and greatly-daring din'd;
Dropt the dull lumber of the Latin store,
Spoil'd his own language, and acquir'd no more;
All Classic learning lost on Classic ground;
And last turn'd *Air*, the Echo of a Sound!
See now, half-cur'd, and perfectly well-bred,
With nothing but a Solo in his head"
(IV, 11. 317-324, *Poems*, pp. 782-783).

Omniphagia produces aphasia: the *Dunciad*'s last book concludes with a feast which is followed by the "yawn" of the Goddess, the silence of the scribblers, and the end of the poem itself. The goddess of Poetic Justice, in the poem's first book, holds up her "lifted scale,/ Where, in nice balance, truth with gold she weighs,/ And solid pudding against empty Praise" (I, 11. 53-55, *Poems*, p. 723). Pope presents "pudding" and "praise" as mutually exclusive alternatives to demonstrate that overindulgence of the gustatory sense leads to the atrophy of the others: that is why the Pope-Warburton note at the poem's beginning defines dullness as "all slowness of Apprehension, Shortness of Sight, or imperfect Sense of things" (*n*. to I, 1. 15, *Poems*, p. 721). The dunces' concern with feeding themselves causes them to confuse two kinds of "grandeur." Preoccupied only with what they eat, they pay no attention to what others, all around them, are "taking in" with all of their senses. They thus believe that their audience's "imperfect knowledge of things" is equal to their own. And this type of megalomania produces writing that is "condescending," mechanical, and obvious—"boring." Their overeating causes them to "find Virtue local, all Relation scorn,/ See all in *Self*, and but for self be born" (*Dunciad*, IV, 11. 479-480). Swift, in a mock-Latin "Love Song," succinctly illustrates the kind of "displacement" that makes them love themselves instead of others: "APUD in is almi des ire,/ Mimis tres I ne ver re qui re" (11. 1-2, *Poems*, III, 1039).

But the starving artist, as portrayed by Swift and Pope, is also one "with nothing but a solo in his head." As is so often the case in Augustan satire, both extremes end up looking very much alike. Pope, in the *Dunciad's* first book, compares the poet's garret with Aeolus' cave for good reason. The writer who starves alone in the garret denies the common human need for food and friends; longwindedness and endless digression result. Taking nothing, and nobody, in, he lacks a viable subject: "Keen, hollow winds howl thro' the bleak recess/ Emblem of Music caus'd by Emptiness" (I, 11. 35-36, *Poems*, p. 722). And because the poems are "empty," they don't sell: thus the scribblers starve because they write and write because they starve. This is what Pope means by portraying them as those "Who hunger, and who thirst for scribbling sake" (*Dunciad*, I, 1. 50,

Poems, p. 723). The phrase exactly describes the *Tale*'s speaker, who confesses that while writing, "I thought fit to sharpen my Invention with Hunger; and, in general, the whole Work was begun, continued, and ended, under a long Course of Physick and a great want of Money" (*Tale*, p. 44). Starvation begets logorrhea, for the same reason—ironically—that surfeit begets silence. Again, it is a case of imbalance: denial of the sense of taste leads to the hypertrophy of the other senses. Thus the *Tale*-teller can talk, through the entire book, about his ability to "inspect beyond the Surface of Things" (*Tale*, p. 66) and then conclude by saying he has written on *"Nothing"* (*Tale*, p. 208). Starvation is necessary to perform this "Experiment very frequent among Modern Authors," which he describes as "to let the Pen still move on, by some called, the Ghost of Wit, delighting to walk after the death of the Body" (*Tale*, p. 208). The *Tale* is filled with scraps of other people's wit and other people's learning because the speaker has abandoned food to eat words. This is also the condition of the "supperless" Bays, who, in the *Dunciad*, recalls all the words he has eaten: "Next o'er his Books, his eyes began to roll,/ In pleasing Memory of all he stole,/ How here he sipp'd, how here he plunder'd snug,/ And suck'd all o'er, like an industrious bug./ Here lay poor Fletcher's half-eat scenes . . ." (I, 11. 126-131, *Poems*, p. 726). But, as Swift tells us, *"Words are but Wind;"* "Learning *puffeth Men up"* (*Tale*, p. 153). The replacement of food with words produces another type of megalomania whose stylistic sign is catachresis—the substitution of private for public meanings of language. Because he does not eat, the starving writer also confuses two kinds of grandeur; he also assumes that his own private version of reality is the same as everyone else's. This is the point of Pope's gloss on the word "supperless": it defends the word choice by asserting that "to represent a critic encompast with books, but without a supper, is a picture which lively expresseth how much the true critic prefers the diet of the mind to that of the body, one of which he always castigates and often totally neglects, for the greater improvement of the other" (*n.* to I, 1. 109, *Poems*, p. 360).

Both extremes, then, produce equally bizarre stylistic aberrations because both represent an unbalanced assessment of the mind's and the body's demands. The antidote to these extremes, as seen by Swift and Pope, lies in the predictable "middle way." "Between excess and famine lies a mean/ Plain, but not sordid, tho' not splendid, clean" ("Imitations of Horace," *Sat.* II, ii, 11. 44-46, *Poems,* p. 620): Pope's prescription for the ideal diet deliberately parodies Denham's description of the ideal style to emphasize that both literary and dietary "good taste" derive from following "nature." Swift expresses the ideal in similar terms in the fourth book of the *Travels,* when Gulliver, eating the Houyhnhnms' diet of oats and milk, learns "how easily nature is satisfied" (*Prose,* XI, 233). The diet's conformity to nature is reflected in the stylistic purity of the Houyhnhnms' poetry, "wherein the Justness of their Similes, and the Minuteness, as well as Exactness of their Descriptions, are indeed inimitable" (*Prose,* XI, 273). Both Swift and Pope eulogize the Horation means as the graceful but utilitarian satisfaction of instinct. Early in his career, Pope counsels simplicity, "Since not much Wine, much Wine, much Company, much Food,/ Make Entertainments please us as they should;/ But 'tis of each, the *Little,* and the *Good*" ("Lines added to the Conclusion of 'The Bill of Fare'" *Poems,* p. 276, 11. 28-30). The autodescription in the last line of the triplet suggests Swift's self-portrait as "Of Size that might a Pulpit fill,/ But more inclining to sit still" ("Part of the Seventh Epistle of the First Book of Horace, Imitated," 11. 11-12, *Poems,* I, 170). As in his verses for the women who cry apples, herrings, onions and the like, Swift's self-portrait advocates an aesthetic of the *à propos.*

But between mind-space and body-space there is no middle ground. We are either "in" or "out," "within" or "beyond." Swift and Pope meet this predicament by looking where we might expect—behind. As Pope puts it, "Now Wits gain praise by copying other Wits,/ As one Hog lives on what the other Sh——" ("Couplet on Wit," *Poems,* p. 295). Swift, in a riddle on the posteriors, asks, "Shall man presume to be my master,/

Who's but my *Caterer* and *Taster?"* (11. 17-18, *Poems*, III, 918).
Starving, like stuffing, is therefore an aggressive act—an attempt
to deny the riddle's truth. The so-called "excremental vision" of
the Augustans is thus inseparable from their alimental vision, as
Swift makes clear when, in "A Panegyric on the Dean," he attributes anal repression to Gluttony: "But, when at last usurping
Jove/ Old Saturn from his Empire drove;/ Then Gluttony with
greasy Paws,/ Her napkin pinn'd up to her Jaws,/ . . . This bloated
Harpy sprung from Hell/ Confin'd Thee Goddess to a Cell" (11.
253-256, 269-270, *Poems*, III, 895). The "Goddess," of course,
in Cloacine, who also presides at the *Dunciad*'s "heroic games."
Swift and Pope thus portray excretion as both analogue and
necessary precondition of art: that is why the *Tale*'s narrator
writes during "a long Course of Physick" (*Tale*, p. 44), why
Bays tells the Goddess of Dullness that "Me Emptiness and
Dulness could inspire/ And were my Elasticity and Fire" (*Dunciad*, I, 11. 185-186, *Poems*, p. 729). Excretion, like starving,
is thus for Swift and Pope a way of denying the body, a way
"out." Pope's dunces are "renew'd by Ordure's sympathetic
Force" (*Dunciad*, II, 1, 103, *Poems*, p. 739); they starve because they have to. Swift's satiric creations, however, starve because they want to, and this difference suggests that Swift, more
than Pope, is preoccupied with the human ambivalence toward
the need to have to eat at all. In an imitation of Donne, Pope
takes this attitude toward "corpority": "But oh! What terrors
must distract the Soul/ Convicted of that mortal Crime, a hole!"
(Satires of Dr. John Donne, IV, 11. 244-245, *Poems*, p. 686).
Swift's riddle on the posteriors shows how we avoid these "terrors": "By all the World I am *oppress't,/* And my *Oppression*
gives them *Rest*" (11. 9-10, *Poems*, III, 918). Scriblerus turns
out to be right after all: repression is a matter of lying to ourselves about the "seat of the soul." Swift knows, as we do, what
these lies produce: on Christmas day, 1710, he writes to Stella,
"I tell you a good pun; a fellow hard by pretends to cure *Agues*,
and has set out a sign, and spells it *Egoes;* a gentleman and I observing it, he said, "How does that fellow pretend to cure *Agues?*
I said, I did not know, but I was sure it was not by a *Spell.*"[47]

The puns speak truth: the ego is an ague of which language is
the symptom, not the cure. In an illiterate shopkeeper's window,
Swift glimpses the human condition in a misspelled word. The
puns show, finally, that Descartes was both right and wrong: extension is the stuff of which our thoughts and dreams are made;
quacks, meanwhile, tell us who and where we are.

Notes

1. *Memoirs of the Extraordinary Life, Works, and Discoveries of
Martinus Scriblerus*, ed. Charles Kerby-Miller (New Haven, Conn.: Yale
University Press, 1950; rpt. New York: Russell and Russell, 1966), p. 137.
Subsequent references to the *Memoirs* are to this edition.

2. See Richard B. Onians, *The Origins of European Thought about
the Body, the Mind, the Soul, the World, Time, and Fate* (Cambridge:
Cambridge University Press, 1951), pp. 115ff; George Sarton, *A History of
Science: Ancient Science Through the Golden Age of Greece* (Cambridge,
Mass.: Harvard University Press, 1952), pp. 517ff.

3. *The Philosophical Works of Descartes*, trans. Elizabeth S. Haldane
and George T. Ross, 2 vols. (Cambridge: Cambridge University Press,
1911), I, 345.

4. For the protest quoted, see *A Tale of a Tub, to Which is Added
the Battle of the Books and the Mechanical Operation of the Spirit*, ed.
A. C. Guthkelch and D. Nichol Smith, 2nd ed. (Oxford: Clarendon, 1958),
p. 3. Swift's mockery of Descartes' theory is to be found on p. 277 of this
edition.

5. *Miscellaneous Works of the late Dr. Arbuthnot*, 2nd ed., 2 vols.
(Glasgow: James Carlile, 1751), I, 180; cited hereafter as *Miscellaneous
Works*. On the disputed authorship of works in this edition, see Lester
M. Beattie, *John Arbuthnot: Mathematician and Satirist* (Cambridge,
Mass.: Harvard University Press, 1935), pp. 308-317; Marjorie Nicholson
and G. S. Rousseau, *This Long Disease, My Life: Alexander Pope and the
Sciences* (Princeton, N.J.: Princeton University Press, 1968), p. 121. Rous-
seau and Nicholson discuss Pope's antipathy toward Woodward's practice
of curing disease by "vomitation" on pp. 118-119.

6. For Prior's treatment of the theme, see *The Literary Works of
Matthew Prior*, ed. H. Bunker Wright and Monroe K. Spears, 2nd ed. in
2 vols. (Oxford, Clarendon, 1961), I, 471-514. This edition is cited hereafter as *Literary Works*. Kerby-Miller quotes the anti-Cartesian couplet
from Fenton's *Fair Nun* (1717) in his edition of the *Memoirs*, p. 287.

7. *The Spectator*, ed. Donald F. Bond. 5 vols. (Oxford: Clarendon, 1965), II, 571, for Tuesday, January 15, 1712.

8. *The Guardian*, 2 vols. (London: Longman *et al.*, 1797), I, 196–199 (No. 32, for April 21, 1713); I, 219-223 (No. 39, for April 25, 1713). The phrase quoted is on p. 219 of this volume.

9. *Memoirs*, ed. Kerby-Miller, p. 137.

10. *The Denial of Death* (New York: Free Press, 1973), p. 3; see also pp. 41–43.

11. This quotation, from Lord Forbes of Pitsligo's *Essays Moral and Philosophical, on Several Subjects* (London, 1734) appears in John Barker, *Strange Contrarieties: Pascal in England During the Age of Reason* (Montreal and London: McGill-Queen's University Press, 1975), p. 174.

12. "Science and the Discovery of the Imagination in Enlightened England," *Eighteenth-Century Studies*, III (1969-1970), 134.

13. "On the Trinity," *The Prose Works of Jonathan Swift*, ed. Herbert Davis. 16 vols. (1938-1965; rpt. Oxford: Blackwell, 1964-1974), IX, 164. Subsequent references to *Prose* are to this edition.

14. *An Essay on Man, Ep.* II, 11. 9-10., *The Poems of Alexander Pope*, ed. John Butt (New Haven, Conn.: Yale University Press, 1963), p. 516. Subsequent parenthetic line and page references to *Poems* are to this edition.

15. *Miscellaneous Works*, II, "supplement," 24.

16. For one treatment of solipsism in the work of Berkeley, Sterne, Wordsworth, and later writers, see A. D. Nuttall, *A Common Sky: Philosophy and the Literary Imagination* (Berkeley and Los Angeles: University of California Press, 1974).

17. "The Passions of the Soul," *Philosophical Works*, trans. Haldane and Ross, I, 345.

18. For a cogent summary of these concepts, see Albert Einstein's preface to Max Jammer, *Concepts of Space*, 2nd ed. (Cambridge, Mass.: Harvard University Press, 1969), xiii-xv.

19. *The Guardian* (1797), I, 170 (No. 35, for April 21, 1713).

20. *The Metaphysical Foundations of Modern Science*, 2nd ed., revised (London: Routlege and Kegan Paul, 1934), p. 115. I am indebted to Burtt's discussion, pp. 96-154 and 301-324, for clarifying many implications of these different concepts of space.

21. "The True Notion of A Spirit," Sect. XXI, *The Philosophical Writings of Henry More*, ed. Flora Isabel MacKinnon (New York: Oxford University Press, 1925), p. 212. Subsequent references to *Philosophical Writings* are to this edition. For the differences between More and Descartes, see Alexander Koyré, *From the Closed World to the Infinite Universe* (Baltimore, Md.: Johns Hopkins University Press, 1957), pp. 110-154.

22. "The True Notion of a Spirit," sect. XXI, *Philosophical Writings*, p. 211.

23. *"Atque ita per eam ipsam januam per quam Philosophia Cartesiana Deum videtur velle e Mundo excludere, ego, e contra, eum introducere rursus enitor et contendo,"* quoted from More's *Enchiridion Metaphysicum* (1671) by Jammer, *Concepts of Space*, p. 42.

24. "The Immortality of the Soul," II. xvii. 4., *Philosophical Writings*, p. 159.

25. "The Immortality of the Soul," II. xvii. 4., *Philosophical Writings*, p. 158; cf. II. xv. i., pp. 152-153.

26. "The Immortality of the Soul," II. xvii. 4., *Philosophical Writings*, p. 158; cf. II. vii, viii.

27. *An Essay Concerning Human Understanding*, ed. Alexander Campbell Fraser, 2 vols. (1894); rpt. New York: Dover, 1959), II. xiii. 27, I, 236. Subsequent paranthetic references to the *Essay*, by book, chapter, and section, are to this edition. Locke's explicit distinction between "extension" and "expansion," added to the *Essay*'s fourth edition, is not completely maintained elsewhere. See. e.g., II, xv., "Ideas of Duration and Expansion, Considered Together" in vol. I of this edition, 257-269.

28. *The Works of Richard Bentley, D.D.*, ed. Alexander Dyce (London: F. MacPherson, 1838), III, 35. This edition is hereafter cited as *Works*.

29. *Works*, ed. Dyce, III, 38.

30. *Works*, ed. Dyce, III, 38-39.

31. *Works*, ed. Dyce, III, 48.

32. *Works*, ed. Dyce, III, 49.

33. *Essay*, II, 327, *n.* 3.

34. *The Denial of Death*, pp. 2-3.

35. *The Poems of Jonathan Swift*, ed. Harold Williams, 2nd. ed., 3 vols. (Oxford: Clarendon, 1958), II, 554, 11. 13-16. Subsequent parenthetic references to *Poems* are to this edition.

36. *Literary Works,* ed. Wright and Spears, I, 222, 11. 198-201.

37. This treatise, formerly attributed to Swift but rejected as inauthentic by Herbert Davis, appears in *The Prose Works of Jonathan Swift, D.D.,* ed. Temple Scott (London: G. Bell and Sons, 1907), XI, 30-43. The passage quoted is on p. 34.

38. This trope is probably best known from the title of George Chapman's poem "Ovid's Banquet of Sence" (1595).

39. *Miscellaneous Works,* I, 69.

40. C. J. Rawson quotes these lines, in a discussion of cannibalism as a theme in Swift's work, in *Gulliver and the Gentle Reader: Studies in Swift and our Time,* (London: Routlege & Kegan Paul, 1973), p. 63.

41. *A Philosophical Dissertation Upon the Inlets to Human Knowledge* (London: T. Cooper, 1739), pp. 42-43.

42. Patricia Meyer Spacks discusses this, and some of Pope's other alimentary images, in *An Argument of Images: The Poetry of Alexander Pope* (Cambridge, Mass.: Harvard University Press, 1971), pp. 117-121.

43. *The Art of Cookery, in Imitation of Horace's Art of Poetry* (London: B. Lintott, [1709]), p. 113.

44. *The Prose Works of Jonathan Swift, D.D.,* ed. Scott, XI, 35.

45. [George Duckett and John Dennis], *Pope Alexander's Supremacy and Infallibility Examin'd; and the Errors of Scriblerus and his Man William Detected* (London: J. Roberts, 1729), p. 3, 11. 21-22.

46. *Pope Alexander's Supremacy . . . ,* p. 3, *n.*

47. *Journal to Stella,* ed. Harold Williams, *Prose,* XV, 139-140.

The Metaphor of Time as Space

Louis T. Milic

In our day, everyone understands that the concepts of space
and time are not any longer discrete, cannot be placed in separate compartments. This is true to some extent even for those
who understand nothing of relativity. The term "space-time
(continuum)" warns all who come near that these are deep
waters, in which time has been demoted to a mere fourth co-
ordinate. *Space* on the other hand has expanded. Apart from
the many uses of the word in everyday language—a blank between words, newsprint sold for advertising, the alternative to a
line in music notation, a seat on a plane, train, or bus—it has acquired a visibility it did not have before, no doubt owing to the
space program and related discoveries in astronomy. It is an
impressive intellectual event that *space* can be defined both as a
boundless entity extending in all directions without limit and
including all material bodies in it, and, as well, the same even if
all material bodies in it are destroyed. The concept of curved
space, as in a Klein bottle, is accepted without murmur by today's literate (numerate?) person.

  There is no question that space has emerged and that time

has lost some importance especially since everyone has become aware of the finite speed of light and the consequent result that any look at the stars is in fact a look at the past. When time lost its immediacy, it lost its most obvious quality. It became a function of space. Science fiction, which probably affects the history of popular ideas more than the discoveries of astrophysicists do, has played with this notion in the form of the "time-warp," "time tunnel" and "time machine," all of which proclaim the spatialization of time. The history of science during the past few centuries has largely witnessed the degradation of time. Of course, time has no science of its own to support its claim, merely a set of hackneyed symbols and metaphors: the hourglass, the reaper, the buds of spring, the falling leaves of October, the infant new year. In Newton's day, one might well suppose, things were different and space and time occupied different mental categories, i.e., had non-overlapping semantic fields.

To some extent, such a supposition would be accurate. One can easily find treatises on space and discussions of time in separate seventeenth and eighteenth century volumes. One may even find the distinction between them made in a single sentence, like this one from Samuel Clarke's *Being and Attributes of God* (1705):

> Infinite space is nothing else but an abstract idea of immensity or infinity, even as infinite duration is of eternity: and it would be not much less proper to say that eternity is the essence of the supreme cause than to say that immensity is so.

A more interesting conjunction is found in William Whiston's *New Theory of the Earth* (1696):

> 'Tis now evident, that every one of the planets, as well as that on which we live, must have a right in its proportion to share in the care of heaven, and had therefore in all probability a suitable space or number of days allow'd to its proper formation. . . .

Whiston evidently conceives of space and time as equivalent commodities, of equal importance to the objects being created. That is, the Creator presumably spent as much time on the creation of other planets as on ours, or perhaps should have, though Genesis clearly states that the earth was made on the first day and "the lights in the firmament of heaven," i.e., the sun, moon, stars and planets, on the fourth. Apart from its revisionism, the statement is remarkable for its evident faith in the equivalence and perhaps convertibility of space and time.

Something of the same type is observable in the everyday utterances of the later contemporaries of Clarke and Whiston, the Augustan essayists. Thus Addison remarks: "But of all the diversions of life, there is none so proper to fill up its empty spaces as the reading of useful and entertaining authors."[1] Elsewhere: "I would, however, recommend to every one of my readers, the keeping a journal of their lives for one week and setting down punctually their whole series of employments during that space of time."[2] Life is visualized by Addison as a sequence of spaces, which may be left empty or may be filled with various activities. Because of his use of this model, Addison senses no contradiction in the expression "space of time."

Addison's partner and co-editor, Sir Richard Steele, just as easily falls into this strain. In a later *Spectator*, he speaks of a nymph who "had wings on her shoulders and feet, and was able to transport herself to the most distant regions in the smallest space of time."[3] In an essay on Alexander Selkirk, the progenitor of Robinson Crusoe, there are many reflections on solitude, which is simply duration of time in a restricted space. So, Steele begins with a revealing analogy: "When we consider how painful absence from company for the space of but one evening is to the generality of mankind, we may have a sense how painful this necessary and constant solitude was to a man bred a sailor . . ."[4] Again, "after the space of eighteen months, he grew thoroughly reconciled to his condition," and "he made a stretch to seize a goat, with which under him, he fell down a precipice, and lay senseless for the space of three days, the length of time he measured by the moon's growth since his last observation."[5]

From this last citation, in particular, it can be seen that Steele also perceives time to be a linear measure of distance or an area (the moon's surface). The space of eighteen months exists on a calendar as well as in the mind. It should not be supposed from these citations, however, that Addison and Steele were the only practitioners of this conversion, the only interpreters of time in spatial terms. It can be found in numerous other prose works of the period. And their contemporary, Alexander Pope, was capable of the same thing in his poetical works. The new concordance of Pope's poetry,[6] which covers a total of nearly half a million words, shows that he used the word *space* on some seventy-three separate occasions, sixteen of which were temporal, for example:

> How short a space our wordly joys endure? (II, 38)[7]
> Such, such a man extends his life's short space (VI, 166)
> So short a space the light of heav'n to view! (*Iliad*, 1, 114)
> Shot thro' the battel in a moment's space (*Iliad*, 11, 50)

Of the total occurrences of *space* in Pope's verse over four-fifths are in his translations of Homer. Only three of the temporal ones are in his non-Homeric work. And, perhaps most important, in well over a third of the lines (28) *space* occurs in last position, as the rhyme word. It seems reasonable to infer that Pope's use of *space* was influenced by his prosodic needs, especially his temporal use of it in his translations of Homer. Still, his use is consistent with that of his age. *Time*, incidentally, occurs 180 times in Pope's poetical corpus, but usually in the sense of occasion rather than duration.

Milton, it might be expected, since *Paradise Lost* deals with the design of the cosmos, had frequent occasion to refer to the vast emptiness around the earth and between the celestial bodies. Indeed he refers, but he does not use the word itself as often as one might suppose. In *Paradise Lost* and *Paradise Regained*, the word occurs thirteen times, eleven in the former.[8] Seven of this total can be considered temporal, though it is sometimes difficult to tell because here, as in everything, Milton continues to be original:

> Nine times the space that measures day and night
> To mortal men, he with his horrid crew
> Lay vanquisht . . . (*P.L.*, I, 50-52)

It is not difficult to find in this quotation an awareness of the relation between space and time which informs our modern conceptions, strangely enough associated with the most medieval of ideas, a monstrous figure symbolizing the embodiment of evil. This citation can be paraphrased thus "nine days he lay vanquished." But this simplification appears to exclude any realization on Milton's part that day and night are separated on the globe by a travelling line of light. One could argue that Milton's circumlocution conceals no awareness of astronomy were it not for a later use which leaves no possible doubt:

> By night he fled, and at midnight returned
> From compassing the earth, cautious of day,
> Since Uriel, regent of the sun, descried
> His entrance, and forewarned the Cherubim
> That kept their watch; thence full of anguish driven,
> The space of seven continued nights he rode
> With darkness, thrice the equinoctial line
> He circled, four times crossed the car of Night
> From pole to pole, traversing each colure;
> On the eighth returned, and on the coast averse
> From entrance or Cherubic watch, by stealth
> Found unsuspected way.

The inter-relation of space and time here is undeniable.

The Bible itself, in its King James version nearly contemporary with Milton, contains numerous temporal uses like "the space of seven sabbaths," "the space of two full years," "about the space of three hours." In this it appears to reflect accurately the usage of its time and a century forward. To go back one more step, we find that in Shakespeare's thirty-two uses of *space*[9] at least thirteen are routinely temporal. In most of these, the simple substitution of the word *time* would modernize the line:

> Stay here in your court for three years' [time] (*LLL*, I. i. 52)
> Within what [time] hop'st though my cure? (*A WW*, II. i. 159)
> From Egypt, 'tis a [time] for farther travel (*A&C*, II. i. 31)
> If you require a little [time] for prayer (*PER*, IV. i. 67)

Chaucer's usage, perhaps the most significant of all because of its location in a developmental stage of the language, is clouded with uncertainty. His fifty recorded uses[10] break down as follows: ten spatial, forty temporal, of which eight are instances of the expression "litel space," eight are such doublets as "time and space," "leisure and space," and two are instances of "furlong way of space" (the time required to ride or walk a furlong). A careful study of Chaucer's relation to *space* shows a decided preference for its temporal senses (duration, opportunity, occasion, interval). *Space* proper in his works has as synonyms most often *place* and rarely *room*. It is not surprising to find that larger quantities of time (months, seasons, years) were perceived as astronomical representations (e.g. "the yonge sonne hath in the Ram his halve course yronne") in that era.

Rather than continue backward any further through the literary monuments of the past in search of the origin of this confusion, it might be preferable to leap directly to the source of our word. The Latin *spatium* ultimately derives from an Indo-European root which means *draw* or *stretch* and which is kin to our *span*. Although its literal meanings all deal with extended objects and concepts of extension, a major division of its figurative senses it concerned with time as interval, period, leisure, opportunity, year, or poetical meter. One example from Caesar's *Gallic War* illustrates the point nicely: "nec fuit spatium tali tempore ad contrahenda castra: ("Nor was there time in such a crisis to reduce the camp").[11] It is striking that Caesar uses *spatium* for *time* and *tempore* for a kind of time or occasion. The confusion between space and time evidently has ancient roots and perhaps the relationship becomes more inevitable the earlier we look.

Apparently it is no solution to the puzzle which this confusion represents to say that *space* in Latin is taken figuratively and applied to *time* (which incidentally also derives from a word meaning "stretch" in Germanic). But Latin *tempus* is never applied to space and the two dozen senses of *time* recorded in the *Oxford English Dictionary* all refer to points or durations of time and never to any extended object or idea of extension. A semantic explanation, which would account for the regularity with which the figurative leap has been made in this particular direction by generations of mankind, is as difficult to provide as any attempt to describe the thought processes of the human brain. To say that it is a metaphor is to assert a perception of resemblance. To say that it is a natural metaphor is to suppose that the resemblance is so powerful that it is repeatedly rediscovered and so becomes part of the language. Such *topoi* as the analogy between human life and a single day or the cycle of the seasons occur without instruction or prompting even to those who are not poets, as do similarities between the state and the family, the ruler and the father, the mind and a machine.

Paradoxically, our experience is much more with time than with the abstract idea of space. But time, however familiar, has always remained incomprehensible, especially when men have reflected on the fate of human beings who seem to decay for no good reason but duration, whose reward for survival is the stigmata of old age. Even more inaccessible has been the notion of time without a beginning, though endless time is, if not conceivable at least acceptable. Abstract space, on the other hand, has an obvious relation to perceptible space, the thing we move around in. Thus until space itself became the awesomely complex entity modern astrophysicists say it is, we felt comfortable enough with it and in it to use it to explain time, which retained its mystery. According to the *Oxford English Dictionary*, this event seems to have happened around the beginning of the last quarter of the nineteenth century. The entry for *space* is divided into two parts, one denoting time, the other area of extension. The latest date of a citation in any of the four temporal senses is 1880 (interval, as in "for a space"). The dozen spatial senses have twelve citations of a later date, of which the last is 1908. It has been suggested that *space* had the general meaning of extent, of either duration or extension, until the seventeenth century; that the new sense (presumably limiting it to extension) developed in the eighteenth century; and that the old meaning still continues.[12] A careful inspection of the OED's citations under *space*, n. shows that the two senses have co-existed from a very early date, as the poetical quotations I have displayed above also indicate. The "new" sense is present in, and contemporary with, Chaucer. That the old meaning has yielded to the new is surely revealed by the lack of temporal citations after 1880. It may be argued that the OED is a nineteenth-century dictionary and that all its citations end around 1880, but it is a fact that the section which includes the word *space* was prepared for publication in December 1913, allowing plenty of time for the accumulation of citations slips bearing dates later than 1880. It is doubtful that many could be found, for this was the moment in history when something happened to time. Between Fizeau's attempt to determine the velocity of light in 1849, Foucault's in 1850, and the Michelson-Morley experiment in 1887, the very nature of time was in question. In some vague sense, time had been shown to be inadequate to reach the limits of space. Space was so vast it was *insensitive to time!*

Though today space cannot be casually understood any longer, in Newton's era a great stability of understanding appeared to have developed concerning the relation between space, time, and force. It was believed that these concepts helped to explain certain beliefs and especially that they supported the possibility of an all-powerful God. The unsatisfactory implications of a mechanical universe were not clear to the general in the time of Pope or Swift, or Voltaire, who appeared to think that a wide popularization of Newton would inevitably forward the social plans of the *philosophes.* Addison's ruminations on this theme set in a proper light the Augustan understanding of Newton and of space:

> Were the Sun, which enlightens this part of the Creation, with all the Host of Planetary Worlds, that move about him, utterly extinguished and annihilated, they would not be miss'd more than a grain of Sand upon the Sea-shore. The Space they possess is so exceedingly little, in Comparison of the whole, that it would scarce make a Blank in the Creation. The Chasm would be imperceptible to an Eye, that could take in the whole Compass of Nature, and pass from one End of the Creation to the other, as it is possible there may be such a Sense in our selves hereafter, or in Creatures which are at present more exalted than our selves. We see many Stars by the help of Glasses, which we do not discover with our naked Eyes; and the finer our Telescopes are, the more still are our Discoveries. *Huygenius* carries this Thought so far, that he does not think it impossible there may be Stars whose Light is not yet travelled down to us, since thier first Creation. There is no Question but the Universe has certain

Bounds set to it; but when we consider that it is the Work of infinite Power, prompted by infinite Goodness, with an infinite Space to exert it self in, how can our Imagination set any Bounds to it?[13]

Addison notes the effect of the velocity of light and admits that space has boundaries but, carried away by the theological implications of his essay, asserts the infinity of space as an aspect of God's infinite power. Newton's absolute space and time (as seen by his contemporaries) have yielded to our relative ideas. Metaphors of absoluteness have given way to relativity and relativism just as absolute correctness and linguistic purism have yielded to context-determined meaning and an alarming permissiveness in expression. These vagaries of space illustrate how the slightest variation from common usage or literal meaning may conceal whole worlds of contending ideas.

Notes

1. *Spectator* No. 93, 1711.

2. Ibid., No. 317, 1712.

3. No. 514, 1712.

4. *Englishman* No. 26, 1713.

5. Ibid.

6. *A Concordance to the Poems of Alexander Pope,* compiled by Emmett G. Bedford and Robert J. Dilligan, 2 vols. (Detroit: Gale Research Co., 1974).

7. Numbers in parentheses refer to volumes in the Twickenham edition. For the *Iliad*, the numbers refer to books and lines, rather than volumes and pages.

8. This information is drawn from the excellent *Concordance to Milton's English Poetry,* edited by William Ingram and Kathleen Swaim (Oxford: Clarendon, 1972).

9. Here I have depended on Marvin Spevack, *The Harvard Concordance to Shakespeare* (Cambridge, Mass.: Harvard University Press, 1973), which is based on his monumental six-volume work.

10. Based on *A Concordance to the Complete Works of Geoffrey Chaucer* by J. S. P. Tatlock and A. G. Kennedy (Gloucester, Mass.: Peter

Smith, 1963), my count excluding 19 occurrences in *Boece* and *Astrolabe* as well as two textual errors.

11. Book VII, Paragraph 40.

12. Ivor Leclerc, "Concepts of Space," above, pp. 209–210.

13. *Spectator* No. 565 (1714).

Berkeley, Newtonian Space, and the Question of Evidence

Richard B. Schwartz

Newton's "scholium on absolute time, space, and motion,"
H. S. Thayer writes, "has occasioned a great wealth of scientific
and philosophic literature, representing a wide range of points
of view and various interests."[1] My interest is neither scientific
nor philosophic but rather literary; I wish to see Berkeley's criticism of Newtonian absolute space within a pattern of thought
which may be used to elucidate certain literary texts. Here I in-
tend to sketch the outlines of the issue, treat the question of
evidence which arises when one attempts to put Berkeley's remarks to other than scientific uses, and hint at the manner in
which one might utilize Berkeley's approach in a literary context.

Berkeley's criticism requires no extensive summary, for he
states and restates his objections consistently and succinctly.
Newton had begun the *Principia* with a series of eight definitions followed by a scholium in which he treated, among other
things, the matter of "absolute space":

> Absolute space, in its own nature, without relation to anything ex-
> ternal, remains always similar and immovable. Relative space is some
> movable dimension or measure of the absolute spaces; which our senses

determine by its position to bodies; and which is commonly taken for immovable space; such is the dimension of a subterraneous, an aerial, or celestial space, determined by its position in respect of the earth. Absolute and relative space are the same in figure and magnitude; but they do not remain always numerically the same. For if the earth, for instance, moves, a space of our air, which relatively and in respect of the earth remains always the same, will at one time be one part of the absolute space into which the air passes; at another time it will be another part of the same, and so, absolutely understood, it will be continually changed.

But because the parts of [absolute] space cannot be seen, or distinguished from one another by our senses, therefore in their stead we use sensible measures of them. . . . And so, instead of absolute places and motions, we use relative ones; and that without any inconvenience in common affairs; but in philosophical disquisitions, we ought to abstract from our senses, and consider things themselves, distinct from what are only sensible measures of them.

It is indeed a matter of great difficulty to discover, and effectually to distinguish, the true notions of particular bodies from the apparent; because the parts of that immovable space, in which those motions are performed, do by no means come under the observation of our senses.[2]

The length of Newton's discussion, from which I have taken brief excerpts, contrasts sharply with Berkeley's curt replies:

And so let us suppose that all bodies were destroyed and brought to nothing. What is left they call absolute space, all relation arising from the situation and distances of bodies being removed together with the bodies. Again, that space is infinite, immoveable, indivisible, insensible, without relation and without distinction. That is, all its attributes are privative or negative. It seems therefore to be mere nothing. (*De Motu*, IV, 45)[3]

And perhaps, if we inquire narrowly, we shall find we cannot even frame an idea of *pure space*, exclusive of all body. This I must confess seems impossible, as being a most abstract idea. (*Principles of Human Knowledge*, II, 93)

Concerning absolute space, that phantom of the mechanic and geometrical philosophers. . . , it may suffice to observe that it is neither perceived by any sense, nor proved by any reason. . . . (*Siris*, V, 127)

In short, "absolute space" is an abstraction. Because Berkeley considers the process of "abstraction" impossible, "absolute space" is best, though clumsily, described as "nothing."

Cajori claims that Berkeley's objections are based on religious fears.[4] Because Berkeley's overriding concern is always religious, the judgment has some validity. Berkeley is troubled by the application of epithets reserved for divinity (infinite, immovable, indivisible) to something inconceivable, but his religious objections are also presented in more general terms. In *The Analyst*, for example, he deplores the fact that science, especially mathematics, is leading to infidelity. In offering a "real" alternative to evanescent faith, the scientist overlooks the fact that the nature of his inquiry is really no more rigorous than the theologian's and the demands which he places on his student's faith are no less great: "He who can digest a second or third fluxion, a second or third difference, need not, methinks, be squeamish about any point in divinity" (IV, 68). The work concludes with a series of queries designed to challenge the haughty scientist. Query 8 is as follows:

> Whether the notions of absolute time, absolute place, and absolute motion be not most abstractedly metaphysical? Whether it be possible for us to measure, compute, or know them? (IV, 96)

The importance of this response to Newton for Berkeley's general philosophic posture has not been overlooked. Colin M. Turbayne comments that "as a philosopher, Berkeley's enduring merit lies in his profound and incisive analysis of the errors present in the basis of the Newtonian world view."[5] Turbayne isolates four errors in particular. Many scientists and their philosophic fellow travelers: (1) mistake abstractions [such as "absolute space"] for realities; (2) regard daily things as unreal, unperceived things as real; (3) attribute active power to bodies; and (4) attribute physical characteristics to mind.[6] In his criticism of, among other things, Newtonian absolute space, Berkeley is often seen as a vindicated precursor of Mach and Einstein[7] and is commonly recognized as a figure of immense influence on Whitehead.[8] S. P. Rosenbaum's judgment that "it is difficult to overestimate the influence of Whitehead's theory on English literary studies"[9] brings us, if only temporarily, to our subject.

It is commonly argued that among the eighteenth-century philosophers Berkeley offers the position most genial to poets and poetry. His focus on valuation, his study of the subjective nature of perception, his interests in language and vision, and his refusal to divorce man's mind from man's physical world have been noted again and again, with good reason. However, Berkeley's comments on Newtonian absolute space are relatively conventional. They are based, to an important extent, on standard scientific ideology and point up divisions within Newton's own methodology. In a sense Berkeley is reminding Newton rather than attacking him.

Basically, Newton's mathematical procedures had brought about a clash with his empirical ones. The use of such notions as "absolute space" conflicts, in ways which Berkeley perceived, with Newton's usual methodological stance, the position essentially the same as that of the Royal Society and its ideologists, a position which (with proper stresses) Berkeley shares. The problem is intensified by the fact that Newton's methodological pronouncements are neither as frequent nor as clear as one might wish and by the fact that some later "Newtonians" tended to follow Newton in those areas where he is most vulnerable to criticism.

The most frequently quoted statement of Newton's position is to be found at the conclusion of the *Opticks*:

> As in Mathematicks, so in Natural Philosophy, the Investigation of difficult Things by the Method of Analysis, ought ever to precede the Method of Composition. This Analysis consists in making Experiments and Observations, and in drawing general Conclusions from them by Induction, and admitting of no Objections against the Conclusions, but such as are taken from Experiments, or other certain Truths. For Hypotheses are not to be regarded in experimental Philosophy. And although the arguing from Experiments and Observations by Induction be no Demonstration of general Conclusions; yet it is the best way of arguing which the Nature of Things admits of, and may be looked upon as so much the stronger, by how much the Induction is more general. And if no Exception occur from Phaenomena, the Conclusion may be pronounced generally. But if at any time afterwards any Exception shall occur from Experiments, it may then begin to be pronounced with such Exceptions as occur.[10]

This formulation is complicated by the fact that the procedure of mathematics is compared with that of empirical science; in

Newtonian practice the two are often joined. Basically Newton presents the Royal Society methodology, what Popkin and others have termed "constructive skepticism," the movement from data to principles (formulated in mathematical terms if at all possible) followed by the testing of the principles by further experiment and observation, a method by which one attains a descriptive rather than an explanatory account of nature, an account always open to revision and valued in proportion to its usefulness. No explanations of ultimate causes are claimed; a course is steered between uncritical dogmatism and radical skepticism.[11]

In this connection, Karl Popper comments that

> The great historical importance of Berkeley lies . . . in his protest against essentialist explanations in science. Newton himself did not interpret his theory in an essentialist sense. . . . But soon after him the essentialist interpretation of his theory became the ruling one. . . . Essentialism . . . implies the idea of an *ultimate* explanation. . . . Yet we know, at least since Einstein, that explanation may be pushed, unexpectedly, further and further.[12]

In his celebrated study of Newton's methodology, Professor Randall notes that Newton sought a system of mathematical laws which could be experimentally verified, but a system which did not pretend to reveal the physical or mechanical *cause* of those laws. Such an explanation, in the eyes of the Royal Society, is simply beyond human capability. However, while Newton fully admits that he has found only the law, not the cause of gravitation, he thought that he did know the cause of the laws of motion, namely the force of inertia.[13] A further methodological split bears on the first. His practice collides with his theory over the issue of his "absolutes" and his use of mathematics, his mathematics pushing him beyond that which may be experienced. Here is Randall:

> Newton's real world is therefore made up of absolute masses endowed with an absolute force of inertia, and perhaps with a force of 'gravitation,' in absolute motion in absolute space and time; while sense experience supplies no evidence for any of these concepts.
> Newton's procedure implied that the concern of science was with mathematical relations in the experienced world. Yet his empirical logic drove him to assume that the terms of those relations are not in

the experienced world at all, and yet are the only reality. The absolute masses of classical mechanics, instead of being taken as mathematical abstractions or isolates, were regarded as the sole components of Nature. Here is the cardinal illustration of what Whitehead has called the 'fallacy of misplaced concreteness.'[14]

Hence Berkeley's criticism. The problem is exacerbated, the misplaced concreteness reinforced, by the fact that so many of Newton's marmoreal statements are mathematical ones. L. L. Laudan comments that the *"Principia* seemed to have established, almost overnight, new standards for rigour of thought, clarity of intuition, economy of expression and, *above all*, the certainty of its conclusions."[15] Here we must resist the enthusiasm of Newton's followers and remind ourselves of Voltaire's definition of Newtonian fluxions, "the art of exactly numbering and measuring that of which we cannot even conceive the existence,"[16] and Einstein's judgment that "as far as the propositions of mathematics refer to reality they are not certain, and in so far as they are certain they do not refer to reality."[17]

In a sense this Newtonian waywardness represents a departure from the important Baconian principle of utility, for Newton has valued the inconceivable at the expense of the here and now and seemingly opted for an unattainable "certainty" in lieu of a description which could prove to be of heuristic value. Berkeley, on the other hand, stresses the notion of utility. He is highly critical of the mechanical, materialist paradigms that dominate science but he welcomes the fruits of such science. As he admits of only spiritual causation he denies the ability of the mechanists to attain knowledge of ultimate physical causes. He wars with some scientists over the theoretical underpinnings of their work but welcomes the work (properly understood) and its results. Scientific accounts, for Berkeley, are best described by Plato's *Timaeus:*

> You must be satisfied if our account is as likely as any, remembering that both I and you who are sitting in judgment on it are merely human, and should not look for anything more than a likely story in such matters.[18]

The "likely story" is all that the Royal Society promised. Scientific "explanations" are, at best, analogies of actual processes. D'Alembert's formulation summarizes the matter nicely:

> Doomed as we are to be ignorant of the essence and inner contexture of bodies, the only resource remaining for our sagacity is to try at least to grasp the analogy of phenomena, and to reduce them all to a small number of primitive and fundamental facts.[19]

Hume writes that "all our reasonings concerning matter of fact are founded on a species of *analogy*"[20]; Kant comments that we study things "according to the analogies of experience which determine in general all real combinations in experience."[21] Berkeley's limited expectations are conservative in that they are rooted in seventeenth-century ideology; they are forward-looking in that they reveal an English skepticism, wary of the search for certitude and trust in mathematics commonly associated with Descartes and Galileo in the seventeenth century and now, in the eighteenth, with Newton, their great English successor.[22]

We may now introduce the evidential problem which arises when one attempts to apply Berkeley's thought to eighteenth-century literary texts. In recent decades approaches to Berkeley have changed significantly. Here is Donald Davie, writing in 1955:

> Berkeley ... until twenty or thirty years ago, was regarded as a proto-Romantic philosopher, one of the fathers of subjective idealism. ... Yeats became interested in him at just about the time when Berkeleyans began to challenge this reading of him, and to take seriously his own claims to be a philosopher of common sense.[23]

Rhetorically as well as philosophically, Berkeley's pose is often that of crisp, clear, good sense. It is his opponents who indulge in fanciful notions concerning such matters as "primary qualities," "absolute space," and "abstraction." His good sense has not, however, always been apparent. He is a thinker who tends to be vindicated rather than immediately understood. As such, for the philosophers, his reputation has risen as Locke's has waned. Not so with teachers of literature, for while Berkeley may be most useful in a theoretical context, Locke's historical impact is far more easily demonstrated. We find Locke everywhere. To detect demonstrable Berkeleian influence, as, for example, Donald Greene has in his important article on Christopher Smart, is a real accomplishment.[24] There is good reason for this. Harry Bracken has shown the manner in which Berkeley's thought was twisted, misunderstood, and exaggerated: "Berkeley was maligned and his views distorted not in philosophical refutation, but in exceptionally partisan intellectual warfare. Aligned with no side, he was attacked by all sides."[25] Like Hume after him, he was forced to rewrite his work in simpler, more digestible form, and still remained misunderstood. The situation is perceived as so extreme that one must now have it demonstrated that Hume himself even read Berkeley.[26]

At least three problems present themselves. First, there is the question of actual historical impact: can we use Berkeley to discuss works by writers who clearly misunderstood him? Second, there is the unique source question: can we talk about Berkeley's influence or usefulness when a certain Berkeleian principle is available elsewhere, for example, in Bayle's challenge to the primary/secondary quality distinction which anticipates Berkeley's?[27] (If we see these problems in tandem, the second largely disappears. Those who misunderstand Berkeley's thought will probably not do well with, for example, Bayle; and those who are aware of, for example, Bayle's anticipation of Berkeley probably understand Berkeley, at least to some extent.) The third problem is most intriguing, namely, the question of whether we should even concern ourselves with the historical context. If Berkeley represents a point of view which has always, to some extent, been germane to the interests and activities of literary figures, then we should be able to apply his thought, provided that we are wary of making claims concerning historical impact. Put another way, the question of later vindication and ensuing use of a figure's thought does not necessarily smack of Whig history, i.e., if Berkeley (or Hume or Kant) have described intellectual processes accurately, we should be able to apply their thought to earlier literature (or to the works of contemporaries who misunderstood them) without being accused of falsification.

All literary history slants; the question is one of extent.

"Slanting" really means egregious slanting; and when we operate in an area that is essentially gray, as we usually do, we must be wary of approaches which either cast aside all rules or follow them without deviation. For example, those who consistently demand evidence of impact or influence frequently err by exaggerating the importance of influence when it is demonstrable. They assume that a text is best approached in the framework of contemporary theoretical commentary and are suspicious of those who seem to be playing fast and loose with such evidence. They guard us against truly absurd approaches ("A writer in 1773 could not have seen things in that way") and aid us in understanding works of secondary quality ("It is Thomson who chiefly influenced these figures; their work is best read in terms of his") but their approach may reduce the range of the important work by the important writer to the conventional presuppositions of unimportant writers or it may canalize our response to the significant work by limiting us to the approach of only one or two contemporary theorists.

The rigorous literary historian is properly cautious in these matters. Those who would use one writer's theories to elucidate another's practices without adducing evidence of actual influence may be straying toward *zeitgeist* or osmosis arguments, a problem which seems particularly acute in the case of Berkeley, for the period which produces the most dazzling triumphs of British philosophy simultaneously produces a large number of writers (many of them formidable ones) unable to appreciate that philosophy. The demonstration of connections seems more difficult than the demonstration of disjunction.

These questions can hardly be answered in detail, but I can outline my response. The notion that important writers transcend historical parameters is a truism more easily accepted than applied. It is, however, regularly applied. Just as important writers outstrip contemporary thought, they anticipate later thought; the application of later thought to earlier works may be objected to in individual cases, but very few would rule it out on principle. The dangers to be avoided are fuzziness on the one hand and narrow rigorism on the other. In the case of Berkeley, it seems to me, one has the benefit of both historical vindication (to an extent Berkeley does describe actual processes) and contemporary analogues (what he says corresponds to what others—both scientists and epistemologists—are saying). Moreover, when one wishes to use him as I do, there is a further analogue, later literary theory. Essentially my response in the case of Berkeley is that writers may operate like Leibnizian monads, independently of one another but in parallel; and though the practitioner may misunderstand the theorist, the theory may still be used to elucidate the practice.

The example I would offer is that of Boswell, not to show Berkeleian influence but rather the usefulness of Berkeley's orientation as a gloss on Boswell's practice. I share Ian Watt's judgment that we most admire those eighteenth-century works "which are closest to being direct records of the life and attitudes of the period. . . ."[28] One of the finest of those works is Boswell's *Life*, but a work which has posed problems generated by Boswell's hesitation to formulate a systematic theory of biography. Approaching the work through the context of eighteenth-century theory does not get us very far. Even Johnson's comments, which constitute a kind of fulcrum in the history of biographical theory,[29] do little to elucidate Boswell's—and indeed Johnson's own—biographical practice. A far more useful approach is the application of the modern distinction between the "definitive" biography, whose virtues are precision, completeness, and authenticity, and the "artistic" biography which seeks to portray the biographee in terms of a unified image, the type of work in which the shaping of facts is of far greater importance than the accumulation of them.

Curiously, most of the recent studies of Boswell have focused on his shaping, while nearly all of his own praise of his work concerns his diligence, authenticity, and hard facts. In a sense he mimics the "Newtonian" desire for rigor and completeness. Here I would introduce Berkeley and argue that the writing of a "definitive" biography is as vain a hope as the desire for "certitude," "completeness," and "essential" explanations which Berkeley criticizes in contemporary science. In the case of life writing, only the autobiographer—as Johnson points out—knows the facts; and few of us are as sanguine as Johnson concerning the extent to which those facts will be manipulated. Moreover, the separation of facts from the shaping of them involves a false dichotomy. Irreducible facts are ultimately trivial. In the moment at which one puts pen to paper, one is already at an advanced stage of the shaping process. There is no real distinction to be made between "objective" facts and "subjective" perceivers, between reality and dreams (especially in the case of a figure like Boswell), between "real" life and art, for we reify dreams (as Berkeley and Blake encourage us to do) and shape reality (as Hume shows we must). If dreams are of value, they are real (in the sense that students and soldiers speak of a better world as the real one) to us. The accomplished life-writer must deal with both fact and form, and his primary task is to so shape his material as to provide his readers with an image of the biographee, an "image" in the form of a book, a book that can be read in a limited space of time, a book whose relation to the life of its subject is at best analogical. All that we may require of the biographer, as of the Berkeleian scientist, is a descriptive account—a likely story—rather than an essential explanation or a marshalling of *all* the data of the biographee's life. The image of the biographee in the mind of the biographer must affect the selection and use of his material. It is the basis of the shaping process and should, to a considerable extent, correspond with or epitomize the multiple dimensions of the biographee which are accessible through the totality of the material. Here, it seems to me, is a useful entrée into the *Life*. The degree of Boswell's success in the *Life* is not my concern here, but I would say that his success in this regard is not as great as the book's reputation would suggest.

Berkeleian science also provides a means of approaching one aspect of eighteenth-century literature which is particularly difficult to describe. Eighteenth-century artists often achieve striking effects by establishing a line of separation between art and life and then traversing that line—in dizzying fashion—with great subtlety and finesse. Here Fielding, Sterne, and Hogarth are particularly adept, and their locale is often the stage; for the eighteenth-century stage often epitomizes the process: peopled by personages in a play who are real people playing artificial characters with tag names who yet represent "real" human beings whose lives are so artifical as to justify caricature.

The process is one of rapid interaction and alternation and finds its analogue in eighteenth-century scientific ideology where one establishes (or should establish) a relationship of successive alternations. Data are taken; principles are shaped; principles are tested by new data; new principles are shaped, etc. In epistemology, an interaction occurs as well. With Berkeley the valuation of the external is intimately bound up with perceiving spirit; with Hume all decisions (based on judgments of causal relationships) are determined by the shape of the individual perceiver's experiences. Finally, with Kant, we see that "nature" depends on human "categories." Human equipment assimilates nature through the categories. We do not perceive or explain ultimates. "We have always to deal with our representations only; how things may be by themselves (without reference to the representations by which they affect us) is completely beyond the sphere of our knowledge."[30] Both in the scientific and in the epistemological context, the focus is on ordered shaping and on a continual interaction of perceiver (or experimenter) and subject. This holds true for the writer as well. Using the example of Boswell, this pattern could be applied to individual scenes while the "image making" pattern concerns the larger architectonics of the book. In Boswell's case, we find a continual mingling of perceiver and subject, of art and life; and Boswell's successes here are considerable. They are not, however, consistent; for all too often Boswell's point of view is grafted on to Johnson. In the art/life process of interaction, our norm concerns the extent to which the writer is in constant control of the procedure. Does he perceive the proper similarities and differences between life and art? Is his manipulation of them purposive and conscious? If he confuses them his skill is questioned, his usefulness minimized.

In the *London Journal*, for example, Boswell's construction and manipulation of his roles and guises and his retrospective choreographing of events is masterful. In a sense we learn far more about Boswell in this, the most successful section of his journal, because of the way he manipulates rather than reports "reality," for the manipulated London, the long-passed world of Mr. Spectator and Macheath is *Boswell's* London. It is not, however, Johnson's, and when we move from the journal to the *Life* (or, sometimes, to Johnson within the journal), we find that confusions concerning setting are a prime source of falsification. To give but a single example, Boswell's exaggerated and romanticized accounts of Johnson's rooms are largely useless as an index to Johnson's life; here John Wain is far better. As an index to Boswell's life and values, they are most useful, but the unconscious substitution of autobiography for biography signals a lack of control.

Boswell's philosophic affection is often reserved for minor figures such as Thomas Reid, and this affection is demonstrable. I would argue, however, that it is Berkeley (and for that matter, Hume) who provide the most useful analogies for discussing his work, partly because their "common sense" often exceeds that of the philosophers to whose names the "common sense" label is usually affixed.

Notes

1. Thayer, ed., *Newton's Philosophy of Nature* (New York: Hafner, 1953), p. 183.

2. Florian Cajori, ed., *Sir Isaac Newton's Mathematical Principles of Natural Philosophy and His System of the World* (Berkeley: University of California Press, 1960), pp. 6, 8, 12.

3. All references to Berkeley's works are to the edition by A. A. Luce and T. E. Jessop, 9 vols., (Edinburgh, 1949–1957), with title, volume, and page numbers.

4. Cajori, p. 641. On this, see also F. E. L. Priestley, "Newton and the Romantic Concept of Nature," *University of Toronto Quarterly*, 17 (1948), 331–332.

5. Berkeley, *A Treatise Concerning the Principles of Human Knowledge*, ed., Colin M. Turbayne (Indianapolis: Bobbs-Merrill, 1957), p. xiii.

6. Turbayne, pp. xiv–xvi.

7. See, for example, Karl Popper, "A Note on Berkeley as Precursor of Mach and Einstein," in C. B. Martin and D. M. Armstrong, eds., *Locke and Berkeley: A Collection of Critical Essays* (Garden City: Doubleday, 1968), pp. 436–449 (first published in 1953; variously reprinted). For another point of view, see W. A. Suchting, "Berkeley's Criticism of Newton on Space and Motion," *Isis*, 58(1967), 186–197.

8. See, for example, Turbayne, p. xxi; John Herman Randall, Jr., "Newton's Natural Philosophy: Its Problems and Consequences," in F. P. Clarke and M. C. Nahm, eds., *Philosophical Essays in honor of Edgar Arthur Singer, Jr.* (Philadelphia: University of Pennsylvania Press, 1942), pp. 353–354; S. P. Rosenbaum, ed., *English Literature and British Philosophy* (Chicago: University of Chicago Press, 1971), pp. 5–8.

9. Rosenbaum, p. 6.

10. Newton, *Opticks: or a Treatise of the Reflections, Refractions, Inflections & Colours of Light* (New York: Dover, 1952), p. 404 (based on 4th edition, London 1730).

11. Among the many studies of these issues, one of the most useful is Henry G. Van Leeuwen, *The Problem of Certainty in English Thought, 1630–1690* (The Hague: Nijhoff, 1963).

12. Popper, p. 447.

13. Randall, pp. 340–344 and passim.

14. Randall, pp. 350, 353–354.

15. Laudan, "Thomas Reid and the Newtonian Turn of British Methodological Thought," in Robert E. Butts and John W. Davis, eds., *The Methodological Heritage of Newton* (Toronto: University of Toronto Press, 1970), p. 103.

16. *Philosophical Letters*, trans. Ernest Dilworth (Indianapolis: Bobbs-Merrill, 1961), p. 79.

17. Quoted by I. Bernard Cohen, *Franklin and Newton* (Cambridge, Mass.: Harvard University Press, 1966), pp. 3–4.

18. Plato, *Timaeus and Critias*, trans. H. D. P. Lee (Harmondsworth: Penguin, 1971), p. 41.

19. Quoted by Henry Guerlac, "Where the Statue Stood: Divergent Loyalties to Newton in the Eighteenth Century," in Earl R. Wasserman, ed., *Aspects of the Eighteenth Century* (Baltimore: The Johns Hopkins University Press, 1965), p. 330.

20. *An Inquiry Concerning Human Understanding*, ed., Charles W. Hendel (New York: Liberal Arts Press, 1955), p. 112.

21. *Critique of Pure Reason*, trans. Max Müller (Garden City: Doubleday, 1966), pp. 174–175.

22. See Bruce Sheldon Silver, "The Status of the Sciences in the Philosophy of George Berkeley," Dissertation, University of Colorado, 1971, passim.

23. Davie, "Yeats, Berkeley, and Romanticism," in *English Literature and British Philosophy*, pp. 278–279.

24. Greene, "Smart, Berkeley, the Scientists and the Poets," *Journal of the History of Ideas*, 14(1953), 327–352. Berkeley's impact on Romantic writers is far more easily demonstrated. For a pertinent comment, see Leonard N. Trawick, ed., *Backgrounds of Romanticism: English Philosophical Prose of the Eighteenth Century* (Bloomington: Indiana University Press, 1967), pp. 19–20.

25. Bracken, *The Early Reception of Berkeley's Immaterialism, 1710–1733* (The Hague: Nijhoff, 1959), p. 6.

26. See Michael Morrisroe, "Did Hume Read Berkeley? A Conclusive Answer," *Philological Quarterly*, 52(1973), 310–315. (He did.)

27. See, for example, Bayle, *Historical and Critical Dictionary: Selections*, ed., Richard H. Popkin (Indianapolis: Bobbs-Merrill, 1965), p. 197 (s.v. Pyrrho), p. 359 (s.v. Zeno of Elea).

28. Watt, "Two Historical Aspects of the Augustan Tradition," in R. F. Brissenden, ed., *Studies in the Eighteenth Century: Papers presented at the David Nichol Smith Memorial Seminar, Canberra 1966* (Canberra: Australian National University Press, 1968), p. 84.

29. In the sense that he consolidates previously existing views and is later used as preeminent theoretical authority.

30. *Critique of Pure Reason*, p. 155.

Emma: *Dancing Without Space to Turn In*

Raymond F. Hilliard

Readers of *Emma* are particularly fond of that moment at the end of Chapter II, Volume III, when Mr. Knightley finally invites the heroine to dance. The occasion is the long-delayed ball at the Crown Inn, and the pairing of Emma and the hero foreshadows their union at the end of the story. The ball becomes possible only after its planners have overcome considerable impediments of space and time; and just as the dancing of Emma and Mr. Knightley prefigures their marriage, so the discussions, preparations, and uncertainties which precede the ball point to the novel's concern with various forms of "confinement."

The idea of dancing is introduced by Frank Churchill, whose first questions upon first visiting Highbury are whether it has a "large neighbourhood," whether it "afforded society enough," and whether there are ever any balls (191).[1] He receives what should be disheartening answers when Mrs. Weston and Emma give him the history of a large room that had been added to the Crown. The inn itself is "an inconsiderable house, though the principal one of the sort" in Highbury, and the large room "had been built many years ago for a ballroom, and while the neigh-

275

bourhood had been in a particularly populous, dancing state . . . but such brilliant days had long passed away" (197). Time has witnessed a decline in the population and vitality of the village, and the space that was once needed for what the narrator calls "the felicities of rapid motion" (247) is now given over to the sedentary occupations of a whist club. The young people of Highbury have "few opportunities of dancing" (262). Far from discouraged, however, Frank chides Emma for not having "revived the former good old days of the room," and even when she points out the "want of proper families" in Highbury, and tells him of her "conviction that none beyond the place or its immediate environs could be tempted to attend" a ball, he is not satisfied. Still "very much bent on dancing" (198), he alarms the rank-conscious heroine by suggesting that people from every sphere of Highbury society might be invited to a ball, and she quite rightly attributes to "an effusion of lively spirits" his "indifference to a confusion of rank."

Sometime later it is Frank who proposes the ball that actually does take place. The initial plan is to have it in the larger parlor at Randalls and to invite five couples, but when Frank and Emma set about "pacing out the room . . . to see what it could be made to hold," "portioning out the indispensable division of space to every couple" (248), they begin to doubt that the room can accommodate so many people. The problem is complicated when the organizers decide that at least ten couples must be invited, and after Mr. Woodhouse scotches Frank's suggestion that both Randalls parlors be used, "the space which a quarter of an hour before had been deemed barely sufficient for five couples was now endeavoured to be made out quite enough for ten" (249). Emma, protesting that there will be "a sad crowd," asks "what could be worse than dancing without space to turn in" (249). But Frank goes on measuring with what seems "unreasonable" persistence.

The following day he returns to Emma with still another plan to solve the space problem, one that will make the ball a more public affair and require "a larger council" of Highbury folk to organize it. This new plan is to hold the ball in the old dancing room at the Crown, but even there space is a problem. The room is not large enough for both dancing and dining, and the only other room in the inn which might be used for supper is separated from it by a long, draughty passage. When it is finally agreed that the passage is not so forbidding, Frank's plan seems feasible. Emma is delighted at "the prospect of the ball" (257), and Jane Fairfax unusually "animated—open-hearted" (258). Yet time proves to be an even more insurmountable obstacle to the would-be dancers. Frank had written "to Enscombe to propose staying beyond his fortnight," but when Mrs. Churchill characteristically withdraws her permission soon after granting it, Emma is left to lament "the loss of the ball" and "the loss of the young man" (259). She foresees a great "loss to their society from his absence," for "his being at Randalls had given great spirit to the last two weeks—indescribable spirit" (262). The same loss leaves Jane "particularly unwell" (263), and because the ball is postponed, many weeks stand "between the young people of Highbury and happiness" (318).

Though generally neglected by Austen's critics,[2] the episode I have summarized is central and paradigmatic, for it mirrors in detail the "situation" of the characters in *Emma* and their typical responses to it: in the world of this novel, human vitality is threatened with confinement and extinction. Dancing is a symbol of that vitality, "playfulness" its most conspicuous form of expression.[3] The pervasive spatial metaphors in the novel point to its underlying concern with those characters—Emma, Jane Fairfax, and even Frank Churchill—whose given social situations do not allow them an adequate outlet for their abundant mental energies. The word "mental" is particularly appropriate to a description of the characters in a novel which is commonly said to have a meager plot, for Austen's predominant verbs describe the characters as "thinking," "wishing," "suspecting," "imagining," "guessing," and so on. As in the ball episode, such activity often betrays an effort of the mind to overcome the restraints placed upon it by space and time, or, to be more precise, by social "conditions" which, in the world of *Emma*, determine a person's sense of space and time. In other words, the subject of the novel is the behavior of the mind—that is, of "life" or "spirit" for Jane Austen—in reaction to confinement.[4]

I

For all the characters, Highbury society is the principal field of action. Although much has been written about the "idyllic" quality of Austen's representation of village life in *Emma*, and about the heroine's sins against the social order, virtually none of the novelist's critics has drawn sufficient attention to the negative side of life in the "confined society in Surrey" (145).[5] As the history of the Crown Inn suggests, the village is no place for the young, the vigorous, and the intellectually gifted, or, as we shall see, at least not for those whose social situations demand only a portion of their energies. Not only is there a want of properly genteel families, and not only can outsiders (dancers, at any rate) not be tempted to visit Highbury, but an Emma Woodhouse can find in the usual "conversation" of most of its inhabitants only "dull repetitions, old news, and heavy jokes" (219). "Not in the habit of judging," the village takes the fatuous Mr. Elton for its "standard of perfection . . . both in person and mind" (174), and believes that his wife "must be as clever and agreeable as she professed herself" (281). For Jane Fairfax, visiting Highbury means living with Miss Bates, who, whatever her virtues, is the tiresome purveyor of Highbury's foolish opinions. Emma's sense of confinement in the village— and the habitual need of her mind for an object to which its full attention can be directed—is suggested by one of Austen's few detailed descriptions of physical space in the novel. Growing impatient with Harriet Smith's dawdling over muslins at Ford's, the heroine

> went to the door for amusement.—Much could not be hoped from the traffic of even the busiest part of Highbury;—Mr. Perry walking hastily by, Mr. William Cox letting himself in at the office-door, Mr. Cole's carriage horses returning from exercise, or a stray letter-boy on an obstinate mule, were the liveliest objects she could presume to expect; and when her eyes fell on the butcher with his tray, a tidy old woman

travelling homewards from shop with a full basket, two curs quarelling over a dirty bone, and a string of dawdling children round the baker's little bow-window eyeing the ginger bread, she knew she had no reason to complain, and was amused enough; quite enough still to stand at the door. A mind lively and at ease, can do with seeing nothing, and can see nothing that does not answer. (233)

The ambiguousness of this passage is typical of the novel in that it forces us to judge the heroine's excesses in relation to the very real limitations of the Highbury community. Emma's friendship with Harriet is confining, but it had begun at a time when Highbury society afforded her no intellectual equals.

Writing of the enjoyment people find in looking backward and forward in time, Gibbon observes that "Our imagination is always active to enlarge the narrow circle in which nature has confined us."[6] In *Emma*, just as the planners of the ball find themselves "hoping in uncertainty," and just as Emma, in looking out the door of Ford's, "hoped" and "expected" to find amusement, so several of the characters in the novel spend much of their time thinking of the future, as if the present moment, with its dull repetitions, were not enough to occupy their minds. If the usual activities in the world of the novel are mental in nature, they also typically involve the characters in "looking forward"—in "hoping," "expecting," "foretelling," "foreseeing," and "speculating." Full of "curiosity," the characters are as preoccupied with other people's "prospects" as with their own. Highbury as a whole feels a great "curiosity" (270) over Mrs. Elton before she first arrives, and an equally "lively curiosity" (17) to meet Frank Churchill: "Cannot you imagine," Emma asks Knightley, "what a *sensation* his coming will produce?" (149). The villagers thirst continually for an "importation of novelties" to "enrich their intellectual stores" (352). If Frank "looked forward with the hope of coming to Randalls" (he has his secret reasons), Emma lives for a time on "the amusement afforded her mind by the expectation of" (124) meeting him. The very day of his first coming to Highbury, Emma, in "mental soliloquy" (189) at Hartfield, imagines in detail his arrival at Randalls "four hours hence" (190). Her mind continually seeks such extension.

II

In their actual or prospective social roles, neither Churchill nor Emma nor Jane Fairfax has sufficient space to turn in. Like the heroine, Churchill is kept at home by a possessive hypochondriac.[7] He "cannot command his own time" (119), and feeling "thwarted in everything material" (365), which for him means being able to marry Jane, he itches frequently to "go abroad" (364). Although Emma is playfully disingenuous in urging Mr. Knightley to make allowances for Frank's behavior to the Westons ("It is unfair to judge of any body's conduct, without an intimate knowledge of their situation"), neither she nor Knightley is aware of the difficulty in the young man's "real situation" (427): while Mrs. Churchill lives, he does "not have a hope, a chance, a possibility of" (398) marrying a Jane Fairfax. As for Emma, it is no mere coincidence that she is the only Austen heroine who does not travel away from home in the course of her story. She has never seen the sea (a symbol of vitality here, as in *Persuasion*), never visited Bath, and never been to Box Hill, which is only seven miles from Hartfield. The beginning of the novel finds her "living alone with her father," who can occupy only "half her attention" (177). Without her former governess, her "situation" (15) means "privations" (18); she has no object for her "energy, and spirits" (18), and "since Mrs. Weston's marriage her exercise had been too much confined" (26). While her father lives, she cannot allow her conscious mind to consider seriously a "change of condition" (448) through marriage.[8] Similarly, Jane Fairfax is leading a life of "privation and penance" (217) at the Bateses'. Her "wearied spirits" are the result of "prospects" which are "closing" (389), for she thinks herself destined to a demeaning situation in the governess-trade.

In other words, an individual's sense of confinement depends as much on the scope of his particular "situation" as on the intellectual limitations of his neighbors. To Emma, Highbury may seem stultifying and moribund, yet to Frank, who comes from Enscombe (the name suggests the word "entomb," and the mistress of the house does indeed die), it holds out the promise of release, of personal extension through the "playing" (as false suitor to Emma) or filling (as true suitor to Jane) of spacious social roles in relation to people as young and talented as he. According to the attitude they take to their social situations, the characters can be divided into three groups: those who withdraw from life by contracting the social space they have to turn in, and who thus find Highbury too large; those whose situations are demanding enough to absorb their energies; and those who feel a need to enlarge the scope of their social roles. This last group includes both people who earn enhanced social status through what the novel sees as valid kinds of self-"improvement," and people who seek self-extension in roles to which they have no true commitment.

To varying degrees, Mr. John Knightley, Mr. Woodhouse, and Mrs. Churchill try to limit their own social activities and those of others. All three seek physical confinement, and all pay a price for their withdrawal from social life in imperfect physical or mental health. Mrs. Churchill's is the most extreme case. She spends her life "stationary" (307) on a sofa at Enscombe, "a retired place" (307) where the Churchills' "visitings were among a range of great families, none very near; and . . . even when days were fixed, and invitations accepted, there was an even chance that Mrs. Churchill were not in health and spirits for going; . . . they made a point of inviting no fresh person; and . . . though Frank had his separate engagements, it was not without difficulty . . . that he could get away, or introduce an acquaintance for the night" (221). More than a stroke of good luck which "opened" to Frank "the happiest prospects" (440), Mrs. Churchill's death is thematically apt, for it points up the danger in such confinement.

Although Mr. John Knightley and Mr. Woodhouse are treated more gently, both are neurotically ill-tempered. The first limits his extra-domestic social intercourse to his work as a lawyer ("Business, you know, may bring money, but friendship never does"). He urges Jane Fairfax to wait for mail at the Bateses' rather than venture as "far" (293) as the post office, and complains unjustly that Emma is too "engaged with company" in what he sees as an "increasing" (312) neighborhood. While Jane's trips to the post office bring her the promise of an end to concealment and thus "a glow of both complexion and spirits," his deliberate withdrawal from society results in irritable and even sadistic outbursts (93). Emma is quite wrong in telling Harriet that it is a narrow income which contracts a person's mind and sours his temper; yet even though she does not have her father or brother-in-law in mind, she is right in saying that people who live "in a very small and generally very inferior society, may well be illiberal and cross" (85). In a novel that concerns itself with "suitable" marriages, Isabella Knightley is no "match" for her husband.

Like his son-in-law, Mr. Woodhouse deliberately confines himself to a small, inferior society. Of the Bateses he can say that "It is a great pity that their circumstances should be confined," but though his own circumstances should be liberating, he stays indoors as much as possible, never walking "beyond the shrubbery" (26) at Hartfield, and having no "intercourse" with Highbury families outside "his own little circle" (20).[9] We learn that he has not been to Donwell Abbey for two years, that he refuses to visit his family in London, and that he has never been to the Crown "in his life" (251). Nor will he be at the inn when the ball takes place: he has never been a dancer. We picture him being safely conveyed to Donwell "in his carriage, with one window down, to partake of [an] alfresco party" (357). We think of his frequently "depressed" "spirits"(275) and of his "fidgitiness" (93), or of his suffering from conversations at dinner parties ("to be sitting long after dinner, was a confinement that he could not endure"). We note that he lives in the past ("My dear papa," Emma says of Frank, "he is three-and-twenty. —You forget how time passes."), and that he tries to keep other people as restricted as himself. "Hating change of every kind" (7), and "no friend to matrimony" (256), he would keep Miss Taylor fixed forever in her office as governess.

By contrast, Isabella Knightley, her brother-in-law George,

and Miss Bates occupy situations suited to their capacity for social and intellectual activity. Although Isabella shares her father's fear of "change" (94), and although she is "wrapt up in her family" (92), she is, to the extent that her narrow domestic role keeps her "innocently busy" and does not require a "strong understanding" (92), "a model of right feminine happiness" (140). Mr. Knightley keeps equally busy in his more varied and more demanding roles, not only as a kindly neighbor to the Bateses or as a counselor to Mr. Woodhouse, but as farmer and magistrate; while Emma has only her father, Knightley has "all the parish to manage" (225). We learn that Donwell Abbey has a "respectable size, a good deal of ground" (358), and that Knightley's activities are sufficient to "fill up his time" (225). At another extreme, Miss Bates finds happiness in the most reduced circumstances. With only "what limited means could command" (163), she and her mother are losing hold of their place in genteel society. Yet their "little" (243) sitting-room is a place of "tranquillity" (240), for Miss Bates is as undiscriminating as she is good-hearted: "I think there are few places with such society as Highbury. I always say, we are quite blessed in our neighbours" (175).

To at least some of those more energetic characters who feel cramped in their given situations, even the confined society of Highbury seems to provide an opportunity for what the novel depicts as workable forms of self-extension. The Westons, the Coles, and the Martins are busy enhancing their claims to gentility. Mr. Weston has known a great deal of "change" in his life; having quit the militia to engage in trade after his first wife's death, he has worked hard enough and long enough to be able to purchase Randalls and marry Miss Taylor. Open and lively, he divides his time "between useful occupations and the pleasures of society" (16). He delights in enlarging the list of those to participate in the ball ("One cannot have too large a party"), and spring is his favorite season because it is "always inviting one out" (309).[10] His marriage to Miss Taylor gives her a new role as mistress of Randalls, where she will have "the exercise and variety which her spirits seemed to need" (361). Despite their origins in trade, the Coles, too, are becoming more than moderately genteel: "With their wealth, their views increased; their want of a larger house, their inclination for more company" (207). They have added a dining room to their home, and purchased a piano, which betokens an opportunity for the talented individual both to "play" and to develop her "powers." Significantly, however, the Coles, like Mr. Weston, owe their increasing social status to their business activities outside Highbury; they and he had not settled permanently in the village when young.[11] Of the social-risers in Highbury, only Robert Martin has not had to leave the community in order to improve himself: living on a "large farm" (23), he spends some of his free time reading the *Elegant Extracts.*[12] Self-improvement is the one form of self-extension of which the novel entirely approves, for it allows the individual to enlarge the psychic or social space in which he has to turn without impinging upon that of others. A gradual process, it allows for healthy "change," both personal and social.

III

Standing in contrast to the Coles or the Martins are Mr. and Mrs. Elton, who merely pretend a commitment to their chosen social roles, and Emma, who fancies herself a real "friend" to Harriet, and who "plays" at being the object of what she imagines to be Frank's amorous attentions. Both Mr. and Mrs. Elton profess to be seekers of personal extension for themselves and other people, but both are self-confined, and Mrs. Elton endangers the personal freedom of others. Because Mr. Elton marries only in order to "aggrandize and enrich himself" (135), his marriage brings him no improvement beyond the monetary; it leaves him "talking only of himself and his own concerns" (182). His wife "thought herself coming with superior knowledge of the world, to enliven and improve a country neighbourhood" (281), and she calls herself "an addition to the society of Highbury" (307). Although she boasts that her "acquaintance is so very extensive" (272), she has known only "one set of people"; Maple Grove, her brother-in-law's home, is "shut out from everything in the most complete retirement" (282). In Jane Fairfax, her vanity finds an object, someone for whom she can pretend to provide the opportunity of personal self-extension; she would place her in a gentleman's family where Jane would "have as many rooms as you like" (301). She urges Emma to join with her in assuming the role of friend or extender (282), and even to the indignant heroine she presumes to offer an enlarged sphere of activity: "The advantages of Bath to the young are generally understood. It would be a charming introduction for you, who have led so secluded a life; and I could immediately secure you some of the best society in the place" (275). Emma resists, of course, but Mrs. Elton's efforts in Jane's behalf nearly result not in an extension of that young lady's personal freedom, but in confinement at a Mrs. *Small*ridge's.

Emma works to confine Harriet in a similar way.[13] The heroine claims to want to introduce Harriet "into good society" (24), but her real desire is to "appropriate" her. In the very act of trying to destroy Harriet's true friendship with the Martins, the heroine warns her that in marrying Robert "you would have thrown yourself out of all good society" and been "confined to the society of the illiterate and the vulgar" (54). But while Emma justifies her meddling as "woman's friendship," what she tells Mr. Knightley about her motives is far truer than she likes to think: "I want only to keep Harriet to myself" (66). The greatest danger in the heroine's self-indulgent activity as a "friend" is that "the effects of her blunders" cannot "be confined to herself" (134). Emma can extend the range of Harriet's "ambitions beyond" her "own set" (63), but not of her actual possibilities, for there is no real chance that a Mr. Elton or a Frank Churchill will want to marry her.

Like that of several other characters, Emma's desire is as much to extend herself by "appropriating" what is outside herself as it is simply to manipulate other people or to refashion society into a form that will gratify her artistic impulses.[14] She betrays her proprietary attitude when she assures Harriet that Mr. Elton's family is waiting to make her one of them: she speaks of "those pleasantest feelings of our nature—eager curiosity and warm pre*possession*" (56, my italics). The quality of the heroine's relationship with Harriet is suggested by the fact that Harriet is "gradually having a bedroom appropriated to herself"

(57) at Hartfield. Although Emma pretends not to be aware of Mrs. Weston's hope that the heroine and Frank will eventually make a match ("Emma could look perfectly . . . innocent, and answer in a manner that appropriated nothing"), her attitude to Frank is like her attitude to Harriet, even before she meets him: "She had frequently thought—especially since his father's marriage with Miss Taylor—that if she *were* to marry, he was the very person to suit her in age, character and condition. He seemed by this connection between the families, quite to belong to her" (119).

Emma is not the only character who would appropriate other people. In novelty-hungry Highbury, Frank "was looked upon as sufficiently belonging to the place to make his merits and prospects a kind of common concern" (17). Mr. Woodhouse would keep his daughters and Miss Taylor to himself. When Mr. Knightley proposes a strawberry party at Donwell, Mrs. Elton immediately calls it "my party" (354). By contrast, Mr. Weston, though always eager to have Frank "among us again" (304), had given up his son to the Churchills so that Frank could have a privileged up-bringing. Unhappily, the Churchills have tried to appropriate Frank entirely, making "so avowed an adoption as to have him assume the name of Churchill upon coming of age" (17); they wish "to keep him to themselves" (122). As for Jane Fairfax, although Mrs. Elton tries hard to "engross" (299) her, and although Isabella assumes that the Campbells will not "be able to part with her at all" (104), the young lady is fortunate in her relations with the Bateses and the Campbells. "By birth she belonged to Highbury," and at three she had become the "property . . . of her grandmother and aunt" (163); yet those selfless ladies had sent her to the Campbells, to whom she has "belonged" (164) for many years, but who will unselfishly send her out as a governess. The Campbells, in fact, although they never actually enter the story, serve as models of what "a real friend" (163-164) should be: one who offers "mental provision" and enables a person to "enlarge" his "comprehension" (60). By giving Jane "every advantage of discipline and culture," and "all the rational pleasures of an elegant society" (164), they have removed her from confinement at the Bateses' in Highbury and allowed her the sort of "improvement" for which she is suited by "nature" (163). With Harriet, by contrast, Emma only pretends to have "views of improving her little friend's mind" (69); not until late in the story does Emma agree with Mr. Knightley that she has been "no real friend to Harriet Smith" (63). Needless to say, Knightley tries to enlarge Emma's comprehension.

IV

As the end of the novel makes clear, only in true friendship or in marriage to a man who might improve her can Emma assume a fulfilling social role which will take her out of herself and, some day, out of her father's house. That she subconsciously knows this is evident in the fact that she spends much of her time imagining herself Harriet's real friend and Frank Churchill's intended fiancée. Like the "playfulness" of which it is a particular form, Emma's play-acting as an eligible young lady betrays the impulse of her mind to release its energies, to extend itself. In its least dangerous form, in fact, her play-acting is purely mental, for even before she meets Frank she imagines him as a suitor:

> She could not but suppose it to be a match that everybody who knew them must think of. That Mr. and Mrs. Weston did think of it, she was very strongly persuaded; and though not meaning to be induced by him, or any body else, to give up a situation which she believed more replete with good than any she could change it for, she had a great curiosity to see him, a decided intention of finding him pleasant, of being liked by him to a certain degree, and a sort of pleasure in the idea of their being coupled in their friends' imaginations. (119)

She continues this sort of day-dreaming even after she has known him for some time (264).[15] Having determined never to marry, never to undergo a real change of situation, Emma seeks self-extension in a purely imaginary role. Hoping to be "enlivened" on what seems a dull occasion, Emma acts out this role in her "flirtation" (368) with Churchill on Box Hill.

As is well known, such role-playing is typical of many Austen characters, particularly of her villains and fools, but in none of her earlier novels is it imagined as entirely the response of a mind deprived of appropriate activity. In *Mansfield Park*, for example, Mary and Henry Crawford try out a variety of piquant social roles, but the two of them are uncertain about their personal identities in a way that Emma and Churchill are not. The cause of the Crawfords' misbehavior is their sense of unlimited freedom, and their "playfulness," motivated by their desire to "triumph" over others, is altogether reprehensible. Toward "play" in *Emma*, Austen's attitude is more complex. The heroine's initial condition is one of "intellectual solitude," for her father "could not meet her in conversation, rational or playful" (7); in complete contrast to his daughter, he is "distressed by the more animated sort" of "game" (347).[16] Emma's need to play is intense, therefore, as we see in the long episode where she argues with Mr. Knightley over Frank's unwillingness to defy the Churchills by visiting Highbury. She had already taken the opposite side of the argument, Mr. Knightley's side, in a conversation with Mrs. Weston, yet, "to her great amusement," she "perceived that she was taking the other side of the question from her real opinions, and making use of Mrs. Weston's arguments against herself" (145). Although Emma has been condemned by more than one critic for what Marvin Mudrick calls a "fear of commitment,"[17] this is one of many instances in which we observe her most engaging characteristics, a remarkable self-detachment and a delight in the workings of her own mind. On such occasions she gives herself "a saucy conscious smile" (449).

That smile is one symptom of the "energy and style" that Lionel Trilling admired in Emma. Commenting on how we are kept from condemning her for her blunders, he wrote that "we are never permitted to close in for the kill—some unnamed quality in the girl, some trait of vivacity or will, erects itself as a moral principle, or a least as a vital principle, and frustrates our moral bloodlust."[18] What needs to be added is that by using the space metaphor to underline the threat to that vital principle, Austen determines that our response to the heroine will be balanced between sympathy and judgment. We find Emma faultless in spite of all her faults in great part because her vitality and its confinement in Highbury are as convincingly rendered as the social morality which Mr. Knightley preaches and to which the "rational" part of Emma herself becomes committed. To put this differently, because Emma, Churchill, and Jane Fairfax manoeuvre almost involuntarily to find adequate "space" for themselves, there is a dramatic tension between their story ("told" through the space metaphor) and the novel's (Mr. Knightley's) overt espousal of such values as restraint, reasonableness, and neighborly duty. Knightley believes that a young woman should "adapt herself rationally to the varieties of her situation in life" (39). But, though the words are Emma's, the novel applies a less rigid standard to Jane Fairfax, whose secret engagement violates a significant social convention: "If a woman can ever be excused for thinking only of herself, it is in a situation like Jane Fairfax's.—Of such, one may almost say, that 'the world is not their's, nor the world's law'" (400).

Although the novel does not extend quite the same absolution to the exorbitant Churchill, he is, nonetheless, the most ambiguously portrayed of Austen's "villains." From Knightley's point of view, he is guilty of an unmanly selfishness, but to Emma and Jane Fairfax, he is attractive because he embodies the vital principle to which Trilling referred. At their last interview, Churchill and the heroine acknowledge their dangerous affinity as manipulators (478). Though condemned by Knightley for playing a "double game" with Jane Fairfax, Churchill, however, is not disingenuous (or wrong) in claiming never to have thought that Emma had taken him seriously as a suitor: "She received my attentions with an easy, good-humoured playfulness, which exactly suited me" (438). Too much "likeness" of this sort would unfit them for life in society were they to marry, as the flirtation on Box Hill shows. The story celebrates true marriage not as an opportunity for unrestricted play, but as an ideal social relationship in which each participant finds a "space" where his energies will be contained but given suitable exercise: the rational and the playful must balance each other. Ever careful in meting our rewards and punishments, Austen makes this clear in her final disposition of Churchill. Unlike the false suitors in Austen's other novels—John Willoughby or Henry Crawford, for example—he is not left to suffer in a hell of his own making; instead, he is rewarded with the nearly flawless Jane Fairfax. Like Austen's critics, Knightley believes that the gain will be Churchill's, for the young man will find in her exactly the "good judgment" (400), the "forbearance" and "self-controul" (289) he lacks. But those readers who bemoan the anxiety which Churchill's games-playing causes Jane would do well to recall that the reserved, fragile young woman is drawn to him by "his delightful spirits, and that gaiety, that playfulness of disposition" which is almost "constantly bewitching" (419) to her. Churchill has a piano sent to the talented Jane at a time when she has "not anything of the nature of an instrument to amuse herself with" (215–216), and on more than one occasion when he plays his double game, she shows "a smile of secret delight" (243). Only the prospect of becoming his wife can restore her "animation" (453).

V

Angus Wilson has divided readers of Austen into two groups: "social traditionalists" and "lovers of energy, boldness, and freedom of the imagination and the vital spirit."[19] Wilson himself dislikes the fact that in *Emma* Austen tips the scale in favor of social tradition, but tip it she does. In the end the heroine must learn to channel her energies in new directions, for her efforts to extend the dominion of her mind by appropriating Harriet as "friend" and Frank as "suitor" lead only to the threat of increased confinement. This irony is especially apparent in the seemingly circular movement of the plot from the beginning of the novel until the end of Chapter XII, Volume III, by which point she has learned about the engagement between Frank and Jane, and believes that a courtship is developing between Mr. Knightley and Harriet. Emma's meddling in Harriet's life had begun as a reaction to the dread of confinement at the very beginning of the story. Although Miss Taylor's wedding had brought the former governess "every form of happiness," it had meant only melancholy change to Emma:

> It was Miss Taylor's loss which first brought grief. It was on the wedding-day of this beloved friend that Emma first sat in mournful thought of any continuation. The wedding over, and the bride-people gone, her father and herself were left to dine together, with no prospect of a third to cheer a long evening. Her father composed himself to sleep after dinner, as usual, and she had then only to sit and think of what she had lost. (6)

The funereal language in this passage makes fun of Emma's selfishness (neither she nor her father acknowledges that marriage brings new life), but it also underlines a state of confinement which does indeed threaten to extinguish her "life." Yet all her activity with Harriet and Frank seems to lead her, many months later, to the same fearful prospect:

> The evening of this day was very long and melancholy at Hartfield. The weather added what it could of gloom. A cold, stormy rain set in, and nothing of July appeared out in the trees and shrubs, which the wind was despoiling, and the length of the day, which only made such cruel sights the longer visible.
> The weather affected Mr. Woodhouse, and he could only be kept tolerably comfortable by almost ceaseless attention on his daughter's side, and by exertions which had never cost her so much before. It reminded her of their first forlorn tête-à-tête, on the evening of Mrs. Weston's wedding day; but Mr. Knightley had walked in then, soon after tea, and dissipated every melancholy fancy. Alas! such delightful proofs of Hartfield's attraction, as those sorts of visit conveyed, might shortly be over. The picture which she had then drawn of the privations of the approaching winter, had proved erroneous; no friends had deserted them, no pleasures had been lost.—But her present forebodings she feared would experience no similar contradiction. The prospect before her now, was threatening to a degree that could not be entirely dispelled—that might not be even partially brightened. If all took place that might take place among the circle of her friends, Hartfield must be comparatively deserted; and she left to cheer her father with the spirits only of ruined happiness.
> The child to be born at Randalls must be a tie there even dearer than herself; and Mrs. Weston's heart and time would be occupied by it. They should lose her; and, probably, in great measure, her husband

also.—Frank Churchill would return among them no more. . . . All that
were good would be withdrawn; and if to these losses the loss of Donwell were to be added, what would remain of cheerful or of rational
society within their reach? (422)

Intellectual solitude, confinement to Hartfield, the loss of "spirit
and gaiety" (423)—such appear to the heroine the bitter fruits
of her attempts to extend herself in imaginary roles as "friend"
and eligible young lady.

Yet the deeper irony of Emma's situation at this point is not
that her attempts at self-extension have left her in dread of
further confinement, but that she turns out to be wrong even
about that prospect. That is, by the end of Chapter XII, Volume
III, Emma sees no more of the real movement of the plot of her
own story than does the reader on his first encounter with the
novel: her fears are the product of her "imagination." The
heroine is wrong about Mr. Knightley, who will return from
London the next day to propose to her, and about Harriet, who
will soon be reunited with the man she truly loves, Robert Martin. Emma discovers that she has all along been too blind to
what people are really like to be able to manipulate them effectively; her efforts to impose herself on the world by appropriating others have left her confined to her own imaginings. This is
the other meaning of "intellectual solitude." She who sets up
for Understanding does not really know either herself, Harriet,
Mr. Knightley, Frank, or Jane. Only a forced recognition of her
many blunders will bring her toward self-knowledge and toward
the possibility of understanding others. And accepting others as
they really are without trying to fit them into situations for
which they are unsuited will open up the possibility of genuine
self-extension for Emma, of release not only from confinement
to her fancy, but to a life-denying idea of friendship and marriage. It is fitting that the beginning of Chapter XIII, Volume III,
should bring a new day and good weather, and that it should
reveal the heroine seeking freshened "spirits" outdoors, where
Mr. Knightley will unexpectedly appear to propose to her.[20]
The proposal climaxes a gradual "disclosure" of the "truth,"
and because it means an end to "concealment" on Emma's side,

"the superior hopes which gradually opened were so much the more enchanting" (432) to her.

To Emma's credit, it can be said that even before Mr. Knightley's proposal she begins to understand that her only hope for self-extension lies in marriage to him or in true friendship. "Birth, abilities, and education," she realizes, "had been equally marking her as an associate for" (421) Jane Fairfax, not for the inferior Harriet. But Jane is a temporary visitor for whom there is no fitting situation in Highbury society, and Emma's efforts to befriend her—to take her out of the Bateses' home, where Jane is "confined always to one room" (389)—are made too late. In Highbury only Mr. Knightley, who has always watched over her "with an endeavour to improve her" (415), is her equal. In marrying him, Emma, the young woman who had thought her "active, busy mind" would find "enough for every hope and every fear" (86) in the duties of unmarried aunt, enters a situation to which her talents and energies are suited. Mr. Knightley will take her to the sea for a honeymoon, and the grounds at Donwell are spacious.

But the heroine's reformation should not obscure for us Austen's emphasis on the obstacles that stand between her young people and happiness. Although *Emma* is rightly said to be about its individualistic heroine's awakening to the necessity for self-restraint and social responsibility, and although the heroine is at fault for increasing her sense of confinement, the novel's paramount irony is that it is in resisting restraints that she and Churchill and Jane find appropriate situations for themselves. Implicit in *Emma* is another story, which Austen did not choose to write: it concerns a Jane Fairfax who, refusing to enter into a secret engagement, ends up as a governess; a Frank Churchill who, prudent and unwilling to trust "to time, chance, circumstance, slow effects, sudden bursts, perseverance, and weariness, health and sickness" (437), does not attract the one woman capable of improving his character; and an Emma Woodhouse who because she refrains from trying to superintend Harriet's destiny and from play-acting with Frank, never discovers that she loves Knightley, or he her (397). Instead, Austen chose to write about the effects on Highbury of an outsider, the impetuous Frank Churchill, who by his insistence that the village begin dancing again, is unwittingly responsible for bringing together the heroine and Mr. Knightley, that too reluctant, thirty-eight-year-old dancer. In *Emma*, society shows itself capable of revitalization, but only because of the urgent energies of Churchill and Emma, the egoists who, from Mr. Knightley's point of view, seem most likely to undermine its stability. The novel insists that such energies be contained and focused in real rather than imaginary social roles, but it also makes clear that there can be a mutually beneficial relationship between the individual and society only when the individual can find a situation suited to his capacity for social activity, but rational and playful.

On one level this reading of *Emma* suggests only that the ending is true to the comic spirit and form of the story as a whole: the young people achieve their desires by overcoming restrictions placed upon them by effete "blocking agents" (Mr. Woodhouse and Mrs. Churchill), and, as the birth of the Westons' baby and the weddings at the end indicate, Highbury is revivified. On another level we can view the novel as Austen's attempt to examine in fictional form the difficulties faced by the talented individual in the traditional society: only in *Mansfield Park* does she show a similar concern with the possibility of wasted, undeveloped, or misdirected natural abilities, but in that novel, the concern is not central. To argue that the space metaphor implies standards of judgment which elude the rational and comfortably situated Mr. Knightley, however, is not to side with critics who have described Austen as essentially hostile to the society about which she writes. The comic conclusion of *Emma* is proof that she was still able to commit herself to the moral and social values of the traditional society—as Duckworth and Trilling have shown—to everything symbolized by an estate such as Donwell Abbey. But her concern with the theme of confinement does, I think, look ahead to *Persuasion*, a story which is generally seen as marking a sudden turning point at the end of her career. In that last completed novel, the traditional society is represented as unworthy and unwilling to accomodate the hero or the heroine, who ends up commiting herself not to a "fixed" situation in the country, but to the socially unstable life of a sailor's wife. Anne Elliot's eight-year loss of "bloom" suggests the likely fate of a less recalcitrant Emma. Churchill, with "his own situation to improve as he could" (16), reminds us as much of Frederick Wentworth as of Austen's villains, for through energy and a willingness to rely on "luck," he manages to marry a woman from whom he is initially separated. Unlike Wentworth and Anne, the young people in *Emma* find suitable "places" for themselves within the confines of the traditional society, but only barely. In *Persuasion*, Enscombe moves to center stage as Kellynch Hall.

Notes

1. All quotations from *Emma* are taken from *The Novels of Jane Austen*, ed. R. W. Chapman, 3rd ed. (London: Oxford University Press, 1933), Vol. IV.

2. Alistair M. Duckworth, *The Improvement of the Estate: A Study of Jane Austen's Novels* (Baltimore: Johns Hopkins University Press, 1971), pp. 163-164, writes of the planning for the ball as a morally subversive activity similar to the theatricals in *Mansfield Park*.

3. Langdon Elsbree, "The Purest and Most Perfect Form of Play: Some Novelists and the Dance," *Criticism*, 14(1972), 364, notes that "in Jane Austen the dance is the purest kind of play."

4. To my knowledge, only two writers have commented on the matter of Emma's confinement. A. Walton Litz, *Jane Austen: A Study of Her Artistic Development* (New York: Oxford University Press, 1965), pp. 135-136, quotes Shaftsbury, *"Sensus Communis:* An Essay on the Freedom of Wite and Humour" (I, iv), to this effect: the "natural free Spirits of Ingenious Men, if imprison'd and controul'd, will find out other ways of Motion to relieve themselves in their *Constraint. . . .*" And Litz remarks that Emma finds relief "through the play of fancy, illusion-mongering, and irresponsible match-making." He does not develop the point or relate it to the space metaphor in *Emma*. Nor does Richard Poirier, "Transatlantic Configurations: Mark Twain and Jane Austen," in *A World Elsewhere: The Place of Style in American Literature* (New York: Oxford University Press, 1966), p. 154, who mentions the "enclosure of natural vitality within a social situation that threatens to smother it." As for time and space, Stuart M. Tave, *Some Words of Jane Austen* (Chicago: University of Chicago Press, 1973), pp. 1-35, passim, emphasizes that the people in Austen's fic-

tional world must learn to live within the limitations of both. And Francis R. Hart, "The Spaces of Privacy: Jane Austen," *Nineteenth-Century Fiction*, 30(1975), 305–333, discusses spatial metaphors in Austen's novels in relation to her heroines' gradual recognition of a need for privacy and true intimacy.

5. Lionel Trilling, "*Emma*," *Encounter*, 8(1957), 58, writes that Highbury is "an idyllic world." Yasmine Gooneratne, *Jane Austen* (Cambridge: Cambridge University Press, 1970), pp. 138–139, describes the village as "in a state of lively, animated progression." Duckworth, who condemns Frank Churchill entirely, argues, p. 113, that the young man "wishes to introduce movement and flexibility into a landscape of peace and stability." E. Rubinstein, *Jane Austen's Novels: The Metaphor of Rank*, in *Literary Monographs*, 2 (Madison: University of Wisconsin Press, 1969), while conceding that Highbury is "in its last stages as an 'idyllic' setting," sees it, p. 168, as a "place of escape" from the meretricious modern world outside, and, p. 160, "not merely embodying an absence of evil but as embodying an ideal of good." Robert Liddell, *The Novels of Jane Austen* (London: Longmans, 1963), p. 110, comments that Highbury "is rather dull and second-rate, and Emma is quite right in thinking so." Hart, p. 328, notes that "the world of *Emma* is most severely restricted in social size and mobility," but neither he nor Liddell points out that Austen imagines social roles as "spaces," or that she is interested in the threat to the vitality of the gifted individual in the world of the novel.

6. *Autobiography* (London: Routledge & Kegan Paul, 1970), p. 1.

7. Of Austen's critics, only the iconoclastic J. F. Burrows, *Jane Austen's "Emma"* (Sydney, Australia: Sydney University Press, 1968), pp. 58–61, pays sufficient attention to the "psychological realities" of Churchill's situation. As will become clear, I side with Burrows in arguing that Mr. Knightley's legalistic pronouncements are not the sole standards by which we are to judge Churchill and Emma.

8. Emma is capable of weeping over the idea of quitting her father "as a sin of thought" (435). Most of Austen's critics have been seduced by the opening paragraphs of the novel into assuming that the heroine, in Duckworth's words, p. 148, has "complete freedom of action," that her "boundaries are where she wishes to place them." Emma has "too much her own way" (5), but only in a situation that seldom allows her to spend even two hours away from her father.

9. Duckworth, p. 149, points out that Mr. Woodhouse's "stipulation against taking his position 'at the bottom of the table' at the Hartfield dinner party for the Eltons is an index of his withdrawal from social and domestic responsibility."

10. Mr. Weston, for all his good qualities, represents something of a laughable extreme in his unflagging optimism and openness. He takes more pleasure in "prospects" themselves than in their fulfillment. Speaking of Frank, he tells Mrs. Elton that "I do not know . . . whether the uncertainty of our meetings, the sort of constant expectation there will be of his coming in to-day or to-morrow . . . may not be more friendly to happiness than having him actually in the house. . . . I think it is the state of mind which gives most spirit and delight" (309).

11. Rubinstein, 165 ff., writes on the social-risers in *Emma* and notes that the Coles and the Westons have made their money outside Highbury.

12. The full title of this compilation by Vicesimus Knox is *Elegant Extracts: or, useful and entertaining Pieces of poetry, Selected for the Improvement of Young Persons*. Writing (in the 1809 edition) of the value of polite literature to the mercantile classes, Knox observes that "Nothing perhaps contributes more to liberalize their minds and prevent that narrowness which is too often the consequence of a life attached . . . to the pursuit of lucre." Quoted by Edmund Blunden, "Elegant Extracts," in *Essays on the Eighteenth Century Presented to David Nichol Smith in Honour of his Seventieth Birthday* (Oxford: At the Clarendon Press, 1945), p. 227.

13. Marvin Mudrick, *Jane Austen: Irony as Defense and Discovery* (Princeton, New Jersey: Princeton University Press, 1952), p. 194, is one of several critics who discuss Mrs. Elton as Emma's "companion in motive." He does not take up the theme of false friendship.

14. Mudrick, 187 ff., discusses Emma's efforts to manipulate other people; and Duckworth, without developing the point, notes, p. 157, that Harriet is to become "a psychic extension of Emma's self." Kenneth L. Moler, *Jane Austen's Art of Allusion* (Lincoln: University of Nebraska Press, 1968), pp. 175-176, writes on Emma's tendency "to 'fictionalize' the real world around her," as does David Lee Minter, "Aesthetic Vision and the World of *Emma*," *Nineteenth-Century Fiction*, 21(1966), 49-59.

15. For a discussion of Emma's playing at being in love, see Edward M. White, "*Emma* and the Parodic Point of View," *Nineteenth-Century Fiction*, 18(1963), 55-63. He does not relate it to her need for self-extension.

16. Several characters define themselves in part by their capacity for play. Unlike Emma's, Mrs. Elton's theatricality is forced, for it does not derive from a genuine liveliness. Mr. Elton and Mr. John Knightley are caricatures of the "rational" man, the first passing up whist for the "busi-

ness" (68) of getting married, the second losing his temper in the name of reason (93). For a more stringent view of the games-playing in *Emma* see Duckworth, *The Improvement of the Estate,* 163 ff., and also "'Spillikins, paper ships, riddles, conundrums, and cards': Games in Jane Austen's Life and Fiction," in *Jane Austen Bicentenary Essays,* ed. John Halperin (Cambridge: Cambridge University Press, 1975), pp. 292-296.

17. *Jane Austen,* p. 203.

18. *The Opposing Self* (New York: The Viking Press, 1955), pp. 207-208.

19. "The Neighbourhood of Tombuctoo: Conflicts in Jane Austen's Novels," in *Critical Essays on Jane Austen,* ed. B. C. Southam (New York: Barnes & Noble, 1968), p. 186.

20. Edgar F. Shannon, Jr., "*Emma:* Character and Construction," *PMLA,* 71(1956), 647, points out that Mr. Elton's proposal to Emma is made inside a carriage in December, while what Emma imagines is to be a proposal from Frank occurs indoors in February. Mr. Knightley's is, of course, a July proposal.

INDEX

Index

Acatalepsis, 82
Adams, Thomas, 67
Addison, Joseph, 251-252, 256-
257; *Spectator*, 219, 271
Alberti, Leon Battista, 187, 188,
199-200; *Della pittura*, 188
Alcmaeon of Croton, 218
Allen, Ralph, 72
Analogy, principle of, 93-95, 265
Arbuthnot, John, 68, 218-219,
221, 234; *Account of the
Death and Burial of Dr. Wood-
ward* (attributed to), 219; *Dis-
sertation on Dumpling*, 234
Aristarchus of Samos, 235
Aristotelian, 12
Aristotle, ix, 12, 91, 114, 175, 211,
218, 223
Augustinus, Aurelius (St. Augus-
tine), ix, 114, 118, 123, 169
Austen, Jane, 159, 275-295;
Emma, 275-295; *Mansfield
Park*, 288, 294; *Northanger
Abbey*, 159; *Persuasion*, 280,
294-295

Bacon, Francis, vii, 12, 80, 81-91,
93, 95-96, 101, 102, 264; pro-

Bacon, Francis (continued)
gram for reform of philosophy
and the sciences, 81-85; *De
Augumentis*, 82, 84; *Magna
Instauratio*, 83, 84, 91; *New
Atlantis*, 85; *New Organon*,
82, 83, 84, 91; *Parasceve*, 84
Bailey, Nathan, *Dictionarium
Britannicum*, 30, 52, 142-143
Baillet, Adrien, *Vie de Monsieur
Descartes*, 198
Balzac, Honoré de, 152
Barfield, Owen, 143
Barrington, Daines, 80, 81, 104
Baxter, Richard, 170
Bayes, Thomas, 38, 57, 58; *Doc-
trine of Chances*, 38
Bayle, Pierre, 266
Becker, Ernest, 220, 230
Ben Israel, Menessah, 178
Bentley, Richard, 175, 226-228;
*Matter and Motion Cannot
Think*, 226
Berkeley, George, 117, 120-121,
143, 213, 221, 222, 226, 230,
235, 259-271; influence of,
266-271; *The Analyst*, 261;
Guardian, 219, 223

301